FOOTPRINTS OF VICTORY OVER RACISM – VOLUME 2

# RAYS OF VICTORY WORKBOOK SERIES

# RAYS OF VICTORY WORKBOOK SERIES

**This Book Belongs to:**

______________________________

**(Your Beautiful Name)**

*"The LORD executes righteousness and justice for all who are oppressed."*

Psalms 103:6

*"He will redeem them from oppression and violence, for their lives are precious to him."*

Psalms 71:14

**RAYS OF VICTORY WORKBOOK SERIES**

# Footprints of Victory Over Racism:

## *In the Secret Place With God* (Volume 2)

**40 DAYS OF READINGS FROM**

**THE RAYS OF VICTORY SERIES:**

***"NAILING RACISM TO THE CROSS"***

*Illuminating daily guideposts for God's rays of victory over racism*

*Jesus Christ in you is greater than the spirit of racism. Let His Footprints lead you to daily victory over racism.*

*Be free forever from Pharaoh's bitter yoke and move beyond racism*

**Dr. Jacyee Aniagolu-Johnson**

---

*Edited by Chad Steenerson (www.christianeditor.net)*
*Also Edited by Uché Aniagolu (Ebony WoodHouse Productions)*
*Cover design by Marble Tower Publishing, LLC*

**Editing Style:**
*Please note that the editing style presented in this book by the second editor, Uché Aniagolu, is meant to emphasize reverence of God, His Son Jesus Christ and His Holy Spirit. This editing style may differ from what you are accustomed to, but we chose it for the reason noted above.*

---

First Paperback Edition

ISBN 978-0-9789669-6-6

Printed in the United States of America by Marble Tower Publishing, LLCPrinted in the United States of America by Marble Tower Publishing, LLC

Publisher's Cataloging-In-Publication Data
(Prepared by The Donohue Group, Inc.)

Aniagolu-Johnson, Jacyee.
Footprints of victory over racism : in the secret place with God / Jacyee Aniagolu-Johnson. -- 1st pbk. ed.

2 v. ; cm. -- (Rays of victory series. Workbook series)

"Illuminating daily guideposts for God's rays of victory over racism."
"Inspirational excerpts from 'Rays of Victory: Nailing Racism to the Cross'"--T.p. verso of both volumes.
ISBN-13: 978-0-9789669-5-9 (pbk.: v. 1)
ISBN-10: 0-9789669-5-3 (pbk.: v. 1)
ISBN-13: 978-0-9789669-6-6 (pbk. : v. 2)
ISBN-10: 0-9789669-6-1 (pbk. : v. 2)

1. Racism--Religious aspects--Christianity. 2. Spiritual warfare. 3. Christian life. I. Aniagolu-Johnson, Jacyee. Nailing racism to the cross. II. Title.

BV4599.5.R33 A54 2011
248.4

# Dedication

This book is dedicated to our Heavenly Father, God Almighty—a God of righteousness, justice, equity and all goodness enveloped in One—our only One and true Living God Who gave us all the gift of eternal salvation through Jesus Christ.

To my dear father, Justice Anthony Aniagolu and my mother Lady (Mrs.) Maria Aniagolu whom I love dearly and who first taught me about God, His profound love, mercy, faithfulness and grace, and His holy justice against any form of evil, wickedness, oppression and injustice.

This book is also dedicated to the memories of Olaudah Equiano (Gustavus Vassa), Saint Katharine Drexel, Malcolm X (Malcolm Little) and his wife Betty X (Betty Shabazz), Reverend Dr. Martin Luther King Jr. and his wife Coretta Scott King, Medgar Wiley Evers, Walter Max Ulyate Sisulu, Steve Biko, James Chaney, Andrew Goodman, Michael Schwerner and Chief Gani Fawehinmi. Also, special dedication to President Nelson Rolihlahla Madiba Mandela, Winnie Madikizela-Mandela, and to all other civil rights leaders, who have boldly stood against injustice, oppression and repression, bad governance and other forms of wickedness in their community, district, borough, county, state or country, that positively impacted the world as a whole.

To all those who dedicate(d) their lives against all odds to the fight against racism or ethnic prejudice, injustice and oppression, and to many others who lived and died for justice and equality; and those who continue to fight for justice in every nation of the world.

Finally, to all those, regardless of race, ethnicity or nationality, who need God's rays of victory to deal with and overcome racial prejudice or discrimination—may your individual victory through God's beams of justice come speedily as you abide in His Holy Word and presence through our Lord and Savior Jesus Christ.

# Acknowledgement

My foremost gratitude is to God my Heavenly Father for His free gift of salvation through my Lord and Savior Jesus Christ, and His Holy Spirit Who dwells within me. It is He Who inspires and fuels me daily to overcome any and all challenges, including my experiences with racial prejudice and discrimination.

To my dear father, Justice Anthony Aniagolu and my mother Lady Maria Aniagolu whom I love dearly for being wonderful parents and for all you did for me and my siblings.

My special gratitude goes to my husband, Lamonte, who remains my earthly Rock of Gibraltar, and through whom God continues to teach me His expression of true and unconditional love that has no bounds. I love you very much.

My special gratitude also goes to my sister, Maryanne, a lovely woman of God—thank you for continuing to help me to better understand how to hear the true voice of God and how to spend endless quality time in God's holy presence through prayer, thanksgiving and worship. I love you very much.

To my sister Uché, I thank God for the sweet fragrance of Jesus Christ in you. You are an embodiment of servanthood—selfless sacrificial giving, and it is the greatness of God in you through Christ that empowers you to humble yourself to serve others; I have no doubt that God will magnify His glory in your life through Jesus Christ. I love you very much.

To my sister Chi-Chi who's giving spirit surpasses anyone that I know—May Luke 6:38 remain like a wellspring within you and may God continue to bless you and enrich your life beyond your wildest imagination through Jesus Christ! I love you very much.

To my brother Kizito whose deep and genuine love for God helps me to stay focused on Matthew 6:33; may the power of God's Holy Word continue to promote you from faith to faith and from glory to glory, in the awesome Name of our Lord and Savior Jesus Christ. I love you very much.

To the rest of my family, Tony, Emeka, Chuka, Lolly and Nwachu, I remain forever grateful to God for your lives, individual families and accomplishments. It is my prayer that John 3:16 will be and remain alive in your hearts. I love you very much.

Special thanks to Reverend (Prophet) Michael Galleta at the Genesis Upper Room Church, San Jose, California. Reverend Michael first prayed for the success of the Rays of Victory Series manuscript and has for many years covered my family with powerful prayers of faith. God has spoken to me through him in many profound ways—and may God continue to bless you, your wife Minister Yvonne Galleta and children, and your entire congregation.

My heartfelt thanks to Minister Sarah Allred at the Genesis Upper Room Church, whom God used her prayer ministry to touch me in a profound manner. Thank you, Sister Sarah, for allowing God to use you to help me refresh my walk with Him. May He continue to bless you!

I would like to thank Elder Peyton Grey at the Evangel Cathedral, Upper Marlboro, Maryland, who prayed for the completion and success of the "Rays of Victory Series. Thank you very much for continuing to allow God to use you in the most tremendous ways.

To David and Fortune West and the Ocean of Mercy Prayer Ministry in Cork, Ireland, I would like to thank God for your spiritual covering of the Rays of Victory project through your prayers and encouragement with the Holy Word of God. As you continue to spread the good news of the Gospel of Jesus Christ, may you continue to be seen as manifested light of Jesus Christ onto nations, and may God continue to diffuse the fragrance of Christ through you to win souls.

To my sisters in the Lord Jesus Christ, Chinwe Igwegbe-Lane, Nonye Igwegbe and Cathy Agada, thank you for all your prayers and support and powerful prophetic words that sustained me during the final "birthing" stage of the RAV book series. May our Heavenly Father continue to take you from faith to Faith and from glory to Glory, in the awesome Name of our Lord and Savior Jesus Christ!

To the rest of my friends and prayer partners, who prayed with and for me for the success of this book and the entire Rays of Victory Series—may God continue to bless you immensely in the awesome Name of our Lord and Savior Jesus Christ.

Finally, to the Body of Jesus Christ (believers in Him and all of God's geniune priests and ministers around the world), regardless of denomination, race, ethnicity or nationality, may God's favor and blessings always overflow in your lives as you continue to spread the good news of the Gospel of our Lord and Savior Jesus Christ, and further His powerful ministry that is firmly rooted in true and pure Love, which is God Himself.

## Stereotypes, Prejudice, Discrimination

"The terms stereotype, prejudice, discrimination, and racism are often used interchangeably in everyday conversation. But when discussing these terms from a sociological perspective, it is important to define them: *stereotypes* are oversimplified ideas about groups of people, *prejudice* refers to thoughts and feelings about those groups, while *discrimination* refers to actions toward them; and r*acism* is a type of prejudice that involves set beliefs about a specific racial group. Stereotypes can be based on race, ethnicity…almost any characteristic. They may be positive (usually about one's own group…but are often negative (usually toward other groups, such as when members of a dominant racial group suggest that a subordinate racial group is stupid or lazy). In either case, the stereotype is a generalization that doesn't take individual differences into account…Where do stereotypes come from? In fact new stereotypes are rarely created; rather, they are recycled from subordinate groups that have assimilated into society and are reused to describe newly subordinate groups."

**(Stereotypes, Prejudice, Discrimination. http://cnx.org/content/m42860/latest/content_info#cnx_attribution_header)**

## Power of the Prayer of Jabez

Like God did for Jabez, may He use the pain you have experienced from your racist offenders, the rejection you experienced from those who mocked you, the wicked words of racists who said that you were insignificant and not good enough because of your race, ethnicity, nationality, or any other reason, to bless and anoint you, enlarge your territory, keep you from evil, and make you a blessing to many, and not an instrument of pain to anyone, in the awesome Name of Jesus Christ, Amen.

**Jacyee Aniagolu-Johnson, PhD**

*"Now Jabez was more honorable than his brothers, and his mother called his name Jabez, saying, "Because I bore him in pain." And Jabez called on the God of Israel saying, "Oh, that You would bless me indeed, and enlarge my territory, that Your hand would be with me, and that You would keep me from evil, that I may not cause pain!" So God granted him what he requested."*

**1 Chronicles 4:9-10**

# What the Bible Says About Oppression

*"He who oppresses the poor reproaches his Maker, but he who honors Him has mercy on the needy.*

Proverbs 14:31"

*"Learn to do good; seek justice, rebuke the oppressor; defend the fatherless, plead for the widow."*

Isaiah 1:17

*"If you see the oppression of the poor, and the violent perversion of justice and righteousness in a province, do not marvel at the matter; for high official watches over high official, and higher officials are over them."*

Ecclesiastes 5:8

*"Ransom me from the oppression of evil people; then I can obey your commandments."*

Psalms 119:134

*"LORD, you know the hopes of the helpless. Surely you will hear their cries and comfort them."*

Psalms 10:17

*"At that time I will put you on trial. I am eager to witness against all sorcerers and adulterers and liars. I will speak against those who cheat employees of their wages, who oppress widows and orphans, or who deprive the foreigners living among you of justice, for these people do not fear me", says the LORD of Heaven's Armies.*

Malachi 3:5

*"For this is what the Sovereign LORD says: Enough, you princes of Israel! Stop your violence and oppression and do what is just and right. Quit robbing and cheating my people out of their land. Stop expelling them from their homes, says the Sovereign LORD."*

Ezekiel 45:9

# Table of Contents

# What is Racism?

"A situation in which one race maintains supremacy over another race through a set of attitudes, behaviors, social structures and ideologies. It involves four essential and interconnected elements:

***Power:*** *the capacity to make and enforce decisions is disproportionately or unfairly distributed*

***Resources:*** *unequal access to such resources as money, education, information, etc.*

***Standards:*** *standards for appropriate behavior are ethnocentric, reflecting and privileging the norms and values of the dominant race or society*

***Problem:*** *involves defining "reality" by naming "the problem" incorrectly, and thus misplacing it."*

**-- Women's Theological Center, Boston, MA, 1994**

# Definitions of Racism

*"Any distinction, exclusion, restriction, or preference based on race, color, descent, or national or ethnic origin which has the purpose or effect of nullifying or impairing the recognition, enjoyment, or exercise, on equal footing, of human rights and fundamental freedoms in the political, economic, social, cultural, or any other field of public life."*

**-- The ICERD (International Convention on the Elimination of All Forms of Racial Discrimination)**

∞∞♦ ♦ ♦ ♦ ♦∞∞

*"Racism has not disappeared…we confront forms of racism that are covert or more complex…"*

**-- The International Council on Human Rights Policy**

∞∞♦ ♦ ♦ ♦ ♦∞∞

*"Racism is a system of inequality based on race."*

**-- Tim Wise**

**Reading Racism Right to Left: Reflections on a Powerful Word and Its Applications (http://www.timwise.org/2010/07/reading-racism-right-to-left-reflections-on-a-powerful-word-and-its-applications/)**

∞∞♦ ♦ ♦ ♦ ♦∞∞

*"Racism involves physical, psychological, spiritual, and social control, exploitation and subjection of one race by another race…This means that racial discrimination and injustice are established, perpetuated and promoted throughout every institution of society - economics, education, entertainment, family, labor, law, politics, religion, science and war…"*

**-- Phavia Kujichagulia (Recognizing and Resolving Racism: A Resource and Guide for Humane Beings)**

∞∞♦♦♦♦♦∞∞

*"Racism - Racial prejudice and discrimination that are supported by institutional power and authority. The critical element that differentiates racism from prejudice and discrimination is the use of institutional power and authority to support prejudices and enforce discriminatory behaviors in systematic ways with far-reaching outcomes and effects…"*

**--Enid Lee, Deborah Menkart and Margo Okazawa-Rey (eds.) (Beyond Heroes and Holidays: A Practical Guide to K-12 Anti-Racist, Multicultural Education and Staff Development.)**

# The Reason for this Book

For every person, every child of God to know, understand and use the awesome power of God's Holy Word and His power within him or her through Jesus Christ to slay the goliath racism that they may encounter.

*"You, dear children, are from God and have overcome them, because the one who is in you is greater than the one who is in the world."* (1 John 4:4, NIV)

To receive the spirit of racism is to reject God's Holy Word.
To practice racism is to disobey God's Holy Word.
To reject the spirit of racism is to uphold God's Holy Word.

# How to Use this Book

This book, "Footprints of Victory Over Racism: In the Secret Place With God—Volume 2", contains selected readings from "Nailing Racism to the Cross" and is a continuation of Volume 1." The content of this book is also designed, as in Volume 1, to help you in your daily meditation, as you deal with the negative elements of racism spiritually and in your physical environment.

This book is to be used in a similar manner as Volume 1. Using this book and the Rays of Victory prayer journal, "One-on-One With God for Victory Over Racism" as your guide to powerful Scriptures in God's Holy Book, the Bible, you may choose to perform a 40-day prayer and meditation, which would help you to prayerfully defeat any influence of the obnoxious spirit of racism in your life. The structure of this book is similar to Volume 1 and so I recommend that you read one chapter a day. Meditate on your reading, and especially, spend quiet time in prayer and worship, and reading and dwelling on God's Holy Word, the Holy Bible. At the end of each chapter are simple yet thought provoking questions that are based on God's Holy Word, the Bible. Try to answer all questions and write down your own thoughts and reflections and as well as any revelations from the Holy Spirit that may come to you while you pray. You may choose to use the "Footprints Notebook for Victory Over Racism – Volume 1" to write down your answers to chapter quizzes in this book.

You may also invite one or two friends or family, or your Bible study group if you have one, to join you in your daily meditation and prayer over the 40-day period. You may meet once a week or more frequently with your prayer partner or Bible study group to share your individual testimony about how God is empowering you daily with the "Footprints" of Jesus Christ for victory over every form of racism that you may encounter.

This book is for every person who needs daily victory over racism regardless of race, ethnicity or nationality, especially Christian believers in our Lord and Savior Jesus Christ. It was written with you in mind to lead you in Jesus Christ to God's Holy Word by His Holy Spirit through Whom God anoints and empowers us daily. Through Jesus Christ, God has given you and me authority over every form of evil, including racism. Be assured that when Christ leaves His Footprints for you to walk into and follow Him, He will lead you to sure victory over every form of evil, including racism.

# Preface

At the very core and foundation of the wholeness of our spirit, soul and body, is our spiritual relationship with the Triune God: Almighty God the Father, His Son Jesus Christ and His Holy Spirit. Jesus Christ is the only Mediator (I Timothy 2:5)—and He is our Lord and Savior who reconciled us to God by His death and resurrection. When Jesus Christ is the authentic Foundation of our belief and knowledge of God's Holy Word, we acquire *true* spiritual discernment of who we are in Him—that is, we begin to recognize and see ourselves spiritually in accordance with the Word. Therefore, when we are *truly* anchored to Jesus Christ, we acquire Christ-rooted love and respect for ourselves and others. Also, we develop Christ-rooted self-regard, self-acceptance, self appreciation, self-esteem and self-confidence—and all of these fuel our self-competence, self-efficiency and self-efficacy. First, let's quickly review some secular definitions of these "self" terms.

Self-respect can be defined as having "a proper sense of one's own dignity and integrity…the quality of being worthy of esteem"[2] or regard. Self-esteem is described as "how valuable or worthwhile we see or perceive ourselves"[2]. Self-respect is having "a proper sense of one's own dignity"[1] that cultivates a behavior of honor and proper conduct which stems from one's self-regard and is groomed by self-acceptance and self-appreciation.

Accepting yourself helps you to regard yourself in a positive manner. Self-acceptance can be defined as acceptance of yourself as you are now—to have a favorable perception of who you are and not who you want or wish to be. To be self-accepting is to have "global affirmation of self…to embrace all facets of ourselves..."[2] To be self-accepting does not mean that you overlook your faults and shortcomings; it simply means that you accept and appreciate who you are now despite your imperfections. Self-acceptance cultivates self-appreciation which is to value who you are regardless of any external opinions or circumstances. Self-appreciation is having a positive perception, reception and approval of who and what one is—and this helps one to cultivate a balanced and healthy mindset. Self-acceptance and self-appreciation are foundational components that are essential for developing self-confidence.

*Be aware that racism is designed to fill you with garbage and lies about your true person (John 8:44).*

Self-confidence is "belief in oneself and abilities"[1] and in many ways it feeds our self-competence, self-efficacy and self-efficiency. "Self-competence involves the interrelationship between self-perception of personal worth and efficacy…and the key components of self-competence are self-esteem, self-determination, and successful coping."[3] In the business world, the term self-efficacy can be defined as "a person's belief about his or her ability and capacity to accomplish a task or to deal with the challenges of life."[4] Efficacy is the power to produce a desired effect, while self-efficacy is the belief in one's efficacy. Self-efficacy is used to describe how one judges one's own competence to complete tasks and reach goals.[5]

*You are a new person in Jesus Christ (Galatians 2:20).*

Albert Bandura defines "perceived self-efficacy" as "people's beliefs about their capabilities to produce designated levels of performance that exercise influence over events that affect their lives. Self-efficacy beliefs determine how people feel, think, motivate themselves and behave."[6] "Self-efficacy is linked to specific tasks, such as one's perceived ability to succeed at" performing a certain task "without mistakes…it is concerned only with perceptions of being able to use skills to be successful."[7] On the other hand, self-efficiency is "the ability to accomplish a job with minimal expenditure of time and effort."[8]

To us who are born again believers "self" does not refer to our worldly carnal self, but to our spiritual makeup that is now "wrapped" in the divine nature of Jesus Christ. As born again believers, our self-respect, self-acceptance, self-appreciation, self-esteem, self-confidence, self-competence, self-efficiency and self-effiacy should be founded on the very identity and nature of Jesus Christ, Whom we have now received as our Lord and Savior. We should define ourselves based on God's Holy Word—that is, who we are in Jesus Christ.As a child of the Most High God created in His Image whose true identity and nature is in Jesus Christ, you should have an overall positive and healthy perception of who you are. "Self-perceptions are a person's own beliefs or predictions concerning their abilities and performance."[7]

*God has not authorized you, me, or anyone else to mistreat others.*

Christ-rooted self-respect cultivates a healthy self-esteem leaving no room for arrogance or foolish self-pride. Remember that to us who are born again believers "self" does not refer to our worldly carnal self, but our spiritual makeup that is now "wrapped" in the divine nature of Jesus Christ. Our previous carnal "self" has been replaced by our new spiritual nature in Jesus Christ (Galatians 2:20). Our self-regard, self-respect, self-acceptance and self-appreciation are now based on God's immeasurable and inseparable love for us (Romans 8:35-39) and His justification of us through Jesus Christ (Romans 3:24-25; Romans 5:1,9). Our confidence is in Jesus Christ; therefore, we are made competent through Him and empowered for self-efficiency and self-efficacy by the anointing of God's Holy Spirit Whom we have received through Christ (Acts 1:8, 2:38; John 14:26). We have God's holy power in us through Jesus Christ that has made us more than conquerors (Romans 8:37) of the daily challenges that we face, including racism. Our confidence is Christ-rooted and we believe that we can do all things through Jesus Christ who strengthens us (Philippians 4:13).

The injustice and oppression of racial prejudice and discrimination can have potential destructive effects on you who may be on the receiving end of it. This is because the vile spirit of racism attacks your soul—your heart, mind, thoughts, emotions will and resolve. It tries to control your attitude, actions, behavior, personality and character, by controlling your mind with its racist lies and destructive toxic deposit of bigotry. It attempts to distort your perception of your true person and it attacks your view of your self-image—your self-respect, self-regard, self-acceptance, self-appreciation, self-esteem, self-worth, self-confidence, self-competence, self-efficacy and self-efficiency. Your view of your self-image is the perception that you have of yourself as a whole—and your "assessment of your qualities and personal worth."[5] Racism is designed to de-face you in your own psyche, and it tries to fill you with negativity by constantly bombarding

*God will deliver you from needing to be validated by others.*

your mind with negative images, words and actions about you and your race, ethnicity or nationality. It is designed to distort your view of your self-image. If you are *truly* a new person in Jesus Christ (Galatians 2:20), racism may still attack your carnal "self", but it has no power over your new renewed spiritual mind and person in Jesus Christ—your true spiritual mindset rooted in God's Holy Word.

Be aware that racism is designed to shatter your own positive perception of your self-image and fill you with garbage and lies about your true person (John 8:44). It is designed to strip you of your sense of self-worth and value to society and to the world in general. It defines and rewards you not by your own individual positive actions and accomplishments, but by your non-preferred race and the negative actions of another with whom you share racial or ethnic identity. Within a racist system you are penalized for being of a certain race, ethnicity or nationality. Your God-given race or ethnicity is abhorred and in many subtle ways you are punished daily for it. By the very nature of the unrelenting acts of racial prejudice and discrimination against you, it can bully your carnal psyche into submission to its lies, injustice and oppression. However, you must know and believe that racism originated from the devil, the father of all lies (John 8:44)—and God has said a resounding NO to racism (Exodus 23:9; Leviticus 19:33-34; Acts 10:9-16, 24-29; Galatians 3:26-29).

*God can rebuild your bruised self-image by renewing your mind with His Holy Word.*

The vile spirit of racism controlling your life was never and still is not God's plan for your life. God has not authorized you, me, or anyone else to mistreat anyone, even foreigners who dwell legally or illegally in our nation (Leviticus 19:33-34).

Racism is designed to handicap us mentally and limit our perception of our intelligence, abilities and potential to learn and develop our abilities and skills—and I repeat that racism is a lie of the devil (John 8:44). We can and should shut-out the lies of the vile spirit of racism by renewing our minds daily with God's Holy Word (Romans 12:2; Ephesians 4:22-23). We who are born again believers know that the power of God's grace through Jesus Christ is more than sufficient (2 Corinthians 12:9) to pull us *up and out* of any negative "valley" to victory. God wants to take us to His positive side where we will regain our self-acceptance, self-respect and self-regard, and have a healthy and positive perception of our self-esteem, self-worth, self-confidence, self-competence, self-efficacy and self-efficiency; although in reality we never actually lost any of them. The power of God's Holy Word will renew your mind, if you read and meditate on it daily (Romans 12:2; Ephesians 4:23-24). If you submit your mind to Jesus Christ, His power in you replaces your carnal "mind" with His spiritual mind; that is, a Christlike mind that

*Our previous carnal "self" has been replaced by our new spiritual "self" in Jesus Christ (Galatians 2:20).*

buffers your way of thinking against the destructive and damaging effects of racism (1 Corinthians 2:16).

God can rebuild your bruised self-image by renewing your mind with His Holy Word, giving you spiritual discernment of your new Christ-rooted image, identity and nature (Romans 12:2; Ephesians 4:23-24; Exodus 3:11-15; 2 Corinthians 5:17, Isaiah 43:18-19, Jeremiah 18:3-6, Jeremiah 31:3, Galatians 5:1). So during tough times when you are bombarded with elements of racism, keep your mind focused on Jesus Christ and the victorious power of His precious Blood upon your life, and not on your racist offenders and their negative actions; immerse yourself in God's Holy Word and meditate day and night on it (Joshua 1:7-9; Isaiah 53:3-5, Psalms 69:19-21; Mathew 27:34; Mark 15:23; Luke 23:36; John 19:29, Hebrews 12:2-3).

*The power of God's Holy Word will renew your mind if you believe, receive and accept it and let it "soak" your heart.*

If you are struggling with feelings of low or lack of: self-regard, self-acceptance, self-esteem, self worth, self-confidence, self-competence, self-efficacy, self efficiency, self-love or self-respect, don't despair because God can and will give you positive spiritual discernment of who you are in Jesus Christ, if you ask Him to (Jeremiah 18:1-4; James 1:5). If you are struggling with any negative perceptions of who you are, you need to ask God in prayer to turn your darkness into light (Psalms 18:28; Psalms 119:105).

In the Book of Exodus, God's Holy Word tells us how Moses once felt inadequate because of His speech impairment (Exodus 4:10-11). Moses stuttered and so he felt he was inadequate to speak before the Pharaoh of Egypt. He asked God for a helper to speak for him. Although God gave Moses his brother, Aaron the Levite, He equipped him spiritually to accomplish that which He called him to do. It was Moses who ended up doing all the speaking before Pharaoh and not Aaron.

In the Book of Joshua, we read that Joshua was appointed by God to take on the mantle of leadership from Moses to lead the Israelites to the Promised Land after Moses died (Joshua 1:1-9). Perhaps, Joshua had become accustomed to being in second place to Moses and when God called him and placed the mantle of leadership on him, he became afraid. God knew that Joshua was anxious and He assured Joshua that he had God's support and protection and encouraged him (Joshua 1:7-9). Even though Joshua trusted God and had faith in Him, perhaps, at first he didn't think he measured up to the enormous task that God had transferred to him from Moses. Just like Joshua, we sometimes feel like we cannot do what God has called us to do because we feel inadequate. Perhaps, others have labeled you inferior and insignificant and you believed them. Perhaps, you have allowed elements of racism to

*The spirit of self-negativity and self-destruction start from within your mind and thoughts.*

demean you in your mind. Our experiences with racism can sometimes have negative effects on our hearts and minds to the extent that they attempt to cripple our thinking and make us believe that we are inadequate and unable to achieve God's great purpose for our lives. In Joshua's case he still made himself available to God who empowered him with a new sense of himself. Joshua now had fresh anointing power of God and a renewed sense of who he was spiritually. He answered God's great call and successfully took the mantle of leadership. It was Joshua who led the children of Israel to the Promised Land (Joshua 3:1-17).

What is it that God has called you to do that you believe you cannot do? How much mental damage have you already sustained from racism? What assignment has God given you, which your negative experiences with racism have convinced you in your mind that you are unable to start and complete? How much of what and who you are have you allowed to diminish in your own eyes due to your experiences with racism? What is it that you believe God cannot do for you? How shattered is your self-acceptance, self-appreciation, self-regard, self-respect, self-worthiness, self-esteem, self-confidence, self-competence, self-efficacy or self-efficiency that you think God is unable to rebuild it for you? How shallow is your belief and faith in God and in yourself that you think God's Hand is too short to pull you out of the deep valley of lies and

*Let God's awesome glory through the Footprints of our Lord and Savior Jesus Christ walk you into daily victory over racism.*

distortions in your mind caused by your experiences with racism? Do you lack true spiritual knowledge about your true nature, abilities and capabilities in Jesus Christ? Is this a spin-off or lingering effect of your experiences with racism or other circumstances?

The real solution to all of these questions is simple: God has all power and His Hand is never too short (Isaiah 50:2) to pull you *up and out* of any undesirable situation or cleanse your mind of any impurities of racism or its spin-off or lingering effects (Romans 12:2; Ephesians 4:23-24). There is nothing too hard for God to accomplish for you and on your behalf (Genesis 18:14). Yes, the power of God's Holy Word will renew your mind, if you believe, receive and accept it and let it "soak" into your heart. God's victorious Holy Word, if you believe, receive and accept it in your heart as the truth, meditate on it day and night, apply it in your daily living (Joshua 1:7-9), and know it as the truth, it will *set* you free—and *make* you free (John 8:32,36). God's awesome grace and power are limitless, boundless, and sufficient (2 Corinthians 12:9) to take you out of any valley of poor self-image and your perception of low self abilities and capabilities, regardless of how deep the valley is. Racism may have tried to sink you in the valley of its oppression and injustice, but God's holy crane will lift you *up and*

*Place your footprint over Jesus Christ's as He walks you over the troubled waters created by racism.*

*out* to sure victory (Psalms 27:6; Psalms 34:6-7; Psalms 35:9-10; Psalms 37:12-15; Psalms 102:18-22).

On a daily basis, your experiences with racism try to deface you, but God's grace and power through Jesus Christ nullifies their effects on you. God remains the Greatest Builder and Rebuilder of your true view of your Christ-rooted image. He is the only original Designer of "you", and He alone can remold your mind back into His original masterpiece (Jeremiah 18:1-4) even after racism or other circumstances, racists or others has tampered with it (Genesis 1:27; Romans 8:29; Jeremiah 18:1-7). Jesus Christ replaces our carnal "self" with His spiritual nature; He renews and empowers our spirit and buffers our soul against the potential damaging effects of racism on our hearts and minds. What an awesome gift of His grace, Jesus Christ, Whom God has given to us. His grace that is more than sufficient for us and His strength that is made perfect in our weakness (2 Corinthians 12:9).

*Take a bold step of faith like Jabez did (1 Chronicles 4:10).*

If your view of your true image has been defaced or bruised by your experiences with racial prejudice and discrimination, accept Jesus Christ as your personal Lord and Savior, if you have not already done so, and start today to read and meditate on God's Holy Word to begin the process of daily renewing of your mind (Romans 12:2; Ephesians 4:23-24). Ask God's Holy Spirit in prayer with humility, sincerity and thanksgiving to help you with the process of renewing your mind daily. Let God give you new spiritual esteem, respect and confidence, and remold your view (in your heart and mind) of your true image, identity and nature in Jesus Christ, that would no longer depend on your carnal "self" or external circumstances to thrive, but on the truth of God's Holy Word. God will deliver you from needing to be validated by others—and fortify you with the power of His Holy Spirit—the power of His internal validation through Jesus Christ. God will deliver you from any other elements of self-deprecation. This means that He will also deliver you from self-negativity and self-destruction due to your experiences with racism. The demonic spirit of self-negativity and self-destruction attacks your mind, and it starts its destructive work also from within your mind, fueling your thoughts with negative and unhealthy beliefs and thinking about yourself and others. It can cause you to use negative words against yourself, or to receive negative words about yourself. If you allow this vile spirit of racism to defile your heart, it can pollute your thoughts and cause you to act contrary to God's Holy Word. When a person receives and does not reject the injustice and oppression of racism, it can cause him or her to internalize self-hate and hate for others who may share similar racial or ethnic identity. The evil spirit of racism can cause you to develop and exhibit feelings of racial hostility toward individuals

*You are a beautiful child of God, and you are dearly loved by Him.*

or groups of people who may share similar racial or ethnic identity, and others who may be of a different race, ethnicity, or even nationality.

If you allow God's Holy Spirit Who dwells in you, He will teach you how to rely on His spiritual validation through Jesus Christ, Whom you have received as your personal Lord and Savior, and through Whom God has justified you. Your true spiritual image in God would now depend solely on His original and only blueprint of who you truly are in Christ. You are a beautiful child (son or daughter) of the Most High God who is dearly loved by Him (Romans 8:35-39), is fearfully and wonderfully made by Him, and is a product of His marvelous works (Psalms 139:14).

*Ask God to make you a blessing to others.*

This book, "Footprints of Victory Over Racism: In the Secret Place With God—Volume 2", will guide you to and through the Number One Book, the Holy Bible—God's Holy Word of love, grace, mercy, faith, hope, justice, deliverance, faithfulness, healing, provision, and so much more, all of which are enveloped within Jesus Christ Who is in you. Through Him, you have God's limitless and boundless glory and awesome power for your life. Through Christ, God's holy promises for your life are way beyond the foul spirit of racism—and beyond measure for your purpose-driven life (Jeremiah 29:11; Isaiah 45:3). With God, nothing is impossible in and for your life (Luke 1:37).

From today, in the awesome Name of our Lord and Savior Jesus Christ, take a bold step of faith like Jabez did (1 Chronicles 4:10), and ask God to bless you and expand your coast and influence beyond the limitations of racism and your own expectations and imagination; ask God to anoint you by the power of His Holy Spirit and keep you from all evil, including the wicked spirit of racism; ask God to make you a blessing to others so that you will be a source of joy and not pain to others; ask God to keep you from evil so that you will not be used as a racist instrument against others by the odious spirit of racism. Let God's awesome glory walk you into daily victory over racism through the Footprints of our Lord and Savior Jesus Christ.

*Take a bold step of faith like Jabez did (1 Chronicles 4:10).*

Now, get ready to place your footprint over Jesus Christ's as He walks you over the "troubled waters" that the foul spirit of racism orchestrates against you, and which it manifests as racism-fueled challenges and obstacles in your physical environment. Jesus Christ nailed racism to the Holy Cross, and on your behalf, He canceled all of its charges against you (Colossians 2:14-15). He, Christ, has gained all victory over racism for you. This victory is yours in His awesome Name! (1 John 5:4)

Now, let's begin the powerful journey with Jesus Christ and walk in His holy Footprints to sure victory over racism.

---

Chapter References:

1. thefreedictionary.org or thefreedictionary.com
2. Leon F. Seltzer, Ph.D. (2008). Evolution of Self: On the paradoxes of personality. psychologytoday.com
3. http://www.rnceus.com/adol/self.htm
4. businessdictionary.com
5. Ormrod, J. E. (2006). Educational psychology: Developing learners (5th ed.). Upper Saddle River, N.J.: Pearson/Merrill Prentice Hall.
6. Bandura, A. (1994). Self-efficacy. In V. S. Ramachaudran (Ed.), Encyclopedia of human behavior (Vol. 4, pp. 71-81). New York: Academic Press. (Reprinted in H. Friedman [Ed.], Encyclopedia of mental health. San Diego: Academic Press, 1998).
7. http://edt2.educ.msu.edu/DWong/Archive-ProsemRDP/CEP900F04-RDP/Wilkinson-AcadSelfPercept.htm Academic Self-Perceptions of Elementary School Children: *The Relevance of Student Self-Perceptions to School Psychology.* Anna L. Wilkinson. Michigan State University. December 15, 2004. (**Note:** Definitions from this paper as indicated in this book "Footprints of Victory Over Racism" have been slightly modified without any changes made to the original intended meaning of the definition.)
8. dictionary.reference.com

# Introduction

Racism is a product of Satan's kingdom of darkness and it is orchestrated by "...principalities, powers, the rulers of the darkness of this age, by spiritual hosts of wickedness in the heavenly places..." (Ephesians 6:12) It is perpetrated and perpetuated by the odious spirit of racism, a demonic spirit that inhabits and influences willing human hosts here on Earth. Therefore, since racism has a spiritual origin, it must first be tackled and dismantled spiritually, before we can begin to see positive changes in the physical realm. How then should we born again believers subdue the foul spirit of racism and its evil activities that it continually stages against our lives? We are already engaged in spiritual warfare, an unseen spiritual battle that is raging between God's Kingdom of light and truth and the devil's kingdom of darkness and lies[1,2], and racism belongs to the latter. Remember that Jesus Christ defeated the devil and his evil powers of darkness by His death for all of humanity and glorious resurrection into Heaven, but the devil is not yet destroyed. The devil's destruction is yet to come as God has declared in Revelation 20:10. The ongoing spiritual warfare manifests in our minds, which is the main battle field, and in our lives. Spiritual warfare has been described as the "battle for the mind. [1] As a born again believer, you need to understand how to apply the spiritual weapons of warfare (Ephesians 6:10-18) against evil spiritual elements and domination[1,2], including the vile spirit of racism.

Offensive and defensive spiritual warfare is the key spiritual ammunition that nullifies the negative power of the evil spirit of racism (Ephesians 6:10-18). Offensive rather than defensive spiritual warfare against racism places you constantly on your spiritual guard. Offensive spiritual warfare means that with or without a manifested presence of any form of evil, including racist actions against you, you are continuously in prayer of faith, thanksgiving and worship; meditating on the Holy Word of God for guiding revelation of His Holy Spirit; in spiritual fasting; voicing out and declaring your victory over racism (and other evil manifestations) in the Name of Jesus Christ; praying for all racist individuals to change their ways; offering forgiveness to all racist individuals; consistently focusing your faith on the sovereign power of God, and targeting your fears and anxieties with your faith, and showing authentic spiritual courage and boldness in Jesus Christ. On the other hand, staging defensive spiritual war-

*You should apply offensive and defensive spiritual warfare against racism.*

fare against evil such as racism is when you are experiencing a racist situation and tackling it by spiritual warfare.

Be aware that the devil knows of God's victory that is yours to claim through Jesus Christ, and will attempt to distract you from God's awesome power through negative elements such as fear, doubt, anxiety, lack of faith, no prayer life, scripture-barren life, and so on. He could achieve this by filling your heart and mind with anger towards those who have hurt you by their racist actions. Therefore, while you are applying spiritual warfare against racism, bear in mind that the devil who is the main evil influence propagating racism against you in the spiritual realm, will have strategies to try to frustrate your spiritual warfare through a willing human host, that is, a racist person, in the physical realm.

*You should exercise your spiritual authority over racism.*

The enemy of your soul, the devil, could: spring up new oppositions and negative surprises against you in your physical environment; introduce new potential sources of worry and anxieties in other areas of your life; set up human baits for you in the environment that you are experiencing racism; try to use a racist person as a bait to make you lose your cool and lash out with the fire of your tongue or actions in a negative manner; heighten the actions of your racist offenders against you to discourage you from continuing with your spiritual warfare; attack your mind with negative, discouraging and unproductive thoughts of accepting defeat in your physical environments; bring up logical arguments in your mind about how you are overpowered, outnumbered and marginalized in your physical environment and how you could never gain victory over racism even with spiritual warfare; and stage psychological warfare against your mind using your experiences with racism.

There are so many other examples of counter attacks that could be mounted by the enemy of your soul, the devil, in the spiritual realm and that could manifest in the physical environment against you. This is why you must rely on your daily 'ammunition' against racism, that is, God's Holy Word, and not solely on your own human power. You must be fully clothed in God's armor against racism (Ephesians 6:10-18). If you have accepted Jesus Christ as your personal Lord and Savior, then you have God's holy armor, He Christ in you, against the vile spirit of racism and its wicked activities perpetrated and perpetuated through willing human hosts (1 John 4:4). You must learn to use God's Holy Word in the awesome Name of Jesus Christ, to pull down the walls of racism (2 Corinthians 10:3-6), shatter its stranglehold and uproot it from the evil source (Ephesians 6:10-18). Your total submission to God through Jesus Christ and spiritual warfare will force the evil spirit of racism and its physical elements to submit to God's Word and flee from you

*You must learn to use God's Holy Word to pull down the walls of racism.*

(James 4:7). As you engage in spiritual warfare against the wicked spirit of racism, God will surely send His chariots of fire to protect you and take charge over you as you encounter any racist situations (2 Kings 6:17).

Don't be intimidated by the devil, the enemy of your soul, who stages racist attacks against you through willing human beings. A defensive spiritual warfare should eventually become your daily offensive strategy that will keep your spirit in a heightened state of spiritual vigilance (1 Peter 5:8-9) against the negative spin-off or lingering effects of racism on you. You must constantly mount a spiritual attack (Ephesians 6:10-14) against the negative effects of racism by declaring God's Word of victory over them (Isaiah 40:8; Isaiah 61:1-3; 1 John 5:4). This way, you will exercise your spiritual authority over racism that God has already given you through Jesus Christ (Psalms 8:6; 1 Corinthians 15:27-28; Luke 10:18-19: John 16:33).

*You must constantly mount a spiritual attack against the negative effects of racism.*

For individuals who have over time allowed the foul spirit of racism to invade their soul, my hope is that this book "Footprints of Victory Over Racism: In the Secret Place With God—Volume 2" will help you successfully navigate the treacherous paths that racism creates for you. This book will reveal to you how to free your soul from the daily assaults and stranglehold of racism forever. You have the victory of Jesus Christ which He won for you and I and all of humanity (Colossians 2:14-15). For those of you who face the injustice and oppression of racism, it is my prayer that as you journey through this book and apply God's Holy Word against racism you will be freed forever from the wicked clutches of the evil spirit racism, in Jesus' Name, Amen.

Now, let's say the prayer of salvation (Romans 10:9-10) and receive Jesus Christ as our Lord and Savior (John 3:16) (if we have not already done so); for it is only through Him that we are able to approach God's throne of grace, and ask for help in time of need (Hebrews 4:16). It is only through Christ that we are able to defeat the world and racism that exist in it. (John 16:33; 1 John 4:4; 1 John 5:4).

---

Chapter References:

1. The Beginners Guide to Spiritual Warfare by Neil T. Anderson and Timothy M Warner. Copyright 2000. Published by Regal.
2. Victory in Spriitual Warfare: Outfitting Yourself For the Battle. Copyright 2011. Published by Harvest House Publishers.

# Plan of Salvation

On this day, ______________________, I, _________________ confess with my mouth that the Lord Jesus Christ is my personal Savior; I believe that He shed His precious Blood for me on the Cross of Calvary and that God raised Him from the dead for my eternal salvation. I repent of my sins and ask God for forgiveness through the mighty Blood of Jesus Christ.

On this day, _________________ by my faith, I, ____________________ believe that I am now saved by the precious Blood of Jesus Christ. I believe in the Triune God: God the Father, God's Son, Jesus Christ and God the Holy Spirit. I believe that in the Name of our Lord and Savior Jesus Christ, I will receive the baptism of God's Holy Spirit that will release from my heart the flowing rivers of Living Water, in Jesus' Name, Amen.

Thank you Father Lord God, for on this day, __________, in the Name of Jesus Christ, I, _________ am Born Again

## Scripture Meditation:

*"For God so loved the world that He gave His only begotten Son, that whoever believes in Him should not perish but have everlasting life."*
*– John 3:16*

*'But what does it say? 'The word is near you, in your mouth and in your heart' (that is, the word of faith which we preach): that if you confess with your mouth the Lord Jesus and believe in your heart that God has raised Him from the dead, you will be saved. For with the heart one believes unto righteousness, and with the mouth confession is made unto salvation."*
*– Romans 10:8-9*

*"He who believes in Me, as the Scripture has said, out of his heart will flow rivers of living water."*
*– John 7:38*

*"That which is born of the flesh is flesh, and that which is born of the Spirit is spirit. Do not marvel that I said to you, 'You must be born-again.'"*
*– John 3:6-7*

# Prayer after Profession of Salvation

Dear Glorious Heavenly Father, thank You that I am born again by the precious Blood of Jesus Christ. I accept my renewed spirit in Him.

Dear gracious Father, I thank You for making me aware that I have spiritual and mental shackles from my experiences with racism. Thank You for revealing to me all areas where I am shackled. Thank You for giving me total release and freedom from the intrigues of the foul spirit of racism. I reject the evil tradition of racism and all that it stands for. I forgive anyone who has hurt or offended me in any manner, including my racist offenders.

Dear precious Father, I believe that You have answered my prayers in the precious Name of Jesus Christ. In His awesome Name, Jesus Christ, our enabling grace from You, Lord God, I know that I have gained victory over any form of racial oppression and injustice.

Thank You, awesome Father, for Your marvelous rays of victory over racism on my behalf, and for Your limitless and boundless power within me through Jesus Christ, Amen.

## Scripture Meditation:

*"And whatever you ask in My Name, I will do, that the Father may be glorified in the Son. If you ask anything in My Name, I will do it."*
*– John 14:13-14*

*"Pray without ceasing; in everything give thanks; for this is the will of God in Jesus Christ for you."*
*– 1 Thessalonians 5:17-18*

*"And whenever you stand praying, if you have anything against anyone, forgive him that your Father in heaven may also forgive you your trespasses."*
*– Mark 11:25*

*"Until now you have asked nothing in My Name. Ask and you will receive, that your joy may be full."*
*– John 16:24*

*"Don't copy the behavior and customs of this world, but let God transform you into a new person by changing the way you think. Then you will learn to know God's will for you, which is good and pleasing and perfect."*
*– Romans 12:2*

*"I have been crucified with Christ; it is no longer I who live, but Christ lives in me; and the life which I now live in the flesh I live by faith in the Son of God, who loved me and gave Himself for me."*

*– Galatians 2:20*

# Partnership Prayer

I commit to spending quality time in prayer, worship and thanksgiving, and meditating on God's Holy Word, to receive His powerful and winning strategies for my daily victory over racism. This I shall do only by the grace of God, in the Name of our Lord and Savior Jesus Christ and through daily guidance by the Holy Spirit. I stand in agreement with my prayer partner(s) ______________________ believing that through the redeeming precious Blood of Jesus Christ, God has taken away the burden of racism, its reproach and yoke of destruction from all areas of my life. I stand in agreement with my prayer partner(s) __________________ believing that the precious Blood of Jesus Christ has permanently destroyed and removed the power of the burden of the foul spirit of racism in my life, in Jesus' Name, Amen.

______________________________________

Your Name

______________________________________

Prayer Partner's Name

*Jacyee Aniagolu-Johnson*

---

Dr. Jacyee Aniagolu-Johnson
(Author remains in agreement with you)

*"Again I say to you that if two of you agree on earth concerning anything that they ask, it will be done for them by My Father in heaven."*
*– Matthew 18:19*

*"It shall come to pass in that day that his burden will be taken away from your shoulder, and his yoke from your neck, and the yoke will be destroyed because of the anointing oil."*
*– Isaiah 10:27*

ꝏꝏꝏꝏꝏꝏ♦ ♦ ♦ ♦ ♦ꝏꝏꝏꝏꝏꝏ

## Introduction Quiz

1. True or false: offensive and defensive spiritual warfare in the Name of Jesus Christ is the key spiritual ammunition that nullifies the negative power of the evil spirit of racism. Explain your answer.

---

2. True or false: the devil knows of God's victory that is yours to claim through Jesus Christ, and will attempt to distract you from God's awesome power through negative elements such as fear, doubt, anxiety, lack of faith, no prayer life, scripture-barren life, racism, and so on. Explain your answer.

---

3. While you are in spiritual warfare, why does the devil spring up new oppositions and negative surprises against you in your physical environment?

---

4. Why and how must you prevent or avoid being intimidated by the devil, the enemy to your soul, who stages racist attacks against you through willing human beings?

---

5. Please describe one way that you can exercise your spiritual authority over racism that God has already given you through Jesus Christ?

---

∞∞∞∞∞∞∞∞∞∞∞∞ ♦ ♦ ♦ ♦ ♦ ∞∞∞∞∞∞∞∞∞∞∞∞

## Reflections:

______________________________________________

______________________________________________

______________________________________________

______________________________________________

∞∞∞∞∞∞∞∞∞∞∞∞ ♦ ♦ ♦ ♦ ♦ ∞∞∞∞∞∞∞∞∞∞∞∞

# CHAPTER 1: Christ-Rooted Strategies Against Racism

When you *truly* accept Jesus Christ as your Lord and Savior, you become spiritually positioned to receive God's Holy Spirit (John 7:38; John 20:20-22). As you live by faith in obedience to God's Holy Word (Romans 1:17), God will give you clarity of mind and purpose and excellence in your daily work that will raise you above the wiles and intrigues of racist schemes. Then racism will cease to be a limiting factor in your life—and God will remove or make irrelevant all racist obstacles before you; first in your mind and then in your own physical environment (Deuteronomy 7:21-24). God will level the mountains of racism being orchestrated against your life.

The existence of racism may never end, but in your own life, you can transcend the challenges, obstacles or difficult situations that those who perpetrate and perpetuate racism attempt to place before you. The mountain of obstacles and challenges orchestrated by your racist offenders that previously appeared weighty for you, would become featherweight and be removed by the power of God's radiance and glory.

Try Christ-rooted strategies against the evil spirit of racism and watch your fear of racism and its illicit schemes turn into your victory through a step-by-step walk with our awesome God. Yes, God will order your footsteps as you tread the treacherous paths that racism creates for you (Psalms 32:8). Through Jesus Christ and by the power of the Holy Spirit, you can advance against a troop of racists and scale racist barriers and wall erected to constrain and hold you back (Psalms 18:29; 2 Samuel 22:30). Through Jesus Christ, God has already given you power and authority over racism (Luke 10:17-19), if you just allow His holy light, His brilliant rays of victory to shine permanently within and through you.

*God will transform the mountains of racism into flattened miniature molds.*

Racism is a negative spiritual force that requires positive spiritual resistance and ammunition, God's Word, the Sword of the Spirit, to gain victory over it. Today, start by renaming "RACISM" to mean: "**R**esist (racism), **A**pply (God's Word), **C**reate (holy strategies), **I**nsulate (yourself with God's Word), **S**olidify (God's Word in you) and **M**anifest (holy victory). So, "**R**esist", "**A**pply", "**C**reate", "**I**nsulate", "**S**olidify", and "**M**anifest" against the foul spirit of racism to bring down the anointing power of God's Holy Word against racism." Therefore,

- **Resist** racism by adsorbing within your heart the truth about God's Word, which decrees that racism is wrong and contrary to His Word (Exodus 22:21; Leviticus 19:33-34; Zechariah 7:9-10; Mark 12:31; Matthew 22:39). Fill your mind with only thoughts, words and actions that are in accordance with God's Word, and cancel all things presented to you by racists because they are lies acting contrary to God's Word (2 Corinthians 10:3-6; John 8:44).
- **Apply** God's Word and armor as your spiritual ammunition against racism (Ephesians 6:10-18). Believe and verbalize the truth about God's Word that no weapon [including racism] formed against you shall prosper (Isaiah 54:17). Believe only who and what you really are in Jesus Christ—that you are fearfully and wonderfully made by God, a beautiful product of His marvelous works (Psalms 139:14).
- **Create** strategies against racism based on God's Word. Ask God's Holy Spirit to help you to create positive spiritual strategies against racism (Jeremiah 33:3). Don't battle any form of racism without first taking on the whole armor of God (Ephesians 6:10-18). Effective spiritual strategies include the following:

*God will level the mountains of racism being orchestrated against your life.*

do not confront racism without wearing God's full armor, the covering of Jesus Christ; going in prayer and fasting to call down the conquering power of Jesus Christ and the guidance of God's Holy Spirit within you; when dealing with racism, always listen to and follow the guidance [leadership, direction, supervision] and prudence [carefulness, forethought, good sense, cautiousness, discretion] of God's Holy Spirit within you; embrace God's Holy Spirit of truth at all times (John 16:13); walk with godly integrity in obedience to God's Word (Ephesians 4:1); don't go with the flow of carnal wisdom, but only go with spiritual wisdom that is in accordance with God's Word and guided by His Holy Spirit; let God take over your battles against racism (2 Chronicles 20:15). Never let unrighteous anger fuel your strategy or approach against racism.

- **Insulate** your heart and mind with God's Word against racism. You can only achieve this by meditating daily on God's Word and spending quiet and prayer time with God (Joshua 1:8).
- **Solidify** God's Holy Word in you. Know the Word of God and solidify it within your heart and mind and stand on it at all times. The absolute truth about God's Word will shield (Psalms 18:1-2; Psalms 91:4) and protect your heart and mind from the lies and deceit of racism (John 8:32,36; Ephesians 6:17; Psalms 18:16-19).

- **Manifest** only godly actions against racism (Ephesians 4:1). If you are angry about racism, let it be only righteous and not unrighteous anger (Colossians 3:8,10). If you have words to say let them be non-abusive and non-condemning words (Colossians 3:9); let your thoughts be godly thoughts of faith in God's ability to demolish any form of racism that you may be encountering.

**Chapter Quiz**

1. Why and how must you redefine racism and its attacks on your soul?

---

2. What steps must you take to create positive spiritual strategies against racism?

---

3. Why and how must you insulate your heart and mind against the evil spirit of racism and its nasty product racism?

---

4. Why and how must you solidify God's Word in you against the loathsome spirit of racism and its odious product racism?

---

5. Why and how must you manifest godly actions against the wicked spirit of racism and its vile product racism?

______________________________________________

∞∞∞∞∞∞∞∞∞∞∞∞ ♦ ♦ ♦ ♦ ♦ ∞∞∞∞∞∞∞∞∞∞∞∞

**Reflections:**

______________________________________________

______________________________________________

______________________________________________

______________________________________________

∞∞∞∞∞∞∞∞∞∞∞∞ ♦ ♦ ♦ ♦ ♦ ∞∞∞∞∞∞∞∞∞∞∞∞

# CHAPTER 2: Knowing Who You Are in Jesus Christ

Knowing who you are in Jesus Christ and understanding your spiritual nature in Him is the gateway to knowing God, His Holy Word, and His excellent purpose for your individual life. Your purpose is like an onion bulb. As you get to know God, more of Him daily through His Holy Word, He peels off the outer "onionskin", layer by layer, and gradually reveals the inner core, the "fresh juicy onion", which is where your true purpose lies. Your true purpose finds you as you seek God and place Him as Number One in your life (Matthew 6:33). Finding and knowing your purpose is a by-product of true spiritual knowledge, which is authenticated knowledge in Jesus Christ. Thus, authentic spiritual knowledge is a heavenly key to first, spiritual victory, and then, material success. When we lack or reject true spiritual knowledge we perish (Hosea 4:6).

True self-knowledge stems from authentic spiritual knowledge, deeply founded in the knowledge of God's Holy

Word, Which is God Himself, the Fountain and the original Source of all true knowledge. The only way to get to God the Father is through His Son Jesus Christ, Who is our Lord and Re-Redeemer and the only Mediator between God and us (1Timothy 2:5). God's Holy Spirit gives us deeper understanding of the knowledge of His Living Word; and from God Almighty through His Holy Word and anointing of His Holy Spirit in us, we obtain true wisdom. John 1:1 tells us that: "In the beginning was the Word, and the Word was with God, and the Word was God." (KJV), so God is His Word and His Word is God—He is inseparable from His Word. "And the Word was made flesh, and dwelt among us, (and we beheld his glory, the glory as of the only begotten of the Father,) full of grace and truth." John 1:14 (KJV)

*True knowledge does not automatically translate into power in our individual lives unless we apply it.*

Therefore, God's Holy Word manifested here on Earth in Jesus Christ Who lived as humanity even though He is divine; God offered Him as the Sacrifice and He (Christ) willingly laid down His life for the salvation of all humanity (John 3:16; John 10:17-18). So, for our sake, He was crucified, died and was buried, and by the power of God's Holy Spirit, He resurrected and ascended into Heaven (Acts 2:23-24; Acts 4:10; Acts 5:30-32). When we accept Jesus Christ as our Lord and Savior and begin to know God in a deep and intimate manner through His Holy

Word, He starts to reveal Himself to us—and also our true nature in Jesus Christ begins to unravel to us. God's Holy Spirit, if we allow Him, begins to guide and guard our thoughts, minute by minute, as He leads and guides us to all truth (John 14:26; John 16:13). Once we begin to receive authentic spiritual knowledge, understanding and wisdom from God's Holy Word, no form of racism could shake or rattle our inner core. This is a silent process that does not necessarily require spoken words or outward actions.

God's Holy Spirit directs true knowledge and understanding and is required for us to grasp authentic spiritual truth and their deeper revelation—and divine wisdom is necessary to effectively apply acquired spiritual knowledge. This kind of knowledge is critical because authentic spiritual truth has powerful positive earthly ramifications (John 8:31-36). Likewise, spiritual lies have negative consequences upon our hearts and minds, our individual lives, our communities, states, countries and the world as a whole (John 8:44). Believing spiritual lies builds a negative stronghold in our minds and keeps us bound both spiritually and mentally.

*Do you know who you are in Jesus Christ?*

Perhaps, you have heard the popular saying, "Knowledge is power." Yes, true knowledge is indeed power; however, in reality, even true knowledge does not automatically translate into power in our individual lives unless we believe, receive and apply it. So, I believe that true knowledge must first be acquired, believed, received, and then be applied before it can be transformed into power. Community health workers will tell you that you evaluate the success of a health education program, such as preventing transmission of an infectious disease, by evaluating if the information presented and provided to the people resulted in the appropriate behavioral change or actions required to prevent transmission of the disease. There may be individuals who obtained the information, but did not believe and receive it, and did not take the necessary steps required to prevent transmission of the infectious disease. So, even though they had the right information, it did not empower them because they failed to believe, receive and apply it. Some of these individuals may still end up becoming infected with the infectious disease even though they had the right information to prevent this from happening. I believe that true knowledge is transformed into invisible powerful and positive energy that manifests into something tangible only when it is applied effectively. So, it is possible to have a lot of knowledge and still lack power, if you don't believe, receive and apply it; but it is not possible to believe, receive and apply good knowledge without acquiring its power.

*True spiritual wisdom means application of a godly attitude in a godly course of action.*

The truth is that racism and the odious spirit behind it originated from Satan's kingdom of darkness, and they oppose God's Holy Word. The truth is also that racism is wrong and

God expects us to reject the evil tradition of racism which has become part of the day-to-day culture in many societies (Mark 7:7-9; Colossians 2:8; Matthew 15:9). God promises us that if we know the truth (His Holy Word), it shall *make* us free (John 8:32,36 KJV). Some people like to quote this Bible verse as "…it shall *set* us free;" but there is a difference between being *set* free and being *made* free. A prisoner who is physically released from a prison, that is, set free, may still be bound or locked up in his or her mind, in the captivity of the sin or the crime he or she committed which caused them to be convicted and imprisoned in the first place. Such a person may be physically free but he or she is still locked up with invisible chains and a criminal mindset. If he or she does not truly believe and receive Jesus Christ and know the truth of God's Holy Word and let it soak their heart and mind, they will not be made free of the captivity of sin, their minds will never be unlocked from the world of crime, and they are likely to commit yet another crime and return to prison. On the other hand, if such a person truly believes and receives Jesus Christ as their personal Lord and Savior, and believes and receives God's Holy Word as the truth, and immerses their heart and mind in it, the power of the truth of God's Word will begin renew their mind and break them free from the captivity of sin, from the world of crime and its viscious cycle. They will not just be set free from

*God promises us that if we know the truth (His Holy Word), it shall make us free (John 8:32,36).*

the physical prison, they will be made free forever—and they will never return to the prison from where they were set free.

Do you know God's holy truth, His Word, which is the only real and authentic truth? Have you received God's holy truth in your heart as the only real and authentic truth? Have you allowed God's Holy Word to renew your mind daily (Romans 12:2)—and do you live by God's holy truth and apply it in your daily living (James 2:20)? Rest assured that if you know the truth—God's Holy Word, through Jesus Christ, it will indeed *make* you free from the lies of the devil and you will surely acquire its holy power for daily victory in your life. It will empower you to stand firm in your rightful position in Jesus Christ against the vile spirit of racism.

*God will give you new vision on how to see and deal with racist schemes.*

Another necessary ingredient for transforming true spiritual knowledge into spiritual power is wisdom. The Bible tells us, "By wisdom a house is built, and through understanding it is established; through knowledge its rooms are filled with rare and beautiful treasures." (Proverbs 24:3-4, NIV) True spiritual wisdom means applying godly knowledge in a godly attitude and course of action. Therefore, we should apply a godly attitude in a godly course of action against racism. To gain daily victory over racism, we have to acquire and apply true spiritual wisdom against it.

How can we become spiritually empowered against the vile spirit of racism? How can we acquire God-directed wisdom against racism? How can we become spiritually larger than racism? Can we really become greater than ills such as racism through our carnal nature? Can we achieve this merely by ourselves without God's supernatural guidance, protection and wisdom? The truth is that we have the authority and power of Jesus Christ in us to tread on the serpent and scorpion spirit of racism (Luke 10:18-19). Through Christ, we have the enabling and empowering Holy Spirit of God in us to reach higher spiritual grounds. We obtain God's supernatural guidance, protection and wisdom from God's Holy Word, by the revelation power of the Holy Spirit and under the covering of the precious Blood of Jesus Christ.

Racism has a spiritual origin and so must also be dealt with spiritually first. It is only someone with a death wish who confronts a lion without having the skills to defend him or herself. A hunter who travels the forest without a loaded gun runs the risk of not returning home either intact or at all. If you challenged or confronted racism within the status quo of any society without God's holy protection, it would devour you like a wild beast tears apart its hunted game. Why?—because the hench demons orchestrating racism and the vile spirit behind it, are highly vicious and destructive and their primary goal to is to steal

*Racism has a spiritual origin and so must also be dealt with spiritually first.*

from you and to kill and destroy you (John 10:10a). Through Jesus Christ who has abundant life for you (John 10:10b), God's Holy Word and Holy Spirit empower and equip you against racism and can build spiritual strength and ammunition within you to make you spiritually greater than the evil schemes of the vile spirit of racism (1 John 4:4). When you receive and meditate on God's Holy Word, the power of its divine illumination will give you new vision on how to see and deal with racist schemes being orchestrated against you (Psalms 119:105; Romans 12:2; Ephesians 4:23-24).

God's Holy Word, the Sword of the Spirit (Ephesians 6:17), illuminates our mind and becomes a lamp onto our feet (Psalms 119:105). It is like the "holy rod" which God used to demonstrate His power and might to Pharaoh and his fellow Egyptians, on behalf of the Israelites who were experiencing great oppression and injustice in Egypt (Exodus 2:20,21; Exodus 7). God's Holy Word illuminates your path as you journey through life, enriching you with divine wisdom which shines His brilliant light on your path (Psalms 119:105). His righteous justice determines that His everlasting goodness will overcome any evil that you encounter, and that He will do this for anyone who believes in Him through Jesus Christ, regardless of their race, ethnicity or nationality. Despite racism that exist

*Racism can and must be brought to submission to God's Holy Word.*

around you, God will make all things work together for your good because you love me and you are called according to His purpose (Romans 8:28).

God's Holy Word empowers us through Jesus Christ to pull down strongholds like racism (2 Corinthians 10:3-6). Racism is a stranglehold against your life that can and must be torn and broken down by the power of God's Word; it can and must be brought to submission to God's Holy Word (2 Corinthians 10:3-6). Surely, you can apply the Sword of the Spirit to dismantle the evil activities of the odious spirit of racism which he orchestrates against your own life (Ephesians 6:10-18).

*God's Holy Word empowers us through Jesus Christ to pull down strongholds like racism.*

**Five Essential Steps to Obtain True Spiritual Wisdom:**

1. In your heart and by your own words and actions, love God above all things (Deuteronomy 6:5), believe and receive His Holy Word; accept Jesus Christ as your Lord, Savior and Redeemer, and receive the Holy Spirit (John 3:6-7,16; Romans 10:9-10).

2. Desire and pursue a close relationship with God through Jesus Christ, in prayer, praise and worship, and seek Him by meditating daily on His Holy Word (Matthew 6:33), and prac-

tice spiritual fasting whenever possible, especially as guided by God's Holy Spirit. In the Name of Jesus Christ, pray, offer praise and thanksgiving and worship God always.

3. Invite, believe, receive and accept the Holy Spirit into your life through Jesus Christ, trust and believe Him as your permanent partner and guide to help you live holy and navigate through life each day, and to guide you to all truth (John 16:13). Meditate daily on God's Holy Word and let it soak your heart and mind (Joshua 1:7-9; John 15:7).

4. Activate your mustard-seed faith (Matthew 17:20) and feed it to grow with God's Holy Word, and step into faith-fueled actions. Ask God in prayer for understanding, knowledge and especially wisdom (James 1:5); ask Him to help you to hear His Holy Word and retain it in your heart and obey it (Romans 10:17; Joshua 1:7-9); and nurture and grow your faith by His Word (2 Peter 3:18). Live by faith (2 Corinthians 5:7; Hebrews 11:6) and let your faith reflect in your actions (James 2:20).

5. Ask God for true spiritual wisdom (James 1:5-8) for dealing with racism. Ask Him for His spiritual strategies for applying true spiritual knowledge with wisdom against any form of evil or deceptive knowledge, including the lies of racism.

ထထထထထထ♦ ♦ ♦ ♦ ♦ထထထထထထ

## Chapter Quiz

1. Do you know who you are in Jesus Christ? Explain your answer.

---

2. True or false: knowledge automatically gives you power? Explain your answer.

---

3. How can you transform true spiritual knowledge to wisdom power against racism?

---

4. How do you receive God's power of illumination? Explain your answer.

---

5. How can you break down the stronghold of racism? Explain your answer.

---

ထထထထထထ♦ ♦ ♦ ♦ ♦ထထထထထထ

**Reflections:**

---

---

---

∞∞∞∞∞∞∞∞ ♦ ♦ ♦ ♦ ♦ ∞∞∞∞∞∞∞∞

# CHAPTER 3: Affirming the "You's" of True Self Knowledge

If you are still striving to become a victor over racism and not see yourself as a victim of it, start affirming daily the simple "you's" of true self-knowledge that is based on authentic spiritual knowledge from God's Holy Word. This will gradually settle in your subconscious mind and begin to spring up into your conscious mind whenever you encounter racism. This is a simple Christ-rooted strategy for gaining your spiritual and mental victory over racism. Remember that by the power of Jesus Christ within you, you are more than a conqueror of any form of racism (Romans 8:37). God wants you to see yourself daily as a victor and not a victim of any form of racism that may be directed against you. In your own words, recite these "Yous" of self-knowledge:

- I am deeply loved by God (John 3:16; Romans 8:35-39; 1 John 4:9-12; Romans 5:8; Galatians 2:20; Proverbs 8:17; 1 John 3:1)
- I am lovely and elegant in God's eyes —yes, I am beautiful in the eyes of God (Genesis 1:27; 1 Timothy 4:4-5; Ecclesiastes 3:11).
- I am born equal to every other person (Genesis 1:27; Acts 17:26; Romans 2:11; Galatians 2:6; Galatians 6:3; Romans 12:3).
- I am neither superior nor inferior to any other person (Genesis 1:27; Acts 17:26; Romans 2:11; Galatians 2:6; Galatians 6:3; Romans 12:3).
- I am created and born wealthy because I have many talents, and even one of these talents when utilized properly and efficiently, through the guidance of God's Holy Spirit, in the Name of Jesus Christ, can make me highly successful (Matthew 25:14-30; Luke 19:12-28; John 14:12).
- God has a unique and excellent purpose for my life (Jeremiah 29:11).
- God's positive spiritual power, which He has infused within me through Jesus Christ, is greater than any negative challenge I may face outwardly (1 John 4:4).
- The awesome power of God, which is in me, is greater than racism that exists is in the world. Therefore,

through Jesus Christ, I am greater and larger than racism (1 John 4:4).

- I can conquer racism with God's boundless and limitless power that resides within me through Jesus Christ (Romans 8:37).
- On my behalf, Jesus Christ defeated the foul spirit of racism which comes from the devil, the father of all lies (Colossians 2:14-15; Luke 10:17-20; John 8:44).
- Satan, the father of racism and its vile spirit behind it, is the father of all lies and no truth can ever come from him (John 8:44). Therefore, the vile spirit of racism is a liar; and it lies when it calls me a mishap, coincidence, mistake or shame through its willing human hosts (racists).
- My specific race and ethnicity are God's own special and lovely choice for me (Genesis 1:26; Jeremiah 1:4-5).
- My race or ethnicity is exactly as God intended me to be (Genesis 1:26; Jeremiah 1:4-5).
- I am determined to and can run every mile of my life's journey with excellent success (1 Corinthians 9:24-28; 2 timothy 4:7; Hebrews 12:1-2; Isaiah 40:28-31).
- Only I can stop myself from successfully completing my life's journey by relinquishing the power within

me to racism or other challenges (Luke 9:62; Galatians 6:9).

- Yes, I believe that through Jesus Christ my spirit is greater than any form of racism and empowers my soul to triumph over racism (1 John 4:4).
- I am an intelligent human being created in the perfect Image of the Triune God. Through Jesus Christ and by the power of God's Holy Spirit, I am an efficient and hardworking person, and I am determined to succeed in life through God's instruction, guidance and direction. Racism cannot stop me from becoming a success! (1 Corinthians 9:24-28; 2 timothy 4:7; Hebrews 12:1-2; Isaiah 40:28-31)
- Through Jesus Christ, I have become a full citizen of God's Kingdom (Ephesians 2:19).
- I have accepted myself as the beautiful person God intended and made me to be in His excellent image (Genesis 1:27).
- I shall continue to grow in Jesus Christ and by the guidance of God's Holy Spirit, Who dwells within me, to achieve greater works here on Earth to the glory of God (2 Peter 3:17-18; Philippians 1:9-10; John 14:12).
- God can and will remold me and help me to correct my flaws and imperfections as I grow to know Him more intimately (Jeremiah 18:1-6; 2 Corinthians 3:18).

- I am a work in progress in God's holy hands, perfected in Jesus Christ. God loves me so much that He gave Jesus Christ for my salvation (John 3:16). Nothing and absolutely nothing can ever separate me from God's love (Romans 8:35-39).
- I am simply a neat bundle of God's spiritual power and I have the authority and power of Jesus Christ in me to overcome racism (Romans 8:37; Luke 10:18-19; 1 John 5:4).

God has validated your worthiness through Jesus Christ and the odious spirit of racism cannot change this spiritual truth. God will reveal to you His unique purpose for your life when you draw near to Him; and He too will also draw near to you (James 4:8). If you seek God, you will find Him when you search for Him with all your heart and soul (Jeremiah 29:13; Deuteronomy 4:29), and He in turn will reveal more of Himself to you in His own way. His holy light, His brilliant rays of glory, are for your life's victory and not for your defeat. Now, shake off the dust of defeat from the soles of your feet. Immerse your heart and mind in the Holy Word of God, and begin to learn the real and only truth about who you are in Jesus Christ. This will come through a gradual process of revelation of God's Holy Word by His Holy Spirit Who dwells within you. Let God's absolute truth, His Holy Word, free your soul

*Shake off the dust of defeat from the soles of your feet.*

from captivity, unshackle your mind from mental slavery and oppression (Isaiah 61:1-3; Psalms 47:3; Psalms 102:19-20; Psalms 103:6), and flood you with His spiritual knowledge and wisdom (Proverbs 2:6; James 3:17; Colossians 2:3). So, your mind will never again be fooled by lies about your worthiness, nor will you ever again rely on validation from others. God's validation is complete and enough for you through Jesus Christ. Let His brilliant rays of victory in you radiate permanently from within your spirit and soul.

> *By the Power of Jesus Christ within you, you are more than a conqueror of any form of racism.*

**Chapter Quiz**

1. Why must you affirm the "You's of true self-knowledge? Explain your answer.

___

2. If Jesus Christ in you is greater than racism, what does that make you? Explain your answer.

___

3. You were created and born wealthy? Explain this statement.

___

4. True or false: your specific race or ethnicity is an abomination before God, so you should be ashamed of it? Explain your answer.

---

5. True or false: your specific race and ethnicity are God's own special and lovely choice for you? Explain your answer.

---

∞∞∞∞∞∞◆◆◆◆◆∞∞∞∞∞∞

**Reflections:**

---

---

---

---

∞∞∞∞∞∞◆◆◆◆◆∞∞∞∞∞∞

# CHAPTER 4: Positioning God's Spiritual Bolts Against Racism

Why do we sometimes try to explain our way through our experiences with racism by harboring thoughts like "there is not much that I can do; this stuff has been here a long time and is not going away any time soon"? Do thoughts like these prepare us for spiritual and material victory over racism or do they position us for defeat by beliefs that convince us that we are victims instead of victors of it? Why do we turn deaf ears to God's faithful Word that empowers, strengthens and protects us, and can renew and spur our mind into triumph over any adversity, including racism? Is He [Jesus Christ] Who is in you not greater than he that is in the world (1John 4:4)? Are you not more than a conqueror through Jesus Christ (Romans 8:37)?

If God has already called us everything good through Jesus Christ, why do we open our minds to negativity (1Timothy

4:4-5)? Why do many of us on the receiving end of racism consciously or subconsciously accept daily unfair and unjust experiences as the way things have been and are more than likely to remain? Why do we willfully or by ignorance accept as part of the course of our lives virulent seeds of hostility that are directed against us? Where are our spiritual lightning bolts against racism (Psalms 18:12-14; 144:6)?

When I say spiritual lightning bolts, what do I really mean by that? These are God's spiritual actions of justice on behalf of those made righteous through Jesus Christ. Spiritual lightning bolts are God's actions in response to our praise, holy worship, prayers and spiritual fasting when we are facing evil, injustice, oppression or wickedness like racism from powers that seem mightier than us (Acts 16:25-35). His spiritual actions have visible, invisible, temporary and eternal consequences. When God releases His spiritual bolts of lightning, no one can stop or reverse them except through repentance by the Blood of Jesus Christ. Spiritual lightning bolts are also God's invisible armor and army, which fight against evil on our behalf (2 Kings 6:17; Daniel 10:12-13); they empower us to overcome challenges, obstacles and adversities that are beyond our human strength and capabilities.

*...One who is in you is greater than the one who is in the world (1 John 4:4).*

In the Book of Esther, Mordecai, Queen Esther and all the Jews prayed and fasted (Esther 4:15-17) and spiritually reversed the wicked murderous plan of the racist Haman (Esther 7). This is an example of what we discern from the Word of God to mean "Spiritual Warfare." The Book of Exodus gives the account of the destruction that came upon the ancient Egyptians who had enslaved Israelites for over four hundred years, and who refused to heed to God's command through Moses to release His people; but there was a set-time for their freedom: God declared it and it happened. Many other accounts of God's release of people under bondage and His protection of them, clearly show that God has declared a loud and resounding NO to any form of oppression, prejudice or discrimination and will put an end to it (Exodus 3:7-8; Acts 10:28-29).

God's power and might are seen in all things around us, and this includes the intricate and meticulous design of nature and its flaunting extravagance. His spiritual bolts of lightning appear in a silent thunderhead with immeasurable speed that breaks down racial barriers, obstacles and challenges that humans foster against one another; against manifestations of spiritual wickedness in high places. Here is the good news—God's power, in the Name of Jesus Christ, has defeated racism on your behalf (John 16:33; Colossians 2:14-15); and if you would receive and believe it in your heart and declare it, you too would overcome racism in the world (1 John 5:4).

*Renew, guard and guide your mind with God's Holy Word.*

You need to believe and receive Jesus Christ in your heart as your Lord and Savior to be able to position yourself to apply God's Holy Word—the Sword of the Spirit, as spiritual lightning bolts against racism. You need to "Put on the whole armor of God, that ye may be able to stand against the wiles of the devil." Ephesians 6:11 (KJV) For you to be able to resist any negative effects of racism on your mind, you must constantly guard your heart with the power and truth of God's Word (Proverbs 4:23); and daily, you have to renew your mind with God's Word (Romans 12:2; Ephesians 4:23-24). This means that you must guard against becoming either a spiritual or mental "victim" of racism or a human instrument for fostering it against others. For whatever you allow to be sown in your heart will also be sown in your mind, thoughts, emotions, will and resolve, and will become the source that fuels your beliefs, attitude, actions, personality, behavior, and character (Proverbs 4:23).

*The power of Jesus Christ in you is greater than the spirit of racism.*

Apply spiritual warfare by continuous faith-fueled prayer, immersing your heart in God's Word, performing spiritual fasting, declaring God's Word and its power, praising, worshiping, thanking God and living by faith. Spiritual warfare against racism is the only way to uproot the negative spirit behind racism to render it powerless against you (Ephesians 6:10-18). God's supernatural power released in you, by the anointing power of His Holy Spirit in the Name of our Lord Jesus Christ, will bring down the forces of evil and darkness of the obnoxious spirit of racism. Let Jesus Christ abide in you and He in you (John 15:3-4). Let God's Word, the Sword of the Spirit, always abide within you and let His divine power be released in you. God's awesome power through Jesus Christ and His Holy Spirit within you would then become your constant spiritual weapon; a precision-perfect spiritual missile against the evil spirit of racism, and the only real power that would bear good fruit in your life (John 15:3-4). Allow the flawless power of God's Holy Word to shatter, demolish and consume in a blazing fire of everlasting destruction the evil activities, wicked intent, motives and evil plots of the vile spirit of racism (Hebrews 12:28-29; Revelation 12:10-12).

*Allow the flawless power of God's Holy Word to shatter, demolish and consume the vile spirit of racism.*

∞∞∞∞∞∞♦ ♦ ♦ ♦ ♦∞∞∞∞∞∞

**Chapter Quiz**

1. 1John 4:4; Romans 8:37: What do these two Scripture verses tell you about God's power in you over any adversity, including racism?

---

2. What do you understand to be God's spiritual bolts of lightning against racism?

---

3. According to Acts 10:28-29, what do you believe is God's stand against racial prejudice and discrimination?

---

4. Exodus 3:7-8: What does this Scripture tell you about God's stand against oppression, injustice, discrimination and wickedness, including racism?

---

5. John 16:33: What does this Scripture tell you about God's conquering power over racism in the world on your behalf?

---

6. 1 John 5:4: What does this Scripture tell you about God's conquering power in you through Jesus Christ to overcome racism that exist in the world around you?

---

∞∞∞∞∞∞♦ ♦ ♦ ♦ ♦∞∞∞∞∞∞

**Reflections:**

---

---

---

---

∞∞∞∞∞∞♦ ♦ ♦ ♦ ♦∞∞∞∞∞∞

# CHAPTER 5: Praying Down God's Spiritual Bolts Against Racism

From my own personal experiences with racism, there are crucial steps that you can take to release God's spiritual bolts of lightning (Psalms 144:6) to work on your behalf against any form of subtle or overt racism. These steps are based on principles that are deeply embedded in God's Word and they are:

1. Love God above all things.
2. Accept Jesus Christ as your Lord and Savior.
3. Accept God's Living Word and His Holy Spirit within you, and meditate on God's Holy Word daily.
4. Have unquestioned belief in the power of God, which can accomplish all things for you through Jesus Christ; believe in the power of God's Holy Word over racism.
5. Have unwavering faith and trust in God; believe God, His Holy Word and also in Him. By faith focus your faith

against racism. By faith declare and "fire" God's Holy Word against racism.

6. Accept and receive God's Kingdom Power within you; this means that you will allow God through Jesus Christ to become the only sovereign authority over your life.
7. Live your daily life consecrated to God's Holy Word. Live in the world, but be not of the world (John17:14) and follow the guidance of His Holy Spirit.
8. Develop a deep and honest relationship with God through daily prayers, praise, worship and thanksgiving; be open to the true knowledge of His Word, and practice spiritual fasting as His Holy Spirit directs you to.
9. Practice daily forgiveness of your racist offenders. Basically, in prayer, report them to God in the Name of Jesus Christ, and then forgive them.
10. Practice daily release of your unrighteous anger, and offer Christ-rooted love to your racist offenders, as you ask God through Jesus Christ to demolish all forms of racism that you experience.

I have tried to practice the ten steps daily when I encounter racism and other challenges, and God has never failed me in releasing His spiritual bolts of lightning on my behalf. Even as I still struggled with one or more of the ten keys, He fired against my circumstances (Psalms

*God does not wait for us to achieve perfection before He acts on our behalf.*

18:12-14; Psalms 78:47-49; 2 Samuel 22:13-15). I believe that because of His awesome grace and love for us, He releases His spiritual bolts of lightning on our behalf as long as our daily effort in serving Him remains genuine. God does not wait for us to achieve perfection before He acts on our behalf. If He did, it would be impossible for anyone of us to partake of His blessings. Jesus Christ is the only perfect Man; because He is the Son of God Who visited the Earth in the form of man. God's grace, Jesus Christ, has qualified us for His mercy, forgiveness and deliverance. We have God's victory over racism through Jesus Christ.

God's spiritual bolts of lightning against racism are a spiritual phenomenon, which is hard to explain but better experienced. In quiet and mysterious ways, God will begin to remove the human hosts of the odious spirit of racism that are in your way, break down glass and concrete ceilings in the workplace, and give earned promotions and raises even during a budget crunch. Yes, God's spiritual bolts of lightning accomplish mighty things with quiet splendor. There is no man, woman, situation or demonic power that has the ability or power to obstruct God's spiritual bolts of lightning. They are God's heavenly-guided missiles that are Earth-bound with flawless precision and an unblemished rec-

*There is no man, woman, situation or demonic power that has the ability or power to obstruct God's spiritual bolts of lightning.*

ord. This spiritual power of God manifests in our natural realm with a perfect force that is beyond our total comprehension. His spiritual bolts of lightning come in a silent thunderhead of immeasurable speed and break down racial barriers, obstacles and challenges that humans foster against one another which are the manifestations of spiritual wickedness in high places. When God releases His spiritual bolts of lightning against racism that you face, you can be assured of His victory on your behalf.

**Chapter Quiz**

1. True or False: The right spiritual approach to fighting racism is to confront racism carnally, "grab the bull racism by its horns" and drag it down. Explain your answer.

---

2. True or false: If you rage back at your racist offender matching his or her mean words and actions with yours, God's power will rain down His spiritual bolts of lightning against racism on your behalf. Explain your answer.

---

3. True or False: Fasting and praying is a waste of time. To deal racists a final blow you must fight them one-on-one so they know that you are not intimidated by their racist actions. Explain your answer.

---

4. What is your understanding of God's spiritual bolts of lightning?

---

5. True or False: The right spiritual approach to fighting racism is to first confront the foul spirit of racism by powerful, faith-fueled spiritual warfare; by firing the power of God's Holy Word against it; by drawing nearer to God through prayer, thanksgiving, praise, worship and spiritual fasting; by asking for and receiving God's divine instructions on how to deal with it. Explain your answer.

---

∞∞∞∞∞∞♦ ♦ ♦ ♦ ♦∞∞∞∞∞∞

**Reflections:**

---

---

---

---

∞∞∞∞∞∞♦ ♦ ♦ ♦ ♦∞∞∞∞∞∞

# CHAPTER 6: Redefining Subtle and Overt Racism with God's Word

Your daily experiences with racism are a part of the trials and tribulations that our Lord and Savior Jesus Christ forewarned us that we would face in the world (John 16:33). However, in the midst of such adversities, He also asked you and I to "…be of good cheer; I have overcome the world." John 16:33 (KJV) So we should be cheerful and happy because He has overcome the world on our behalf. We should not allow the troubles of the world to overwhelm us because He [Jesus Christ] has overcome the world and all of its trials and tribulations [including racism] for us. If racism is overwhelming you, ask God through Jesus Christ to activate in you His overcoming power in Jesus Christ (Romans 8:37), which He has already placed within you by His Holy Spirit. Lay down the burden of racism at the Feet of Jesus Christ (Matthew 11:28) and let His Footprints carry yours over the treacherous paths that racism charts for you; Let Him lead you to still waters and restore your soul (Psalms 23:2-3; Psalms 37:23). It is the power of God's Holy Spirit within you that will guide you into the only truth of who you are in Jesus Christ—and transform your mind into a Christlike mind (Romans 12:2; Ephesians 4:23-24) with the absolute truth of God's Holy Word abiding in you. It is the power of Jesus Christ in you (1 John 4:4), that will raise you above racism and all of its negative effects, and take you into triumph and victory—and give you a life of complete success despite racism and all of its ills around you.

In your personal life, you must re-define subtle racism with God's Word to: **S**ubmit, **U**ndertake, **B**ind, **T**hrash, **L**oose and **E**xpose racism by the power of God's Word. **S**ubmit and subject racism to the Word of God (2 Corinthians 10:3-6); undertake racism with the Word of God (Psalms 35, 37, 91); **B**ind racism with the Word of God (Matthew 18:18); **T**hrash racism with the Word of God (Jeremiah 51:20; Isaiah 41:14-16); **L**oose racism to destruction by the power of our Lord Jesus Christ (Revelation 12:10-12); and **E**xpose racism with the Word of God (Hebrews 4:12-13).

Likewise, you must re-define overt racism with God's Word to: **O**vertake, **V**eto, **E**liminate, **R**ebuke/**R**enounce, and **T**hrash racism by the power of God's Word. **O**vertake racism with the Word of God (Psalms 18:29); **V**eto racism with the wisdom of God's Word (John 8:44, 10:10; Isaiah 54:17) **E**liminate racism with the power of God's Word (Exodus

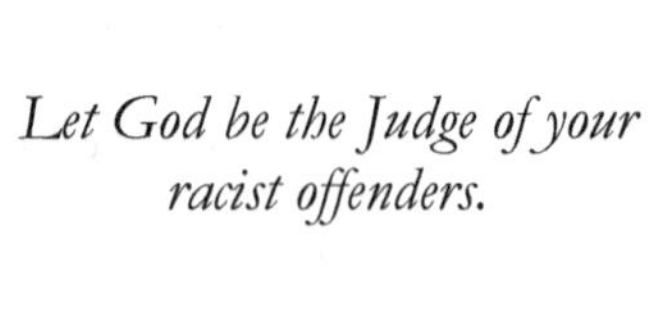

14:13; Luke 10:17-19); **R**ebuke and **R**enounce racism with the Word of God (Luke 10:17-19; John 8:44; Luke 8:24-26; Mark 4:35-41); and **T**hrash racism with the Word of God (Jeremiah 51:20; Isaiah 41:14-16).

Use the Sword of the Spirit, which is the Word of God, to reverse the plans of racists who target you (Ephesians 6:10-18). Use daily, a godly plan of action against racism: start with thanksgiving in prayer, offer repentance and spiritual fasting, worship and praise, and by name, bring your racist offender(s) in prayer before God in the Name of Jesus Christ, offer forgiveness to such racist offender(s), and then let go and allow God to handle the situation and reveal to you if and how He wishes you to respond. Remain obedient to God's Holy Word and let Him become an Enemy to your racist enemies and an Adversary to your adversaries (Exodus 23:22). Let God be the Judge of your racist offenders and let Him bring down the "Pharoah" who is working against your career, progress, promotion, ministry, and so on.

*Overtake racism with the Word of God (Psalms 18:29).*

Through Jesus Christ, God has positioned you victoriously to gain triumph over racism. As you pray, use God's Word as your spiritual ammunition, because His Holy Spirit fires with precision at evil, including the vile spirit of racism and its human recruits. The precision of the fire power of the Holy Spirit will demolish their evil plans against your life. Let your daily battles become God's and cease to be yours (2 Chronicles 20:17). Let your racist offenders become enemies and adversaries of God and let Him oppose them on your behalf (Exodus 23:22; Psalms 35). No man or woman, evil spirit, or any other being, seen or unseen, can withstand God's opposition.

If you trust God, He will either change the racist situation you are facing or change your response to the situation—or do both. God will begin to deal with you spiritually to change your daily responses to any form of racism that may be directed against you. He will cleanse your mind of any defeating negative thoughts of victimization that you may have allowed habitation within you—so you begin to see yourself as a victor rather than a victim of racism (Romans 8:37; Psalms 144:1-2; Numbers 13:30). Then, through his Holy Spirit Who dwells within you, He will give you renewed spiritual wisdom and knowledge through revelation of the knowledge of His Holy Word. At the same time, God will begin to deal with your racist offender(s), through whom the ultimate enemy of your soul, the devil, is working to destroy you, a child of God, using racist actions.

*Seek God in prayer and worship and He will deliver you from those who may seem too strong for you.*

If you are feeling oppressed and manipulated by the foul spirit of racism, it is time for you to fire and expel it with the power of God's Word in you through Jesus Christ. Let God's Holy Spirit empower you to be a spiritual "fire ball" against racism. Know that God does not ignore any form of oppression, and He would not ignore the injustice of racism that you may be facing now (Exodus 3:7-10). As you encounter the perpetrators of racism, seek God in prayer and worship and He will deliver you from those who may seem too strong for you in your physical environment (Psalms 18:16-19, 91:14-16, 144:7-8). He is a God of equity and justice (Psalms 103:6; Psalms 111:7), and He will not allow racism or any other form of oppression to consume you for you are His child and co-heir to His Kingdom through Jesus Christ (Romans 8:14-17).

"Jesus Christ the same yesterday, and today, and forever." Hebrews 13:8 (KJV) and God is our Father Who does not change (Malachi 3:6). He is the same God who delivered Israelites from the brutal and harsh treatment of their oppressors in Egypt (Exodus 3:7-8), and He will deliver you from the stranglehold of the odious spirit of racism, and the wicked activities of its racist human recruits. God will deliver you from the pangs of racism because He is a God Who does not change (Malachi 3:6; Hebrews 13:8), lie or relent on His promises (1 Samuel 15:29). God will surely redeem your life from any form of oppression or violence, and racism is not an exception (Psalms 103:6)

*No power is greater than God's supernatural power!*

∞∞∞∞∞∞∞∞∞∞ ♦ ♦ ♦ ♦ ♦ ∞∞∞∞∞∞∞∞∞∞

## Chapter Quiz

1. How does the following definition of **OVERT** RACISM help you apply God's Word against overt racism and the spirit of racism: **O**vertake, **V**eto, **E**liminate, **R**ebuke/**R**enounce, and **T**hrash?

---

2. How does the following definition of **SUBTLE** RACISM help you apply God's Word against subtle racism and the spirit of racism: **S**ubmit, **U**ndertake, **B**ind, **T**hrash, **L**oose and **E**xpose?

---

3. In what ways could God work on your behalf in order to help you deal with racism and the loathsome spirit of racism? Name and discuss at least two ways.

---

∞∞∞∞∞∞∞∞∞∞ ♦ ♦ ♦ ♦ ♦ ∞∞∞∞∞∞∞∞∞∞

## Reflections:

---

---

---

---

∞∞∞∞∞∞∞∞∞∞ ♦ ♦ ♦ ♦ ♦ ∞∞∞∞∞∞∞∞∞∞

# CHAPTER 7: Daily Positive Affirmations Offset the Vile Spirit of Racism

Now you have true spiritual knowledge, that is, the knowledge that you are equal in creation and humanity to any man or woman; you have a spirit that is greater than the negative actions and words of any prejudiced and racist individual; your race or ethnicity, whatever it may be, is a special blessing from God your Creator; Jesus Christ has defeated the evil spirit of racism and racism on your behalf; you can conquer racial prejudice and discrimination in any situation anywhere once you keep the spiritual warfare within you alive. You must make Christ-rooted positive affirmations to yourself daily—believe them in your heart so that you will eventually overcome the mental and physical battles that are within and around you. By the power of the Holy Spirit of God who dwells within you through Jesus Christ, God would either alter your response to the negative events around you or He would alter the negative circumstances around you. The amazing wonder of God is that He often sneaks in the surprise of altering both, when you submit your life and circumstances, entirely to Him.

A positive spiritual attitude requires that you remain focused on God (Matthew 6:33) and His awesome purpose for your life (Isaiah 26:3-4). Through your spirit, which remains empowered by the Holy Spirit of God, you will constantly be reminded by Him that you are a beautiful creation of God and more than a conqueror of all challenges and obstacles through Jesus Christ. In response to any form of racism, the first and most important change must come from within you. If you allowed your spirit to be awakened by the Holy Spirit of God, He would direct your heart, mind and thoughts, and your inner and outward responses to your environment. Then you would also develop the right positive inner and outer responses to negative situations and environments. You would develop the ability to successfully fight-off the mental strongholds of racism and their potential spin-off or lingering effects. The subsequent changes that would come would be your mental and manifested physical victory over the individuals who direct racism against you. When the predicted negative responses from you to prejudiced and racist attitudes fail over a period of time, you would frustrate the

*You are a beautiful creation of God and a conqueror of all challenges and obstacles.*

perpetrator into change. This change does not mean that he or she would suddenly stop being prejudiced or racist, but change would come in the form of discontinued efforts to degrade or disrespect you by deliberate actions or attitudes fostered by his or her intrinsic habit of practicing racism. Now, receive this daily affirmation as yours as you continue on your path of victory over racism.

## Daily Affirmation

I affirm that through Jesus Christ, the powerful radiance of God's Kingdom Power glows within and through me daily. God's holy light, His brilliant rays of victory, empower me daily through Jesus Christ with the guidance of His Holy Spirit. Daily, I see the manifestation of God's glory and power in my life clearing my paths of any roadblocks, obstacles and challenges placed by racism.

*If you allowed your spirit to be awakened by the Spirit of God, He would direct your soul, your inner and outward responses to your environment.*

Daily, I am more than a conqueror of any form of racism. I affirm boldly with the power of the Holy Spirit of God within me that I am under God's guidance daily. I affirm that His guidance through the paths of my journey will take my hard and sustained labor to great heights of success. I know that I am able, I can, and I have won the ultimate spiritual, mental and physical victory over racism. Thank you, Lord, for your limitless and awesome power in me.

**Chapter Quiz**

1. True or false: There is at least one man or woman who is either superior or inferior to you. Name at least one and explain in what way such a man or woman is either superior or inferior to you. State a Scripture to support your answer.

2. True or False: Jesus Christ has defeated racism and the foul spirit of racism on your behalf. Explain your answer.

3. True or false: In response to any form of racism, the first and most important change must come from within you. Explain your answer.

∞∞∞∞∞∞ ♦ ♦ ♦ ♦ ♦ ∞∞∞∞∞∞

**Reflections:**

∞∞∞∞∞∞ ♦ ♦ ♦ ♦ ♦ ∞∞∞∞∞∞

# CHAPTER 8: Do You Feel Spiritually or Mental Defeated by Racism?

Do you feel spiritually or mentally defeated by racism? Many who are the targets of racist activities feel and become spiritually and mentally defeated by racism because they lack true spiritual knowledge (Hosea 4:6), wisdom and power of God's Holy Word, or they lack true faith in God's Word and power to overcome racism in their individual lives.

Do you believe that on your behalf, Jesus Christ has overcome racism that exists in the world? Are you one of those on the receiving end of racism who believe in God, but do not believe Him and His Word? If you are, then perhaps, you lack readiness to engage racism in spiritual warfare.

You see, you cannot stand in Christ's victory for you without believing the promises of God's Word (1 John 5:4). You cannot become an overcomer of racism without standing in the victory that Christ gained for you. You must believe that God has supernatural power over all evil, including racism.

If you are not spiritually vigilant, you could unknowingly allow your inner person to be invaded and eroded by the wicked lies of the foul spirit of racism, which attacks you through the negative words and actions of other individuals, and institutionalized racist cultures and systems. In First Peter 5:8, Apostle Peter admonishes us to "be sober, be vigilant; because your adversary the devil walks about like a roaring lion, seeking whom he may devour." (NKJV) The foul spirit of racism can devour your soul if you allow it by not being spiritually clear-headed and watchful.

*Racism can be a destructive weapon against your soul, if you allow it.*

Internalizing your daily experiences with racial prejudice and discrimination can become a mental or physical burden that can consume your entire being. In some cases, such a burden can lead to depression or physical ill health or both. Also, if you lack true spiritual knowledge about your real nature and identity in Jesus Christ, then out of spiritual ignorance, you could allow your mind to be subject to racism, its evils and lies, that which racism seeds within anyone who is spiritually complacent ; anyone who is "carnally-minded" and not spiritually-minded (Romans 8:5-7).

In Apostle Paul's letter to the church at Ephesus (Ephesians 6), he admomishes us to: "Be strong in the Lord and in his mighty power." (Verse 10 NLT) How? By faith, we are to "Put on all of God's armor so that you [we] will be able to stand firm against all strategies of the devil." (Verse 11 NLT) By our faith in Jesus Christ, we receive the full armor of God [in Christ], Who embodies the belt of truth, the body armor or breastplate of righteousness, the Gospel of peace, the shield of faith, the helmet of salvation, the Sword of the Spirit, that is the Word of God, and the spirit of unceasing prayer (Ephesians 6:10-18). Our faith in God through Jesus Christ empowers us to stop the fiery darts of the devil against our lives, through various forms of evil, including racism. The odious spirit of racism wants to control your inner man, but it cannot because you are shielded by the covering of the precious Blood of Jesus Christ; so it targets your soul, especially if you are carnally-minded. If the vile spirit of racism cannot control your inner man, it won't be able to control your soul, that is your heart, mind, emotions, thoughts, will and resolve, and it won't be able to control your attitude, actions, personality, character and behavior.

*God's design for you is victory.*

To be able to defy racism, we must submit our inner man entirely to God's Holy Word, and Holy Spirit dwelling in us through Jesus Christ (James 4:7). To defy racism, we need to be spiritually-minded (Romans 8:6). When we meditate on and abide in God's Holy Word, His power will abide in us through Jesus Christ (John 15:7); and we become spiritually-minded and empowered with God's full armor [He Christ in us], to deal victoriously with racism which sets before us daily challenges and obstacles (Ephesians 6:10-18).

Do you sometimes feel emotionally harassed or oppressed by the foul spirit of racism and its willing human recruits? The vile spirit of racism and its racist human hosts are not authorized by God to mock, harrass, attack, oppress or condemn you (Isaiah 54:15)? God is our Creator and even with His immeasurable power, He does not oppress us. So, what gives humans, His creations, the right or authority to oppress one another? If you allowed your experiences with racism to invade your heart, they could become daily destructive weapons that could weaken your mind and your entire soul, limiting and keeping you bound in spiritual and mental defeat, and eventually defeating your career and life; such defeat is not God's design for your life—God's thoughts for you are of peace and not of evil, for you to have excellent future and hope (Jeremiah 29:11); and His plan for you is victory. Yes, you can tap into the awesome power of His Holy Spirit within you through Jesus Christ Who has made you more than a conqueror of racism (Romans 8:37), and Who has overcome the world and its evils on your behalf (John 16:33).

*The vile spirit of racism and its racist human hosts are not authorized by God to mock, harrass, attack, oppress or condemn you (Isaiah 54:15).*

Nothing stays the same indefinitely except the Triune God (God the Father, the Son Jesus Christ and the Holy Spirit) and His Holy Word. God's universal law of nature dictates that the cycle of things will eventually change. However, the change that you have direct control over must come first, because it comes from within you, propelled by your faith in God's Holy Word and the anointing of His Holy Spirit in you. This change that you have control over is mostly your own personal response to your external environment, including your experiences with racism. When you are spiritually-minded, you respond to racism based on God's Holy Word. God will give you true spiritual knowledge of who you really are in Jesus Christ. True spiritual knowledge is the main key to the wisdom door that will lead you first to inner spiritual victory, and then to physical victory over any obstacle or challenge will follow.

True spiritual knowledge is the knowledge of God that leads to authentic self-knowledge and wisdom and this transforms you into a conqueror through Jesus Christ Who gives us strength daily. This knowledge is the only true knowledge of who you are and the purpose for your being and creation. This is knowing that you have the God-given right to be here in this world; to have joy and be whole; to be successful in anything that you put your mind to and to work hard for it, which is according to God's excellent will and purpose for your life (Jeremiah 29:11).

*God's spiritual victory for you will trigger your own mental and physical victory over racism.*

You have to come to understand that the attitudes, behavior and actions of a prejudiced and racist individual are an assault on your soul. However, your spirit which is now renewed in Jesus Christ, and empowered by the Holy Spirit, is higher and greater than any such assault (1 John 4:4). Your spirit, once fortified by God's Holy Word and empowered by the Holy Spirit through Jesus Christ, will then trigger a change on the outside; the change that you do not have direct control over. Basically, God's spiritual victory for you will trigger your own mental and physical victory over racism in your surrounding environment. This means that God's mantle of victory for you over racism lies solely with and within you, and also begins within you.

*God's mantle of victory for you over racism lies solely with and within you!*

**Chapter Quiz**

1. True or false: God's Word wants you to dwell on the negativity of racism and the hurt and pain it inflicts upon you? Explain your answer based on Philippians 4:6-8.

2. True or false: You should apply Ephesians 6:10-18 in your spiritual warfare against racism and the vile spirit of racism. Explain your answer.

3. 1 John 4:4: What does this Scripture tell you about the power of God in regards to your victory over racism?

_______________________________________________

4. 1 John 4:4: How can you apply this Scripture to gain victory over racism and the foul spirit of racism?

_______________________________________________

∞∞∞∞∞∞♦ ♦ ♦ ♦ ♦∞∞∞∞∞∞

**Reflections:**

_______________________________________________

_______________________________________________

_______________________________________________

_______________________________________________

∞∞∞∞∞∞♦ ♦ ♦ ♦ ♦∞∞∞∞∞∞

# CHAPTER 9: Our Spiritual Rock Jesus Christ

Jesus Christ is our immovable spiritual Rock Who sets us on a solid and true permanent spiritual Foundation (Matthew 7:24-27, 16:18). Our faith and belief in Jesus Christ gives us the Foundation of true spiritual courage to press on against racism and other life's challenges with the power of the Holy Spirit of God Who dwells within us. In the absence of true spiritual Foundation—Jesus Christ, our spirit becomes unprotected from the fiery darts of evil like racism.

We would never think of not fortifying the natural and physical environments where we live or not securing our properties: our homes, cars, computers and other electronics, offices, merchandise and so on. With today's high technology inventions, we have choices on what types of protective devices that we can use. Often we try to keep our knowledge up-to-date with new devices on the market so that we can keep pace with the changing technology and stay at least one step ahead of burglars and fraudsters. On the one hand, we invest so much time and money in protecting perishable properties and things in our natural environment. However, on the other hand, we spend little or no time on eternal spiritual things that give life to our inner man and these are far more important than anything we may own in the natural realm. Therefore, we leave our soul wide open to receive negative assaults that permeate us in a manner that is destructive to our hearts, minds, thoughts, emotions, will and resolve. How many of us fortify our soul with the Word of God against the effects of racist assaults that we encounter?

The assaults of racism easily rank as one of the most destructive negative forces on our hearts and minds. Throughout history and in our times such assaults have destroyed and continue to destroy many who are not spiritually equipped to deal with them. We are all born with great potentials and yet so many of us fail to attain great heights, because we allow our souls to become vulnerable to the daily assaults of oppressive, unjust and wicked acts like racism. Many of us who are targets of racism yield to racist lies that we are inferior and under achievers. We, not being spiritually equipped to handle deceptive lies and tricks of racists, also yield to their negative and destructive actions against us. Ultimately, we may loose faith in God, our Maker, and

*Our faith and belief in Jesus Christ gives us the Foundation of true spiritual courage.*

in ourselves, and as well as in others from whom we could draw positive spiritual energy, focus and direction.

There is no doubt that without the awesome protective power of God in our lives, racism has the potential to become a very negative, distracting and destructive tool on our hearts, minds, thoughts, emotions, will, resolve, attitude, actions, behavior, character and personality. Without the protective covering of God's Holy Word by the powerful Blood of Jesus Christ, our hearts, minds, thoughts, emotions, will and resolve yield to the negative and destructive forces of racism. In the process, we become vulnerable to untruthful negative thoughts about who and what we are not. We begin to see ourselves through the eyes and negative views, words and actions directed against us by prejudiced and racist persons within our society, and we allow their attitude and actions to invade our hearts, minds, thoughts, emotions, will and resolve. We begin to listen to such subtle untruth like our race is bad; our skin is ugly, we are unattractive, our brain is smaller; we are less or not intelligent; we are not educated or capable of being highly educated; our excellence deserves less or no reward; we are unequal to another; crime is an integral part of us; we are ultimately prison-bound; we are statistically at higher risk of failure and so on.

*The assaults of racism easily rank as one of the most destructive negative forces on our minds.*

Dear child of the Most High God, reject such racist lies and open up your heart and mind to receive true spiritual knowledge, the knowledge of the absolute truth of God's Holy Word within your heart, and invite in the Holy Spirit of God to reveal to you its deeper meaning. The revelations of God's Holy Word by His Holy Spirit will illuminate your own heart and mind (Psalms 119:105) with His glowing search lamp, His holy light of perfect truth. It is this search lamp that will deeply penetrate your heart and mind, and those of others to expose (Hebrews 4:12-13) and bring to your knowledge clarity about the racist situations that you may be experiencing and the hidden motives and intent of your racist attackers. The Holy Spirit will search deep into all areas of your heart and the hearts others (Proverbs 20:27), and will reveal to you all truth, misconceptions and intent about you and others. He will empower you with godly strategies for your protection from issues like racism and its lies, and give you spiritual and material triumph over them (Psalms 91:14-15). If you desire to gain permanent victory over racism, you need to receive, know and believe God's Holy Word to develop Christ-rooted strategies that will empower and fortify you against it. The awesome, revelation power of God's Holy Word will unravel the truth to you that:

*God's Holy Spirit will empower you with godly strategies for your protection from issues like racism.*

1. Your race or ethnicity, whatever it is, is beautiful and is God's perfect choice for you;
2. Your skin color, shade or tone, however dark or light it is, is lovely—and your skin is exquisite;
3. Your brain is God's right size for you and you are an intelligent person; therefore, you have the capability to become highly educated, and are positioned and empowered to achieve great works in the awesome Name of Jesus Christ (John 14:12);
4. Your hard work and excellence deserves reward and promotion which God will award you (Psalms 75:6-7; 1 Corinthians 3:6-7);
5. You are equal to every other person; therefore, you are neither superior nor inferior to any human being (Genesis 1:27; Galatians 6:3; Romans 2:11);
6. You are not prison-bound for Jesus Christ has made you free and you are free indeed (John 8:32,36; Isaiah 61:1-3);
7. God's most accurate statistics have declared that you are not at higher risk of failure in life; He has great plans for your life (Jeremiah 29:11);
8. The power of God's Holy Word is in you through His Son Jesus Christ and His Holy Spirit (John 15:1-8). Therefore, use it to declare that the foul spirit of racism and its human recruits, that is, racists, are liars! (John 8:44);

9. You have the authority and power of Jesus Christ in you to trample the evil activities of the vile spirit of racism and its willing racist human hosts (Luke 10:18-19); and

10. By faith in Jesus Christ, declare your victory over the odious spirit of racism and its willing racist human hosts (1 John 5:4)

**Chapter Quiz**

1. Who is your eternal spiritual Rock and immovable Foundation? Explain your answer.

---

2. How should you fortify yourself spiritually against the vile spirit of racism and its willing racist human hosts? Explain your answer.

---

3. Philippians 4:6-8: How can you apply this Scripture to ward off any negative effect of racism on your heart, mind, thoughts, emotions, will and resolve?

---

4. Who is your daily spiritual Rock and immovable Foundation against all forms of evil, including racism? Explain your answer.

---

5. What does John 8:44 tell you about the evil spirit of racism and its recruits, racists? Explain your answer.

______________________________________________

∞∞∞∞∞∞∞∞∞∞ ♦ ♦ ♦ ♦ ♦ ∞∞∞∞∞∞∞∞∞∞∞

**Reflections:**

______________________________________________

______________________________________________

______________________________________________

______________________________________________

∞∞∞∞∞∞∞∞∞∞∞ ♦ ♦ ♦ ♦ ♦ ∞∞∞∞∞∞∞∞∞∞∞

# CHAPTER 10: Purge your Mind of Racist Lies

Has racism labeled you a "second class citizen" or a "lower class citizen"? Whoever told you that your race is inferior and that you are a second-class citizen lied to you! (John 8:44) Henceforth, please understand with spiritual clarity and wisdom that anyone who tries to make you believe that they can limit your career and life's success is also lying to you. The only person who can limit your career and life's success is you when you allow someone to convince you otherwise. So, if you believe that anyone can limit your career and life's success, then they can; and if you believe they cannot, then they cannot (Proverbs 23:7a). Do you have activated faith and spiritual authority through Jesus Christ to believe that your career and life's success lie solely in the holy Hands of God because of His promise to you in Jeremiah 29:11?

It is important to recognize that racism has the negative power to transform you into a weakened vessel with a defeated mind and an unrighteous angry spirit, and it could dictate the state of your heart, mind, emotions, thoughts, will and resolve and belief about who you are, if you allowed it. As our conscious mind opens up to awful racist lies, our subconscious mind begins to register them first as thoughts, then as beliefs. Through this negative process, we begin to draw more negative thoughts into our mind and the circle of negativity gets even larger. As years go by, subconsciously, we gradually relinquish the potential within us that God our Creator freely gave to us. By and through our own thoughts, we would have willed away our wonderful and great destiny that God designed for us even before we were conceived in our mothers' wombs (Jeremiah 1:4-5).

*The only power that racism has over you is what you allow it to have.*

The negative effects of racism could spur you into a cycle of acceptance of a permanent state of defeat. You could easily forget God's true label on you of being a "first class citizen" through Jesus Christ, a new creation in Him (2 Corinthians 5:17; Galatians 2:20), and not a person who accepts the carnal label of an "inferior being" or a "second or lower class citizen." Don't allow this to happen to you because you are precious in God's sight. He has honored and loved you (Isaiah 43:4). Through Jesus Christ, God had always been there to overtake your negative situations if you would open the door to your heart (Revelation 3:20). If you allow God's Holy Spirit to be your guiding light, He will give new spiritual life to your mortal body (Romans 8:11). God's Holy Spirit will give you great counsel and guidance and lead you to all truth (John 16:13) and no lies. The Holy Spirit will empower you to prosper through your skills and talents, and earnest hard work, and make you victorious over racist intrigues, schemes and evil machinations that are directed against you. If you obey God's Holy Word, He will become an Enemy to your enemies and an Adversary to your adversaries (Exodus 23:22)—He will make you the head over racism and not the tail (Deuteronomy 28:13). God will raise you above racism such that you will always have the upper hand over racist plots and schemes that are directed at you. He, God, our Heavenly Father, will always only raise you above, and never beneath any evil orchestration (Ephesians 1:19-23; Psalms 2:7-9, 3:5-8). Hallelujah!

*God expects you to maximize use of your talents, gifts and abilities to the glory of His Name.*

If you were not empowered by the Holy Spirit of God to reject racism, it would begin to define your belief about who you are, and your state of happiness, joy, hope, peace, love, success and life's fulfillment. Recognize that discriminatory actions that stem from racial bias are demonic attacks on your soul and you must resist such attacks. Do not be afraid of racism, but rather, submit yourself first to God, then by the power of God's Word and His Spirit Who dwells within you, resist the devil and his hench-demon spirit of racism and he will flee from you (James 4:7).

The only power that racism has over you is what you allow it to have. Also, know that this power is illegal and unauthorized by God. Those who attack you do so without God's permission (Isaiah 54:15). The foul spirit of racism attempts to enslave you with its lies and intimidation but Jesus Christ set you free from the entanglement of all evil and demonic influences such as racism (John 8:32,36). Do not allow yourself to be entangled once again with the yoke of bondage of racism (Galatians 5:1). Therefore, nothing and absolutely nothing should you ever allow enslave your mind. The only thing that you are to be a "slave" to is God's Holy Word and righteousness through Jesus Christ (Romans 6:17-18).

*Do not be afraid of racism, but rather, resist it with the power of God's Word and His Spirit that dwells within you.*

The truth is that God is your awesome, beautiful and wonderful Creator and is the only One Who can place limitations on you, if He wishes; He has chosen not to, but rather, He has given you and every child of His unique gifts, talents, abilities and potentials to invest properly—and guess what? God expects you to maximize the use of your talents, gifts and abilities to the glory of His Name here on earth and not to waste or hide them (Matthew 25:14-29). God's Word makes it clear that He, our Heavenly

Father, will not accept any excuse from us for not using our talents and abilities properly here on Earth (Matthew 25:14-29); He will not accept the excuse that our experiences with racism or other challenges was our justification for not trying, for accepting our temporary failures as permanent situations, or for our giving up prematurely and not completing any task that He has given us (Luke 9:62). Through Jesus Christ, God has also taken off any limitations on the possible heights of our achievement that other humans, our own mind or other circumstances in our environment have placed on us. He validated us through the Blood Covenant with His Son, Jesus Christ, our Savior and Redeemer. Through Him God's awesome light, power, grace and guidance dwell within our own spirit.

*Now is the time for you to purge your mind of racist lies.*

Stop at this very moment and recall the many negative thoughts you have had and even believed about yourself. In reality, can you honestly say that these thoughts represent who you really are or were they what another person made you to believe about yourself? Did these thoughts truly originate from you, or are they what society or other circumstance made you believe of yourself? Now is the time for you to purge your mind of racist lies; purge your mind of these negative thoughts and reclaim the only true spiritual knowledge revealed to you in God's Holy

Word through Jesus Christ and by the revelation knowledge of the Holy Spirit Who dwells within you.

We must understand that the purging of our minds and thoughts can only be successfully achieved first by true knowledge of God's Holy Word, that is, God Himself—our Creator. We must also come to a point of understanding the excellence and magnificence of His boundless love for us through Jesus Christ (John 3:16; Romans 8:35-39). Apostle Simon Peter recognized and acknowledged who Jesus Christ really is and Christ revealed more of Himself [the Rock] to Peter and the promise of the power of the Kingdom Keys: "You are the Christ, the Son of the Living God", Jesus then revealed to Peter who he [Peter] truly was: "Blessed are you, Simon Bar-Jonah for flesh and blood has not revealed this to you, my Father who is in heaven. And I also say to you that you are Peter, and on this rock I will build My church, and the gates of Hades shall not prevail against it. And I will give you the keys to the kingdom of heaven, and whatever you bind on earth will be bound in heaven, and whatever you loose on earth will be loosed in heaven." " (Matthew 16:15-19). You see, the gates of Hades will not prevail against you you because you are a member of Christ's Body, the church. The vile spirit of racism is a product of Hades and will never prevail against you.

*God's spiritual knowledge and wisdom empower and sustain you.*

When you acknowledge Who Jesus Christ is—the Son of God and your Lord and Savior, then through Him and His Holy Spirit within you, God will let you know who you are in Christ, and through Him [Christ], He [God] will release in you the awesome fire power of His Holy Spirit to gain triumph over all evil, including challenges like racism. God's spiritual knowledge and wisdom empower and sustain you and reveal His faithful Word and promises to you.

*Cast the burden of your daily experiences with racism at the Feet of Jesus Christ.*

Daily, you need to cast the burden of your daily experiences with racism at the Feet of Jesus Christ Who has all authority over evil and has given you power to defeat evil (Psalms 55:22; Matthew 28:18; Luke 10:18-19). With true spiritual knowledge, you will begin to understand the unlimited boundaries of the awesome power of God, which lies quietly within you through Jesus Christ (Ephesians 1:18-23). God never willed your heart, mind, thoughts, emotions, will, resolve, dreams or aspirations to be controlled by the lies, deception or wickedness of anyone, including any prejudiced and racist person. Through Jesus Christ, He, God, willed you to be more than a conqueror of any such negative force or evil that you may encounter, including racism (Romans 8:37). Claim this holy truth for yourself—it is yours to keep forever!

ꝏꝏꝏꝏꝏꝏ♦ ♦ ♦ ♦ ♦ꝏꝏꝏꝏꝏꝏ

## Chapter Quiz

1. Discuss at least one approach which is based on the Bible that you can apply to purge your mind of racist lies.

---

2. How can you protect your conscious mind from receiving the lies of the despicable spirit of racism?

---

3. How can you protect your subconscious mind from receiving and storing the lies of the foul spirit of racism?

---

4. If you are not sure who you are, what is one sure way to discover who you are and how can you go about getting to know who you truly are?

---

5. Mathew 16:15-17: What does this Scripture tell you about how to discover who or whose you are?

---

6. Mathew 16:15-17: What is the significance of this Scripture in your spiritual battle against racism?

---

ꝏꝏꝏꝏꝏꝏ♦ ♦ ♦ ♦ ♦ꝏꝏꝏꝏꝏꝏ

**Reflections:**

---

---

---

---

∞∞∞∞∞∞∞ ♦ ♦ ♦ ♦ ♦ ∞∞∞∞∞∞∞

# CHAPTER 11: Carnal Superiority or Inferiority is a State of Spiritual Ignorance

God's Holy Word should abide in us. "If you abide in Me, and My words abide in you, you will ask what you desire, and it shall be done for you." (John 15:7) If God's Word does not abide in us, we will not be able to exercise the power of our faith in Jesus Christ and we will not possess His authority and power over evil and demonic powers like the foul spirit of racism (Luke 10:19).

If you lack God's Holy Word in you, the negative power of racism could manifest in or against you. If you are not empowered by the Holy Spirit of God through Jesus Christ to reject racism, it could begin to define what you believe about who you are, and your state of happiness, joy, hope, peace, love, success and life's fulfillment based on the rules and standards of others, the society or the world in general. Recognize that discriminatory actions that are pervasive in society stem from ethnic or racial biases and are demonic attacks on your soul and you must resist such attacks with the absolute truth of God's Holy Word. Do not be afraid of racism, but rather, resist it with the power of God's Word and His Holy Spirit Who dwells within you.

If you are not steadfast in your faith and spiritually vigilant in dealing with racism, it would convince you that you are less worthy and valuable than what God created you to be (1 Peter 5:8-9). Consciously or subconsciously, you would internalize such lies and validate them within your heart and mind, and project those lies onto others around you. Your spiritual fight against racism must be constant and unrelenting because it is a devourer of the human mind, thoughts, emotions, will and resolve, hopes, dreams and aspirations (1 Peter 5:8-10).

Remind yourself daily that you are a creation of an awesome God Who never creates any inferior being. You are created in God's own excellent Image as a human being. We humans are mere mortals and the only man or woman who is superior to another is one who will not die and rot (Psalms 49:10-12). The only man or woman who is superior is one who will not stand in judgment before God, and such a person does not exist (Hebrews 4:12-13). When we feel superior or inferior to any person, we are

*If you are not empowered by the Holy Spirit of God to reject racism, it could begin to define what you believe.*

in a state of spiritual ignorance (Hosea 4:6). It is a weapon of deceit that the devil often uses successfully through one individual against another because he knows how much God abhors arrogance and feelings of superiority (Daniel 5:20; Obadiah 1:3; Isaiah 2:11, 13:11, 23:9; Proverbs 16:5,19; Galatians 6:3).

Education, social class, wealth, race, ethnicity, country of birth, citizenship or other distinction does not make anyone inferior or superior. Superiority or inferiority complex is a lie of the devil (John 8:44). A rich man is neither superior nor inferior to a poor man. Money does not make anyone superior and lack of money does not make anyone inferior because money cannot purchase life and money cannot prevent anyone from going to the grave one day (Psalms 49:5-12). After we die, our spirit having been redeemed in Jesus Christ returns to God (1 Corinthians 15:54), while our mortal flesh rots in a grave under the earth, and we receive a new glorious body (Philippians 3:20-21). So, the mortal flesh of a rich man or woman dies and rots. A poor man or woman, regardless of their earthly status, dies and rots. All men and women of all races, ethnicity and shades die and rot (Psalms 49:10-12, 89:47-48). Who among these men or women are truly inferior or superior to the other and what is the basis of their claim of inferiority or superiority? The answer to this question should be clear to you by now—no one is inferior or superior to anyone. Spiritually ignorant persons have

*Spiritual victory always defies all odds.*

created a racial or ethnic hierarchy to convince individuals or a race or ethnic group of either their superiority or inferiority. Many believe these lies and based on their belief of inferiority to others will give away the greatness of their being to mediocrity or even failure. Others based on this false belief, feel superior and operate throughout their lives as a cruel menace to so many whom they suppress and oppress with their societal powers treating them as unequal in a society that should truly be made of equals. Before God's eyes all human beings are equal in creation and in dignity and humanity. All men and women must stand in judgment before God for their actions—everyone with no exceptions! (Hebrews 4:12-13).

To entertain negative words, actions or attitudes of racist and prejudiced individuals in your mind and thoughts, is to respond to their negative perceptions of whom you are and not to true spiritual knowledge, which is the true reality of whom you are in Jesus Christ. To entertain such negative words, actions, attitudes in your mind and thoughts is to dissipate and disable your inner spiritual power and focus; giving away God's rays of victory within you, and thus empowering the prejudiced and racist individual(s) against you. Your goal should be to invite God permanently in your life in the Name of Jesus Christ and He would empower you through His

*When we feel superior or inferior to any person, we are in a state of spiritual ignorance (Hosea 4:6).*

Holy Spirit Who dwells within you. Then you could claim what is already within you through Jesus Christ—God's awesome grace, power and brilliant rays of victory.

It is up to you as an individual to stage a relentless resistance in your spirit, that is, spiritual warfare against oppression and injustice like racism. This is your spiritual warfare against the devil's design of racial inequality among human beings, adopted by and operated through racist persons, groups and institutions. This spiritual resistance can be sustained once your spirit remains fortified by the power of God's Holy Word and His Holy Spirit Who dwells within you. This is not a physical but a spiritual battle. It is a "fight" that is necessary because the alternative is giving up and accepting the lies of a racist society or any racist individual(s) to prevail over your life. When you are engaged in a spiritual battle wearing God's full armor, Jesus Christ in you (Ephesians 6:10-18), you are shielded by God's invisible and invincible army, and you become God's powerful majority, although you may be outnumbered in the physical environment (2 Kings 6:14-17). It wasn't just a physical pebble or stone that David aimed at, hit and killed Goliath with; rather, it was the unquenchable power of God loaded within David, propelled by his faith that fired the stone and destroyed the giant, Goliath (1 Samuel 17:45-47). In your case, the Goliath may be racism you face.

*It is up to you to stage spiritual warfare against the foul spirit of racism.*

You too possess the power of God's Holy Word in you; fire it against racism with your faith in God through Jesus Christ, and turn it into a fallen and dead Goliath.

God's spiritual power has supernatural dominion that governs your physical environment. Spiritual victory always defies all odds. It takes you from the valleys of racist deceit and lies to triumph—God's holy truth that leads you to authentic spiritual knowledge, and ultimately, to material success. In the awesome Name of Jesus Christ, God's spiritual army will overtake the vile spirit of racism and its unholy army (2 Kings 6:14-17). Do you believe this?

*By your faith in Jesus Christ, fire God's Holy Word against racism and turn it into a fallen and dead Goliath.*

**Chapter Quiz**

1. True or false: Carnal superiority is a state of spiritual ignorance. Explain your answer.

---

2. True or false: God created some inferior human beings. Explain your answer and provide at least one Scripture to back up your answer.

---

3. True or false: God created some superior human beings. Explain your answer and provide at least one Scripture to back up your answer.

---

4. True or false: God created all human beings in His own image. Explain your answer and provide at least one Scripture to back up your answer.

---

5. True or false: Your daily battle with racism can be easily won by you without you dwelling in God's Holy Word and applying it daily. Explain your answer.

---

∞∞∞∞∞∞ ♦ ♦ ♦ ♦ ♦ ∞∞∞∞∞∞

**Reflections:**

---

---

---

---

∞∞∞∞∞∞ ♦ ♦ ♦ ♦ ♦ ∞∞∞∞∞∞

# CHAPTER 12: Quenching the Fiery Darts of Racism

Racism is a tool of the demon spirit of racism to cause you spiritual and mental defeat, and render you an ineffective vessel through which God's awesome power cannot work. Through the elements of racism, such as individuals, groups and systems within a society, the devil wants to turn you into a pack of ineffective "dry bones" (Ezekiel 37:1-3). Racism originated from and is perpetrated and perpetuated by spiritual wickedness in high places. It is designed to make you uncomfortable and unhappy in a world that Jesus Christ has overcome for you (John 16:33). If you have, over the years, allowed racism to turn you into "dry bones", all hope is not lost; you still have your faith in Jesus Christ and the power of God's Word and Holy Spirit in you to speak life into the "dry bones" to come alive once again (Ezekiel 37:1-14).

Don't be fooled for one moment; for the vile spirit of racism wants to steal, kill and destroy you, but Jesus Christ has given you life more abundantly and you can claim it by faith (John 10:10). Racism wants to steal your peace and joy permanently. It is a direct assault on God's individual purpose for your creation and existence (Jeremiah 29:11) . It creates illusions and lies about who and what you are, and attempts to distort in your mind your view of your true image in Jesus Christ. Racism is an assault on every human race and ethnicity; it is an assault against your own ethnicity and race, whichever it may be, because all humans are made in the Image of an excellent, holy, perfect and awesome God. The foul spirit of racism attacks your heart and mind—especially your perception of yourself—and even your physical state, especially your health through stressful situations, and it is against God's excellent purpose for your life (Jeremiah 29:11).

Daily, as one believes, accepts or fosters practices of racism, subtle or overt, it takes conscious acceptance of racism for it to nurture and grow in one's subconscious mind. Being spiritually receptive to the belief of inequality of human races gives the evil spirit of racism access to one's soul. Thus, every time you experience racism and do not spiritually resist it with the power of God's Word in your heart and mind, you are allowing the evil spirit of racism to successfully invade God's holy altar, which is

*Racism is a tool of the demon spirit of racism to cause you spiritual and mental defeat.*

you and your whole body. God has not authorized racism, anything or anyone else to defile you for you are a temple of His Ho-Holy Spirit Who dwells in you (1 Corinthians 6:19-20).

As you experience racism and do not apply spiritual resistance, subconsciously, it will begin to dominate your heart and mind, rule over your thoughtlife, and then control your life. Never ignore the reality that racism was designed to defeat and make you uncomfortable in a world that Jesus Christ has already defeated on your behalf. Racism is designed for you to react negatively to it in a manner that would be self-destructive to your heart and mind, and your entire soul. So, your main godly plan of action against racism should be to always reject racism and its lies by applying God's Word against it. You are a precious work of genius of an awesome God and He has not authorized anyone or anything [not even you] to defile your body that is His temple. Yes, God has not authorized anyone to defile or destroy His temple, but you can allow it if you lack God's Word in you. His Hands formed and created you for His glory (Isaiah 43:7). God's glory can only manifest through you when you are not subdued by evil, including the foul spirit of racism. You are God's great work of artistic genius, created in Jesus Christ for good works that God has preordained for you (Ephesians 2:10), and not for you to be condemned by racism. You are in Christ and racism cannot condemn you (Romans 8:1).

*Racism is an assault on every human race and ethnicity.*

Racism twists and repackages "truth", which it presents to you as well-packaged lies and deceptions (John 8:44). If you are "naked" without Jesus Christ, without the full armor of God, either as the perpetrator or as the target of racism, it would trespass against your spirit and invade your soul. You need to know that the Sword of the Spirit, the Holy Spirit-fueled Word of God, is your greatest spiritual weapon against racism. God's supernatural spiritual armor is greater than any form of racism, and it can release you from any spiritual and mental stranglehold of racism (Ephesians 6:10-18).

In Apostle Paul's letter of encouragement to the Ephesians, he explains what God's invisible armor is (Ephesians 6:10-18). We, too, know that it is a formidable and indestructible holy spiritual force of precision, the power of Jesus Christ, God's Living Word in us, that can and will target and destroy any form of evil fashioned against our lives (1 John 4:4). God's Holy Word—His power in us through Christ will expose and demolish all forms of racism, subtle or overt (Hebrews 4:12-13). The central core of God's full armor is Jesus Christ through whom God has given us the anointing power of His Holy Spirit, which dwells in us. So, do you have God's full armor in Jesus Christ Who dwells in you? Do you possess?

*Racism twists and repackages "truth" that it presents to you as well-packaged lies and deception.*

1. The Sword of the Spirit, God's Holy Word;
2. The power of the truth of God's Word within you;

3. The Breastplate of Righteousness;
4. Feet covered with the preparation of the Gospel of Peace, and the peace of God;
5. The Shield of Faith;
6. The Helmet of Salvation; and

Are you in constant prayer with God's full armor? If you, then you can withstand the fiery darts of Satanic forces, including those orchestrated by the despicable spirit of racism. It is the anointing power of God through Jesus Christ that breaks every yoke of hindrance of evil, wickedness, oppression and injustice such as racism (Isaiah 10:27). So we can take on His yoke that is easy and His burden that is light (Matthew 11:28-30). There is no weight that Jesus Christ has not carried for you; no burden He has not removed for you. Is there anything too hard for God to accomplish in your life and on your behalf (Genesis 18:14; Jeremiah 32:27)? It is by faith in the victory that Christ gained for us, that we put on God's full armor for daily spiritual warfare and apply them against the foul spirit of racism and its evil activities orchestrated through willing human hosts. Now, let's review the elements of God's invisible armor that Apos-

*Walk and work within God's grounds of integrity (Ephesians 4:1).*

tle Paul presented to us in Ephesians 6:10-18, and how you can apply them against the vile spirit of racism:

1. The Sword of the Spirit, God's Holy Word powered by the Holy Spirit. God's Holy Word: the Written Word is the Bible, and the Living Word is Jesus Christ. God's Word is the most powerful ammunition you can fire against the odious spirit of racism and the racist activities of its human recruits. By faith in Christ, speak God's Word and bind the foul spirit of racism! Allow God's Word to dismantle the activities of racist elements that have gathered against you (Jeremiah 1:19; Isaiah 54:15,17)
2. The power of the truth of God's Word (within you), which suffocates the lies of the devil. The power of the truth of God's Word stands forever and cannot be destroyed. When the devil lies to you through elements of racism, the truth of God's Holy Word in you cancels the lies.
3. The Breastplate of Righteousness; virtue, morality, justice, decency, honesty and uprightness of Jesus Christ protects you from the lies and wicked intrigues of the devil.
4. Feet covered with the preparation, training or grounding by the Gospel of Peace; a willingness and eagerness to allow God's Holy Word to clothe your spirit and soul, and His Holy Spirit to take you into a higher spiritual realm, equipping you to be able to spread the Word of God, giving no room to any evil force, including the vile spirit of racism.

5. The Shield of Faith that we gain and fortify by hearing God's Holy Word (Romans 10:17) and by its constant application (James 2:17). Without faith in God's Holy Word and Jesus Christ, and the empowerment of God's Holy Spirit, you become a defenseless open target for the devil and his wicked plots through racism and other devious means.
6. The Helmet of Salvation, Jesus Christ Himself; to take the Helmet of Salvation is to receive Jesus Christ in our hearts, and redemption and deliverance through Him. The covering of the powerful Blood of Jesus Christ prevents the spirit of racism from attacking your spirit.
7. The Peace of God which is a product of all of the above, generates God's calm, quiet, stillness, tranquility, silence, harmony and serenity within you, displacing the internal or external uproar that would have been caused by any form of evil, including racism. The presence of the peace of God is not the absence of difficulties, challenges, obstacles, accusations and so on. It is the presence of God's peace that surpases all understanding (Philippians 4:6-7)—calmness and stillness within us that is of Him through Jesus Christ in the face of negative and difficult situations.
8. Constant prayer, which includes thanksgiving, praise and worship of God; faith-fueled prayer activates God's spiritual armor and continual prayer keeps it activated

within you for effective spiritual warfare. Remember that the effective prayer of the righteous person avails much (James 5:16).

The true nature of racism is a manifestation of spiritual wickedness in high places of unseen dimensions. Therefore, we must have a Word-based and Christ-rooted response (not reaction) to racism. As born again believers in Jesus Christ, we encounter and battle racism daily, but we are positioned in the righteous and victory of Jesus Christ. Therefore, we should walk worthy before God (Ephesians 4:1), even as we face daily challenges with racism. A Christ-rooted response to experiences with racism should not be an exception; we must also respond in a Christ-like manner to other adversities that we may encounter in life including those like racism, which are orchestrated and controlled by evil influences. Although the fiery darts of racism are directed against you, the truth of God's Holy Word will be your shield and buckler (Psalms 91:4)—and the precious Blood of Jesus Christ in which you are covered will repel each dart into its destined destruction (Revelation 12:10-12). Through Jesus Christ, God has given you the power to bind and loose anything here on earth (Matthew 18:18).

*God's invisible armor and army are formidable and indestructible holy spiritual forces of precision that can and will target and destroy any form of evil.*

Now, by your faith, exercise that power to bind and loose anything according to the Word of God (Matthew 18:18), and to be able to overcome the evil spirit of racism (Revelation 12:10-12). By the precious Blood of Jesus Christ, the foul spirit of racism has been marked by God through Jesus Christ for the everlasting destruction. Know that the fiery darts of racism, which target your life, hopes, dreams, aspirations, career and so on, are not authorized by God; such fiery darts are trespassing against God's holy temple, "you", whom God has not authorized to defile.

*The shield of faith extinguishes **the** fiery darts of the devil.*

The shield of faith extinguishes the fiery darts of the devil who orchestrates racism through the odious spirit of racism. So now, will you take up your God's full armor against racism? Will you stand in Christ's victory over the vile spirit of racism and its willing racist human hosts? This is your personal decision to make.

**Chapter Quiz**

1. Ephesians 6:10-18: How can you apply these Scripture verses against racism?

2. What is God's full armor which you are to apply in spiritual warfare against any form of evil, including racism?

___

3. True or false: We don't have the choice to respond to racism in a godly manner because racism is a wicked and divisive tool of the devil. Explain your answer.

___

4. True or false: Your body is not a temple of God and the vile spirit of racism has every right to dwell in it. Explain your answer.

___

5. True or false: Your body is a temple of God and the vile spirit of racism has no right to dwell in it. Explain your answer.

___

ꝏꝏꝏꝏꝏꝏ ♦ ♦ ♦ ♦ ♦ ꝏꝏꝏꝏꝏꝏ

**Reflections:**

___

___

___

___

ꝏꝏꝏꝏꝏꝏ ♦ ♦ ♦ ♦ ♦ ꝏꝏꝏꝏꝏꝏ

# CHAPTER 13: Essence of Racial Diversity

The seed of racial hostility bind many people and this grows from the seedsof racial prejudice sown by our enemy, the devil, in the hearts of willing individuals (Matthew 13:38-40). The hostility may appear as race-biased attitudes deeply rooted within people's hearts, and for some, having gone unchecked for generations racism has become tradition, a way of life for them (Mark 7:7-9, 13; Isaiah 29:13). Many who follow a long tradition of racism do so without a single thought about what they do and why they do it and the devastating impact that it can and does have on other individuals—and some simply don't care. Unfortunately, racial discrimination has become institutionalized in many societies. It has become deeply rooted in the day-to-day activities of society.

Legally speaking, in most societies, racism is not acceptable; there are penalties for any overt, racially motivated, prejudicial or discriminatory actions against anyone. However, in many respects, culturally and socially, racism has an unspoken and unwritten stamp of approval in many circles, and there are no penalties for it, especially in its subtle forms. In such circles, there is an unspoken acknowledgment among those who are participants and beneficiaries of racism, an age-old tradition. And yet God's Word has specifically instructed us not to conform to ungodly traditions of the world (Mark 7:7-9, 13; Isaiah 29:13) and rather to renew our mind with God's Holy Word (Romans 12:2; Ephesians 4:23-24).

Unfortunately, seeds of racial hostility have been watered daily by a culture that has for centuries offered fertile ground to grow them. Everyday, the seeds bear new, unhealthy fruits of negative thoughts, beliefs, words and actions. The seeds of racial hatred become planted deeply in the soil of the heart, and over time they are nurtured and are gradually accepted, first within individuals, and then collectively within society. Such seeds of racial hatred grow into vast, unending acres of unfruitful fields of superiority or inferiority complexes, hostility, resentment, anger, bitterness, unforgiveness, wickedness, oppression, injustice or meanness within the hearts of many. We who are in Jesus Christ should know that He has already freed us from any bondage, including the stranglehold of racism (John 8:32, 36). If we accepted Him in our hearts and sur-

*The spirit of racism perverts the hearts and minds of people and blinds them to the truth of God's Holy Word.*

rendered our experiences with racism to Him, He would give us daily victory over them.

Racism is a form of spiritual perversion that turns willing and available individuals away from God's holy truth, diverting them from the true intent of God's Word. Thus, they act in an unrighteous manner [turning from God and twisting God's Word] to suit their carnal, human purpose (Mark 7:13). This is what the evil spirit of racism does to those who open the door of their souls to it; it perverts their hearts and minds and blinds them, men and women alike, to the truth that God created us equal in humanity in His excellent Image and in dignity, and no one is either inferior or superior.

Crystallize the truth within you that you and I and all humanity are made in the Image of a perfect, beautiful, lovely, wonderful, marvelous and awesome God. Know the truth that God created a variety of races and ethnic groups as a blessing of diversity to the world. Likewise, being male or female of any specific race or ethnic group was not designed to cause divisions or be used to enslave one group or declare another superior and free.

> *You have been sanctified and made holy through Jesus Christ.*

Your race is not the purpose for your existence—it is only the shade of the physical form of your body. Your race is not your identity—your true identity is in Jesus Christ Who is in you.

Your spirit is expressed within and through your soul and physical body; and it defines who and what you are. First, you are made in God's excellent Image, and as a believer who is "reborn" in Jesus Christ, you are a new man in Jesus Christ (Ephesians 4:20-24; 2 Corinthians 5:17)—you have been sanctified and made holy and blameless through Him (Hebrews 10:10; Colossians 1:21-24; Ephesians 1:3-6).

The truth is that human diversity was designed by God to bring a variety of people; male and female alike, all under the banner of the precious Blood of Jesus Christ as seeds of Abraham and heirs according to the promise of God (Galatians 3:26-29). Know this truth and let no man or woman convince you of the superiority or inferiority of any ethnic group, race or nationality. This is a lie of the devil; the enemy of your soul. Remember that Jesus Christ has named the devil "…the father of all lies…", declaring that no truth can ever come from him (John 8:44). Do not believe Satan, the enemy of your soul who packages lies in various forms, including racism, and presents them to you. Immerse yourself in the absolute truth of God's Word in Jesus Christ, then, the truth shall make you free from the trickery of the enemy, which comes against you in the form of racism and its perpetrators (John 8:32,36).

*The seeds of racial prejudice are sown by our enemy, the devil (Matthew 13:38-39).*

ꝏꝏꝏꝏꝏꝏ ♦ ♦ ♦ ♦ ♦ ꝏꝏꝏꝏꝏꝏ

## Chapter Quiz

1. Galatians 3:26-29: What does this Scripture tell you about racism and the spirit of racism?

---

2. True or false: Your race, ethnic identity or nationality is your true spiritual identity and you must uphold it above all others. Explain your answer.

---

3. True or false: Racism is a form of spiritual perversion that turns willing individuals away from God's truth. Explain your answer.

---

4. True or false: Racism perverts the minds of those who receive it and blinds them to the truth that God created us all in His excellent Image. Explain your answer.

---

ꝏꝏꝏꝏꝏꝏ ♦ ♦ ♦ ♦ ♦ ꝏꝏꝏꝏꝏꝏ

**Reflections:**

---

---

---

---

ꝏꝏꝏꝏꝏꝏ ♦ ♦ ♦ ♦ ♦ ꝏꝏꝏꝏꝏꝏ

# CHAPTER 14: Are You Harboring the Spirit of Prejudice or Racism?

When a person believes in their cultural or racial superiority, they tend to also believe that their race or ethnicity should have superior advantage, dominance, pre-eminence, power, control, upper hand, authority, supremacy or ascendancy in society. This is called ethnocentrism. In the context of race or ethnicity, ethnocentrism can be defined as the belief that one's own racial or ethnic group is superior to all others[1].

An excerpt from a piece on "Ethnocentrism" written by an anthropologist Ken Barger defines ""Ethnocentrism" as "thinking one's own group's ways are superior to others" or "judging other groups as inferior to one's own." "Ethnic" refers to *cultural heritage*, and "centrism" refers to the central starting point...so "ethnocentrism" basically refers to judging other groups from our own cultural point of view. But even this does not address the underlying issue of *why* people do this. Most people, thinking of the shallow definition, believe that they are not ethnocentric, but are rather "open minded" and "tolerant."...To address the deeper issues involved in ethnocentrism calls for a more explicit definition. In this sense, ethnocentrism can be defined as: making false assumptions about others' ways based on our own limited experience. The key word is "*assumptions,*" because we are not even aware that we are being ethnocentric... we don't understand that we don't understand.[2]"

Basically, ethnocentric individuals interpret and see the world only from the perspective of the assumed superiority of their own race and culture. Such individuals foolishly believe in the lie of inborn supremacy of their own race. Based on this false belief, they show blind loyalty or allegiance to their race and culture, which they view as the norm and standard. To them, right or wrong and good or bad is based on race, and their race is superior, always right and all good; and every other race and culture is all bad and somewhat inferior to their own.

*Do you interpret and see the world only from the perspective of the assumed superiority of your own race and culture?*

A prejudiced individual who believes in such superiority affirms in his or her mind the stereotyping or illogical and negative judgment of an individual or group of another race, ethnicity or nationality. "A "stereotype" is a generalization about a person or group of persons. We develop stereotypes when we are unable or unwilling to obtain all of the information we would need to make fair judgments about people or situations. In the absence of the "total picture," stereotypes in many cases allow us to "fill in the blanks."...stereotypes often lead to unfair discrimination and persecution when the stereotype is unfavorable."[3]

Race stereotyping is the belief that all individuals of a specific race act or will act in the same manner, usually in a negative way, or that they have inferior abilities and intelligence because of predetermined and preassigned beliefs about that group of people. Such predetermined beliefs become the basis for prejudging and discriminating against such individuals. "Stereotyping often results from, and leads to, prejudice and bigotry. Unchecked prejudice and bigotry leads to discrimination, violence, and, in extreme cases, genocide. Prejudice can be spread by the use of propaganda and inflamed by demagogues. Language, particularly slang, is often used to dehumanize members of certain groups of people, and this dehumanization is a precursor of discrimination, isolation, and violence."[3]

*A racist person operates under the negative influences of the foul spirit of racism.*

God's Word does not promote one race over another; therefore, He, God, does not judge anyone based on their race, skin color or shade, appearance or ethnic group (1 Samuel 16:7; John 7:24). God is no respecter of persons (Acts10:34-35; Romans 2:11), He loves all people regardless of race, ethnicity or nationality because He created all of humanity in His own Image. So, we know that God in Whose excellent Image and Likeness we are made is definitely and absolutely not racist. God is pleased with anyone who loves, believes, worships, trusts and obeys Him, regardless of race, ethnicity or nationality (I Samuel 2:30; Psalms 91:14-15).

What about you? Are you prejudiced or racist? Do you act justly regardless of race, ethnicity or nationality? Are your actions based on God's Holy Word and not based on race or ethnic bias? Are you on the side of God's holy justice against racial injustice, or on the side of racial inequity? Are you respectful of people's race, ethnicity and nationality? This question refers to being respectful of racial, ethnic or cultural differences. For example, due to historical experiences that people of certain races have endured, using certain words or phrases to address them either as individuals or as a people may be considered mean or racially insensitive. Do your actions show that you have no racial bias or do you say that you are not prejudiced or racist but act or speak in a manner that contradicts your own words?

*Do you believe that your race or ethnic group is superior to others?*

For racism to be perpetrated against anyone, another individual must invite and harbor within him or her, the foul spirit of racism. A racist person operates under the negative influences of the loathsome spirit of racism. A racist person then becomes a yielding vessel to this negative spirit, which takes over his or her heart as its host and territory where it continues to seed more racial prejudice within them; usually in the form of lies that are contrary to God's Word. The foul spirit of racism fosters racial dislike, loathing, hate and cruelty against an individual or a racial group as a whole, and it stands against the Holy Word of God, which opposes any form of oppression and injustice including racism.

So, pause for a moment for a self-check: are you harboring the wicked spirit of prejudice or racism? In humble prayer, ask God's Holy Spirit through the precious Blood of Jesus Christ, to reveal to you any areas where you may be harboring the vile spirit of racial prejudice or racism. If you are harboring the foul spirit of racism, ask God for forgiveness through Jesus Christ and make a permanent change from any further practices of racism (2 Chronicles 7:14).

*What about you? Are you prejudiced or racist?*

## Chapter Quiz

1. Are you harboring the foul spirit of prejudice or racism? Do you believe that you can objectively search your own heart, or do you believe that you need God's Holy Spirit to search your heart and reveal to you if you have any

seeds of racial prejudice or racism?

---

2. Do you feel inferior to anyone either because of your race or for any other reason? What Holy Scripture supports your belief or feeling of inferiority?

---

3. Do you feel superior to anyone either because of your race or for any other reason? What Holy Scripture supports your belief or feeling of superiority?

---

4. Is it possible for a prejudiced or racist person to change his or her ways? Can you suggest one way he or she can go about changing his or her racist ways.

---

ꝏꝏꝏꝏꝏꝏ ♦ ♦ ♦ ♦ ♦ ꝏꝏꝏꝏꝏꝏ

**Reflections:**

---

---

---

---

ꝏꝏꝏꝏꝏꝏ ♦ ♦ ♦ ♦ ♦ ꝏꝏꝏꝏꝏꝏ

---

Chapter References:

1. The Holocust – The Guide for Teachers, Copyright 1990 Gary M. Grobman http://remember.org/guide/History.root.stereotypes.html. Note: The defini-

tion of the term "ethnocentrism" obtained from this reference was further modified to emphasize racial and ethnic ethnocentricism.

2. Ken Barger Ethnocentrism: What is it? Why are people ethnocentric? What is the problem? What can we do about it? Recognition and control of Ethnocentrism as a basic methodology for understanding ethnic behavior... both our own and others. http://www.iupui.edu/~anthkb/ethnocen.htm
3. Stereotypes and Prejudices. http://remember.org/guide/History.root.stereotypes.html

# CHAPTER 15: Always Reject Racism and its Spirit of Racism

God's glory and power are unquenchable, immeasurable and without boundaries, and no one can limit Him. However, while no one can ever limit God's glory and power, we can impede manifestation of His power, glory and promises in our lives by our lack of faith, our unbelief, and ignorance of His Word (Hebrews 11:6; Hosea 4:6). Do you obstruct God's glory in you by being racist or by your reaction to racism? Do you know that you can hinder God's glory shinning through you when you are held down by racist thoughts and negative intent and motives due to your experiences with racism or any other challenges, obstacles or unfavorable situations that you encounter?

Child of the Most High God, resist and reject the vile spirit if racism. You should all learn to resist and reject the lies that others tell you about who or what you are, and don't let such lies penetrate your inner person to pollute your heart, mind, thoughts, beliefs, emotions, attitudes, personality and behavior.

At the same time, discard your own lies to yourself about what racism has defined you to be before your mind becomes an enemy to yourself. Casting out a demon that dwells within you is much harder to do than banishing one that dwells outside of you. The destructive spirit of self-rejection, self-dislike, self-loathing or self-hate is worse and far more lethal than the demon spirit of racism, which gave birth to these elements of a negative mindset.

To sustain permanent spiritual victory over racism, you need to have an effective and efficient defensive and offensive spiritual strategy; that is by staging daily spiritual warfare through prayer, worship and thanksgiving offering to our Father in Heaven, in the Name of Jesus Christ. Spiritual warfare does not require you to visibly scream or kick in anger in response to racism. It is a silent spiritual strategy that requires you to recoil in prayer, thanksgiving and worship to meditate on God's Living Word and practice spiritual fasting as Jesus Christ always did to renew His spiritual strength. Renewing your mind with God's Holy Word is powerful spiritual warfare against the devil's plan to disable your spiritual power and subdue manifestation of your victory in the physical realm (Romans 12:2; Ephesians 4:23-24; Ephesians 6:10-18; 2 Corinthians 10:3-6).

*The spirit of self-rejection is worse than the demon spirit of racism, which gave birth to it.*

Seasoned spiritual strategy will become your invincible tool for calling down the power of God's invisible army that will demolish the fiery darts of any form of racism, which you may be experiencing. When God is on your side, no one can be against you—nothing and no one can over run you (Romans 8:31). By faith, we must receive and believe this spiritual truth, and stand and act on it always when we are dealing with the foul spirit of racism and its offensive product racism.

While many in our society may continue to deny that racial prejudice and discrimination exists, you must however, by spiritual defiance, reject the human illusion of power that it may have over you. This rejection is spiritual defiance of evil based on God's Holy Word, principles and promises. In John 10, Christ said "No man taketh it from me, but I lay it down of myself. I have power to lay it down, and I have power to take it again. This commandment have I received of my Father." (John 10:18) When Pilate arrogantly spoke to Jesus Christ and told Him [Christ] that he [Pilate] had the power to either free or crucify Him [Christ] (John 19:10). Immediately, Christ rejected the human illusion of power that Pilate had and answered: "…You would have no power over me if it were not given to you from above. Therefore the one who handed me over to you is guilty of a greater sin." (John 19:11) You and I must learn to apply spiritual warfare to reject the illusion of power that the vile spirit of racism and its willing human hosts try to make us believe they have over our lives.

*Racism is against God's Word.*

The spirit of racism is wrong and contrary to God's Holy Word. It is perverts and corrupts the minds and hearts of its yielding human vessels, convincing them that the material benefit from perpetrating racism outweighs the spiritual gains of resisting it and acting against it. Be cautioned, for these are short-lived material gains made by the perpetrators of racism against the everlasting spiritual gains from rejecting it.

For those who are on the receiving end of racism, the very foundation and basis of your individual resistance against racism must first be Christ-rooted in the absolute truth of God's Holy Word—the holy truth that racism is contrary to God's Word, is from the father of all lies, the devil (John 8:44), and has no truth or everlasting gains in it. Therefore, racism has no real spiritual authority over your life, only imagined power, which you can allow to manifest through the subdued state of your own mind. God has given us the power to speak and attract good or bad into our lives (Proverb 18:21), so exercise that power by the precious Blood of Jesus Christ and rebuke the evil spirit of racism destined for everlasting destruction (Revelation 12:10-11).

*Racism is against God's Holy Word and He has outlawed it.*

Your victorious journey against racism and the foul spirit behind it must start with you. You need to start by asking God if you have any prejudiced or racist tendencies against anyone or people of any specific race, ethnicity or nationality. You must be willing to acknowledge racism as a sin, reject it, and ask God to cleanse you by the precious Blood of Jesus Christ. You must be willing and determined to remain on a new path where you would no longer receive, harbor or foster racism. If you have been on the receiving end of racism, you also need to let go and forgive all of your racist offenders.

On a daily basis, your individual goal should be to resist, defy and conquer any and all negative effects that racially motivated and discriminatory actions may have on you. Your goal should always be to use the spiritual precision of God's Living Word, in the Name of Jesus Christ, to gain complete spiritual and material victory so that your life's dreams and aspirations remain untouched by the evil schemes and intrigues of the foul spirit of racism. Your goal must be to use holy spiritual ammunition, that is, God's Holy Word, prayer, praise, worship, and spiritual fasting, to keep your heart and mind undefeated by the oppression and injustice of racism. Your honest hard work must then remain sustained by your daily-renewed strength in the Living Word of God, with guidance from His Holy Spirit Who dwells within you. By this, your confidence and excitement for your life's journey and success would not become tainted, stifled or controlled by the negative actions or intrigues of any form of racism that may be directed at you.

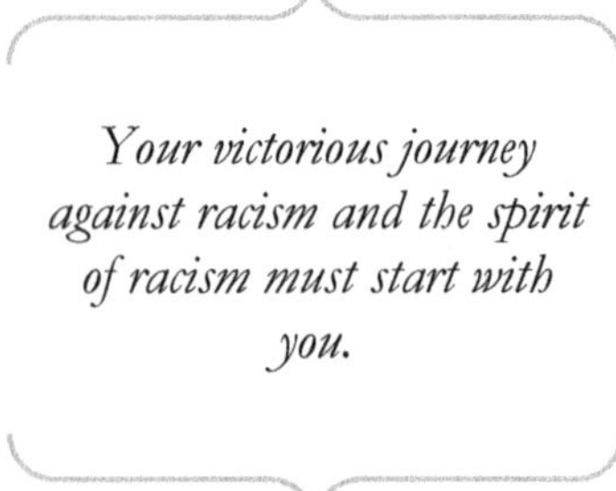

I emphasize that racism is against God's Holy Word. God has outlawed racism and the precious Blood of Jesus Christ has cancelled all charges against you, including racism and all other forms of oppression (Colossians 2:14-15). So, the foul spirit of racism is not authorized in your life and should never be allowed to gain entry into your heart. Therefore, in your mind, you must always reject racism and all that it stands for. However, it is not enough for one's rejection of racism to be politically correct or superficial; the belief that racism, subtle or overt, is wrong must permeate deep down within your heart and mind for you not to become a yielding vessel to the wicked spirit of racism. This is why it is safest to always reject the evil spirit of racism at all times, and by doing so, you keep the door to your heart permanently shut against the demon spirit that originates racism. When a child of God rejects racism, but instead, fills his or her heart and mind with God's holy truth that all men and women are created equal and in God's excellent Image, there will be no room within him or her for temporary or permanent habitation of the demon spirit which controls racism. Essentially, you and I should shut the door to our hearts, thereby preventing the evil spirit of racism from gaining any access. We should allow only the holy truth of God's Word to abide in us and possess our hearts and minds (John 15:1-8).

*Deliverance means that the negative influence of the foul spirit of racism is expelled from within.*

If you have already opened the door to your heart to the obnoxious spirit of racism, or you have become a weakened or defeated target of racism, all hope is not lost. The power of God through the precious Blood of Jesus can still deliver you from the negative effects of racism. How? He, Christ, is the One Who gained eternal salvation and victory over all evil, including the odious spirit of racism—and because you have received Him in yur heart, you too possess the same victory! Deliverance means that the negative influence of the foul spirit of racism is expelled from within a person. The power of God's Holy Spirit within you will battle racism for you so that you can begin to function normally again. God's Holy Spirit within you will reinstate within you, godly love and respect for all humanity.

First, truly profess your faith in Jesus Christ and come under the powerful covering of His precious, redeeming Blood; a simple spiritual step for the beginning of your deliverance from the foul spirit of racism. So, if you have already become a vessel through which racism is being perpetrated, now is the moment to start the process of deliverance from the abhorrent spirit of racism by declaring this statement or another prayer in your own words: *"In the Name of Jesus Christ, I repent of my sins of racial prejudice or racism. I regret and reject any past associations with the loathsome spirit of racism or racists. I reject racism and all that it stands for. I rebuke the despicable spirit of racism in the Name of*

*Do you limit God's glory in you by your reaction to racism?*

*Jesus Christ. I denounce and veto racism and the despicable spirit that orchestrates it. I declare that I will no longer submit to the vile spirit of racism. I believe and declare that racism is contrary to the Holy Word of God and sinful, and as such, is ungodly and an offense against God and all of all humanity. I will not [or will no longer] partake in any kind of racist practices, in Jesus' Name, Amen."*

**Chapter Quiz**

1. Why must you always reject the evil spirit of racism?

______________________________________________

2. True or false: Your individual resistance against racism must first be rooted in God's absolute truth that racism is contrary to God's Word. Explain your answer.

______________________________________________

3. True or false: Before you can successfully defeat racism that surrounds you, you must first purge yourself of any racial prejudice or bias seeded in you by the demon spirit of racism. Explain your answer.

______________________________________________

4. Why must you remain a yielding vessel of God against the odious spirit of racism?

______________________________________________

∞∞∞∞∞∞∞∞∞∞∞ ♦ ♦ ♦ ♦ ♦ ∞∞∞∞∞∞∞∞∞∞∞

**Reflections:**

________________________________________

________________________________________

________________________________________

________________________________________

∞∞∞∞∞∞∞∞∞∞∞ ♦ ♦ ♦ ♦ ♦ ∞∞∞∞∞∞∞∞∞∞∞

# CHAPTER 16: Dealing With the Daily Assaults of Racism?

There are many people who consider themselves "good" people even though they exhibit prejudiced and racist behavior. This is not surprising since most people who exhibit racist attitudes towards others are usually the first to declare that they are not racist. I have heard individuals say things like, "Our children understand that they cannot marry outside of our race or ethnic group, but that does not make us racist." There are individuals who would gladly acquit a person of their own race who assaulted or murdered a person of another race even with video-recorded evidence and at the same time declare to themselves, "We are not racist", or "I am not racist." You see, God's Word tells us that any attitude of wickedness is like darkness which blinds such people to their behaviors in their own minds (Proverbs 4:19; John 3: 19-21; Proverbs 28:4-5). The people become blinded to their wicked ways, declare that they are "good" and continue to act in an unjust manner towards others. Many people who consider themselves "good" and who justify their actions, exhibit prejudiced and racist attitudes towards others daily.

We know that there is only One true God in Whose excellent Image and Likeness we were made (Genesis 1:26-27, and Who in the Beginning was and still is the Word (John 1:1). All races are God's creation, rich or poor, and regardless of race, ethnicity or nationality; and God does not judge us based on our race or outward appearance (1 Samuel 16:7). God's Word clearly declares His stand on any form of oppression and racism being a form of oppression is no exception. For this reason, God delivers the "poor", "lowly" and "weak" from the hands of those who are too strong for them (Psalms 103:6; Proverbs 22:22; Psalms 35:10). The Holy Spirit of God is One in all of us who have received Jesus Christ, regardless of our race, ethnicity or nationality (Ephesians 4:4-6). The Holy Spirit of God is the power of God in us through Jesus Christ.

*It takes a negative spiritual influence in anyone for them to block the path of progress of another.*

God has not authorized anyone to oppress others. On the contrary, God has instructed us to treat others as we wish to be treated—and treat foreigners in our land well (Matthew 7:12; Exodus 22:21-23). A negative spiritual influence is required for anyone to block the path of progress of another, prevent their earned promotion in the workplace, mock, reject and criticize another based on their race, ethnicity ornationality, or develop a permanent mentality of racial or ethnic superiority. When we have a carnal mindset, our minds can easily be controlled by evil spiritual influences. When our mind becomes subject to negative control (Jeremiah 17:9-10), it signals spiritual weakness and ignorance, and a lack of holy spiritual mindedness. Such negative spiritual influence or carnal mindedness, can cause us to become an oppressive weapon against another individual. Individuals under negative spiritual influence of the foul spirit of racism can try to block the path of progress of anyone, intimidate their targets into self-rejection and accept belief in their own inferiority, or force their submission to mentally accept their own racial superiority. However, it is important to understand that when a person says to another that they are nobody and will never become somebody, they too become judged by their own words (Matthew 12:37; Luke 19:22; Job 15:6). When anyone calls another person [perhaps you] nothing good, God has already called you everything good (1Timothy 4:4). He has freed you from the clutches of the oppressor [such as a racist] and reversed their racist actions against you (Isaiah 61:1-3).

*When our mind becomes subject to negative control, it signals spiritual weakness.*

If you were on the receiving end of racism, how could you deal with it in a godly manner? Our daily experiences with racism, subtle or overt, can sometimes be overwhelming and thus make us feel fearful, angry, bitter, vengeful, powerless or hopeless, and may even blur our outlook on the horizon for a successful career and life. During such times, rather than give in spiritually or mentally to the defeating lies of the devil, the arch enemy of your soul who orchestrates racism through humans, and become broken by the injustices and oppression of racism, buckle up with God's Holy Word and girdle yourself with His whole armor (Ephesians 6:10-18). Retreat into God's Word and let it become your fueling ammunition for the full release of God's anointing. Through Jesus Christ Who is God's grace to us, the power of God's holy anointing oil will activate the power of His Holy Spirit in and over your life and against the fiery darts of the devil against your life—and break the yoke of the burden of racism (Isaiah 9:4,10:27; Nahum 1:1-13).

*If you are "naked" without the full armor of God, racism will invade your soul and devour you.*

By the precious Blood of Jesus Christ, the oppressed and unjustly treated have been released from their bondage (Isaiah 61:1-4) and the powerful Blood of Jesus Christ has broken the staff of the wicked. Having come under the Blood Covenant of Jesus Christ, by believing and professing Him as your personal Lord and Savior (Romans 10:9-10), you are spiritually born-again, and your spirit now has full access to God through Christ. John 4:24 (NKJV) tells us that "God is Spirit, and those who worship Him must worship in spirit and truth." Then, by Christ's anointing grace and power, you gain the authority that God has given believers through Him [Christ] to tread on serpent and scorpions and over all the power of the devil—He, Christ, has broken the yoke of all burdens, including racism. Therefore, lay down any burden coming from your experiences with racism at the holy feet of Christ (Matthew 11:28-30).

If you are feeling overwhelmed and defeated by your daily experiences with racism, do not lose hope or your grip on the power of the good news and promises of God's Holy Word. In prayer, ask God to place a hedge of protection around you and begin to lift off your mind, the spirit of defeat or victim mentality, which you acquired from your experiences with racism. God will renew your mind with His empowering and conquering Word by the anointing power of His Holy Spirit through Jesus Christ.

Declare the following statements or another prayer in your own words: *"In the Name of Jesus Christ, I bind all evil forces of the odious spirit of racism and declare them powerless in my life. I am under the covering of the precious Blood of Jesus Christ and will not be overcome by racism. I am a victor and not a victim of racism because I am more than a conqueror through Jesus Christ Who loves me (Romans 8:37), and through Him Who strengthens me I can do all things (Philippians 4:13). In obedience to God's Word, I forgive my racist offenders and I pray for them to change their ways. In the Name of Jesus Christ, I believe and declare that all*

*God's Word clearly declares His stand on any form of oppression and racism being a form of oppression is no exception.*

*racist plans directed against me will fail (Jeremiah 1:19). In the Name of Jesus Christ, no weapon that they have fashioned against me will ever prosper (Isaiah 54:17).*"

Racism originates from the devil's distortion of truth, which it presents to you as well-packaged lies and deception. If you were "naked" without the full armor of God, either as the perpetrator, recipient or target of racism, it would invade your soul and devour you (1 Peter 5:8-9). You need to know that the Sword of the Spirit, which is the Word of God, is your greatest spiritual fire against racism. God's spiritual armor is greater than any form of racism, and can release you from the spiritual and physical stronghold of racism. God's invisible and invincible armor is a formidable, indestructible and positive spiritual force of precision that can and will target any form of evil, including racism; it will expose and demolish all forms of racism; hidden or blatant (Hebrews 4:12-13). God's holy armor is able to stand against and destroy the evil forces of lies, deceit, oppression and injustices that accompany racism.

*Racism originates from the devil's distortion of truth.*

Understand and use the full armor of God against the foul spirit of racism: Ephesians 6:10-18: a) Belt of Truth—the truth of God's Word; b) The Breastplate of Righteousness—the righteousness of Jesus Christ in you; c) Shoes of Peace—inner peace and readiness received from God's Holy Word to share the good news of the Gospel of Jesus Christ; d) Shield of Faith—your own faith in God's Word and living by this faith; e) Helmet of Salvation—the gift of salvation through Jesus Christ; f) Sword of the Spirit—God's Holy Word that will demolish evil deceptions and accusations, such as those presented to and against you by the foul spirit of racism; and g) The power of praying without ceasing (1 Thessalonians 5:17).

ꝏꝏꝏꝏꝏꝏꝏ♦ ♦ ♦ ♦ ♦ꝏꝏꝏꝏꝏꝏꝏ

**Chapter Quiz**

1. What must you do if you are feeling overwhelmed by daily experiences with racism?

---

2. Discuss at least one way that you can apply God's Holy Word against racism and the evil spirit of racism.

---

3. List the critical elements of spiritual warfare in Ephesians 6:10-17 that you can also apply against racism and the foul spirit of racism.

---

4. "I am a victor and not a victim of racism because I am more than a conqueror through Jesus Christ": How can you apply this statement which is based on the Holy Scripture, Romans 8:37, to gain daily victory over racism and the obnoxious spirit of racism?

---

∞∞∞∞∞∞∞∞∞∞∞ ♦ ♦ ♦ ♦ ♦ ∞∞∞∞∞∞∞∞∞∞∞

**Reflections:**

---

---

---

---

∞∞∞∞∞∞∞∞∞∞∞ ♦ ♦ ♦ ♦ ♦ ∞∞∞∞∞∞∞∞∞∞∞

# CHAPTER 17: The Power of Faith and the Sword of the Spirit Against Racism

Racism is a form of evil spiritual and psychological bullying that is designed to impede the progress of your life by negatively affecting your heart, mind, thoughts, will, resolve, attitudes, actions, personality, behavior, health, career and life in general. Racism is pure defiance of God's Word, and as such is an offense against Him. As a child of God who dwells in His Holy Word, who is basking in the grace, knowledge and glory of our Lord and Savior Jesus Christ and is empowered by the Holy Spirit, you should not allow racism to bully your mind or psyche. The believer that you are knows that God is on your side (Romans 8:31) against any form of oppression or injustice (Isaiah 58:6). Jesus Christ has set all captives free from oppression and stranglehold of evil, including racism (Isaiah 61:1-4). So, racism should never stop you from completing with huge success the journey that God has so beautifully mapped out for your life (Jeremiah

29:11; Philippians 3:12-15). Your life's journey starts with you knowing God's designed purpose for your life. Find, know and guard your God-given purpose —nurture it—and do not allow racism to distract you from it.

No mere mortal or circumstance has the power to limit God's purpose for your life unless you allow it by your lack of faith and trust in Him. Have you become mentally defeated by the loathsome spirit of racism? Is your "carnal tank", your soul, "leaking" from the "fiery darts" of racism? Have you allowed racism to "puncture" your soul and is it now "leaky" and "sore" with "open wounds"? It is time to begin to "seal" the "puncture" with the healing touch of God's Holy Word. It is time to nurture yourself back to true spiritual life with God's Holy Word, which will start the process of renewing your mind and healing your wounded and broken heart.

*You must reject racist lies and focus on the absolute truth of God's Holy Word.*

The power of God is in you through Jesus Christ and racism lacks spiritual authority power to limit your desires, goals and ultimate success unless you relinquish your faith, and your heart, mind, thoughts, emotions, will and resolve to it. The ultimate power within and over your life is with God through Jesus Christ and His awesome and energizing Holy Spirit Who dwells within you. Through God's enabling grace and power, you can conquer any form of racism that you may encounter; first in the spiritual realm where racism originates; and then within your heart and mind and finally in your physical environment. In Mark 11:23 Jesus Christ gave us the power and authority to speak to any evil mountain blocking our path to be removed. By faith, it is time for you to begin to exercise that authority over racism, which Christ has already given to you.

You need to apply the power of your faith and the Sword of the Spirit against racism. As you are bombarded with racist lies about who you are and the limitations of what you can do or achieve, you must reject such lies and focus only on the pure and holy truth about your true image in God—your nature and identity in Jesus Christ, and your abilities through Him. You have to tap into God's power and authority that you have received through Jesus Christ. The truth of God's Word cancels all lies and effects of racism (John 8:32-33, 36). Learn to use the Sword of the Spirit, that is, the Word of God, against racism by applying a godly plan of action to reverse the evil plans of racists and the potential effects of racism on you.

*Your life's journey starts with you knowing God's designed purpose for your life.*

The Sword of the Spirit, which is the Word of God, will fill your heart and mind to fortify your faith. God's Word is pure and absolute truth. Like a belt around your waist, you need to buckle or girdle His Living Word in you through your own faith in Jesus Christ (Psalms 91:4; Ephesians 6:14). This becomes your own belt of undefiled truth (Ephesians 6:10-18). God's Word is the only and absolute truth about who and what you are. You must leave no room within you for the loathsome spirit of racism and its negative effects to defile your person through its lies and toxic deposit on your heart, mind, emotions, will and resolve, and in your thoughts, words, actions, behavior or personality.

Take the Shield of Faith—your own faith that you live by, which comes from hearing the Word of God (Romans 10:17), will fortify you with a calm and confident trust in God's supernatural and divine power over all things, including racism. Receive and believe God's empowerment, which comes from hearing, receiving and believing His Word, and He will protect you from false beliefs, fear, anxiety and paranoia of the illusionary power that racism has over your life, which is only a deceptive tool of the devil. But know that you must always exercise faith in God for without faith, it is impossible to please Him (Hebrews 11:6). Without faith you cannot believe the absolute truth of His Holy Word, and therefore, you cannot be empowered by it.

*Jesus Christ is in you and you in Him.*

Your own faith in God's Word will shield you from the lies of the vile spirit of racism, and deflect the fiery darts of blatant or hidden forms of racism directed at you by evil spiritual schemes in the workplace or elsewhere through humans. It is faith in God's Word that will fortify you with the true spiritual knowledge that the Seed of God's Word—Jesus Christ Himself—is in you and you in Him (John 15:1-8); and that He [Jesus Christ], who is in you is greater than any form of racism directed against you (1 John 4:4).

**Chapter Quiz**

1. True or false: The Sword of the Spirit, which is the Word of God, must fill your heart and mind, and you must walk daily with God, to fortify your faith with His Word. Explain your answer.

---

2. True or false: God's power, which also resides in His Holy Word, will protect you from the false belief, fear, anxiety and paranoia of the illusionary power that racism has over your life, Explain your answer.

---

3. True or false: Your own faith in God's Holy Word will shield you from the vile spirit of racism, and deflect the fiery darts of blatant or hidden racism directed at you by evil spiritual schemes at work or elsewhere through humans. Explain your answer.

---

4. How can you apply the power of your faith and the Sword of the Spirit against racism and the evil spirit behind racism?

---

∞∞∞∞∞∞∞∞∞∞♦ ♦ ♦ ♦ ♦∞∞∞∞∞∞∞∞∞∞∞

**Reflections:**

____________________________________________________________

____________________________________________________________

____________________________________________________________

____________________________________________________________

∞∞∞∞∞∞∞∞∞∞∞♦ ♦ ♦ ♦ ♦∞∞∞∞∞∞∞∞∞∞∞

# CHAPTER 18: Jesus Christ Has Defeated Racism

Jesus Christ is our Mediator (I Timothy 2.5)—our immovable spiritual Rock, Who is our solid and permanent spiritual Foundation (1 Corinthians 3:9-15; Psalms 62:5-6). Our faith and belief in Jesus Christ gives us the solid Foundation of true spiritual courage to press on against racism and other life's challenges with the power of God's Holy Spirit in us and His Holy Word..

There is no doubt that in our lives, without God's protective covering through Jesus Christ, racism has the potential to become a very negative and destructive tool against our hearts, minds, thoughts, emotions, will and resolve. This is because it can attack and weaken our hearts and minds, and even our physical body through ill health. Once our hearts yield to racism's destructive forces, our minds, thoughts and emotions yield as well. In the process, our minds open up to negative, untruthful thoughts about who and what we are. We begin to see ourselves in the same way that prejudiced and racist individuals see us, and not as

God sees us—and then, we allow their negative words and actions to invade our entire soul.

You must understand that the purging of your mind and thoughts can only be successfully achieved first by daily renewing of our minds with God's Holy Word (Romans 12:2; Ephesians 4:23-24). However, we must first receive in our hearts Jesus Christ, the Son of God, as our Lord and Savior Who reconciled us to God, and God's Holy Spirit Whom we have received through Christ. God, our Creator, through His Seed and manifested Word Jesus Christ revealed the excellence and magnificence of His boundless love for us and our true identity in Him [Jesus Christ] (John 3:16; Romans 8:35-39; Galatians 2:20). When, by the power of God, the Apostle Simon Peter recognized and acknowledged who Jesus Christ really is: "You are the Christ, the Son of the Living God", Jesus said to Peter : "Blessed are you, Simon Bar-Jonah for flesh and Blood has not revealed this to you, but my Father who is in heaven." (Matthew 16:15-17). Christ also revealed to Peter who He [Christ] is—the Eternal Rock: "And I say also unto thee, that thou art Peter, and upon this rock [Jesus] I will build my church; and the

*God's Holy Spirit within you will illuminate your spirit and soul.*

*Jesus Christ is our immovable spiritual Rock and Foundation.*

gates of hell shall not prevail against it." (Matthew 16:18) In addition, Christ released a promise to Peter and all of us who are believers in Him: "And I will give unto thee the keys of the kingdom of heaven: and whatsoever thou shalt bind on earth shall be bound in heaven: and whatsoever thou shalt loose on earth shall be loosed in heaven." (Matthew 16:19) We, the body of Christ, can stand on Him, Christ, the Rock—and by His authority in us, we can bind the vile spirit of racism!

If your heart is ready and open to receive Jesus Christ as your only Lord and Savior, you will also receive God's Holy Spirit who will reveal Who Christ is to you, and also reveal the deeper meanings of God's Holy Word (Matthew 3:16-17). If we abide in God's Holy Word, the Holy Spirit will continually reveal to us its deeper meanings—He will always lead us to all truth, both spiritual truth and truth in the physical environment (John 16:13). Through holy praise, worship, prayer and spiritual fasting, you will begin to develop a more intimate relationship with God, through Jesus Christ and God's Holy Spirit Who dwells within you. If you draw nearer to God, He will draw nearer to you (James 4:8). By revelation power of God's Holy Spirit through Christ, you will begin to acquire from God true spiritual knowledge, understanding and wisdom of His Holy Word. Simply put—the more you get to know God by knowledge, understanding and wisdom of His Holy Word, re-

*God's Holy Spirit within you will illuminate your heart and mind with God's glorious light of truth.*

vealed to you by His Holy Spirit through Jesus Christ, you will draw nearer to Him through holy praise, worship, prayer and spiritual fasting. When you draw nearer to God, He too will draw nearer to you (James 4:8a). Your true intimacy with God will begin to unravel to you true spiritual knowledge of who you are in Jesus Christ.

When you acknowledge Who God is and His power in your life through Jesus Christ, His spiritual knowledge and wisdom empower and sustain you and gradually reveal God's faithful Word and promises for you. His Holy Spirit within you will illuminate your heart and mind with God's glorious light of truth (Ephesians 5:8). Through Jesus Christ, God will release in you greater power than your own (Matthew 16:18), which will protect you from the evil influences of the foul spirit of racism backed by the destructive attempts of Hades, the devil's place of torment. If you are facing racism, God will empower you to gain triumph over it. You will gradually begin to understand His essence and purpose for your creation, and that His promises for you include abundance of love, joy, hope and success in your life—even in the midst of difficult challenges and obstacles like racism. Realizing God's purpose for your creation is only possible through authentic spiritual knowledge. Revelation knowledge of His Holy Word can only

*Whatever form of racism or any other adversity that you may be facing now, Jesus Christ has already defeated it for you.*

make this clearer to you—through the inspiration power of His Holy Spirit Whom God gave us through His Son Jesus Christ. In simple terms, if you got to know Jesus Christ, you would receive the Holy Spirit Whom would lead you to all truth (John 16:13) and teach you all things (John 14:26), and God would reveal to you whom you truly were (Mathew 16:15-19).

While racism may have the potential to be a destructive and evil force, your Holy Spirit-empowered spirit and soul are well-equipped to handle and disable its malicious and destructive forces, rendering them utterly powerless against your life (Luke 10:18-19). Through authentic spiritual knowledge in Jesus Christ, you would become empowered to deal with and overcome the effects of racism.

All things have been placed by God under the Feet of Jesus Christ (1 Corinthians 15:28), therefore, you then being under the holy covering of His Blood and righteousness have His spiritual authority over the adversities that you face, and this includes racism (Luke 10:18-19). Through Jesus Christ Who has defeated all principalities on our behalf, God has given you spiritual authority to break down evil influences first in the spiritual and then in the natural realm. This means that whatever form of racism or any other adversity you may be facing now, Jesus Christ has already defeated it for you (John 16:33). Thus, if you acknowledged Jesus

*Through Jesus Christ, you would become the head over racism and not the tail under it.*

Christ as the Head over your daily personal affairs, tapped into God's glorious power in His Holy Word through His Holy Spirit, and walked in obedience of God's Word, the victory that He, Christ, has already obtained for you, would begin to manifest in your life (1 John 5:4). Through Him [Jesus Christ], you would become the head over racism and not the tail under it.

*Have you made Jesus Christ the Head over your daily personal affairs?*

**Chapter Quiz**

1. Who is the Eternal Rock of Ages through Whom God delivers you from all evil, including racism and the spirit of racism?

___

2. True or false: Jesus Christ has defeated all forms of racism for you. Explain your answer.

___

3. True or false: Without God's protective covering through Jesus Christ racism has the potential to become a very negative and destructive tool against your heart, mind, thoughts, emotions, words, actions, will, resolve, personality and behavior. Explain your answer.

---

4. True or false: All things have been placed by God under the Feet of Jesus Christ, therefore, you then being under the holy covering of His precious Blood and righteousness have His spiritual authority over the adversities that you face, and this includes racism. Explain your answer.

---

ꝏꝏꝏꝏꝏꝏ ♦ ♦ ♦ ♦ ♦ ꝏꝏꝏꝏꝏꝏ

**Reflections:**

---

---

---

---

ꝏꝏꝏꝏꝏꝏ ♦ ♦ ♦ ♦ ♦ ꝏꝏꝏꝏꝏꝏ

# CHAPTER 19: Power of Dominion Over Racism

God has given us dominion—power, authority, control, command, over the earth, our environment, with all of the challenges, obstacles and situations that it may present to us at various times (Genesis 1:26-28). We, humans, may choose to either preserve the Earth or destroy it; and in many ways we seem to have chosen the latter—to destroy not just the Earth but also our fellow human beings.

Through Jesus Christ, God has given us victory over the world and its evils orchestrated by the devil through its willing human hosts (John 16:33). God has also empowered us individually and collectively through Christ, and so He expects us to surmount the problems that we encounter and not to let the challenges consume us (Romans 8:37). Therefore, you have the mandate from God through Jesus Christ to victoriously overcome racist acts that may be directed against you (1 John 5:4). Racism does not have power over you; rather you have the authority and power of Jesus Christ in you over evil principalities, dark powers, rulers of the darkness of this age and spiritual hosts of wickedness in the heavenly places that perpetrate and perpetuate it (Ephesians 6:12). However, having dominion over evil, like racism, does not mean that you alone as an individual can fight racism in your community, city, county, borough, district, or in the world. It means that you as an individual can gain spiritual and personal victory over racism, and collectively as individuals and Christian believers (the Body of Christ), we can all gain dominion over racism that exists in the world, by standing in the victory that Christ obtained for us. Remember that God has given you and I (us), the church, the Body of Jesus Christ, the authority and power of Christ over every form of evil (Luke 10:17-19). So, exercising personal dominion over racism is gaining your own individual victory over it through Jesus Christ. How can you achieve this?

*God's grace within each of us is enough to give us complete victory over racism.*

To activate God's spiritual authority over our personal problems we must exercise undoubting faith in His enabling power and grace. Our individual faith is powered by God's Holy Word abiding in us—when we read it and meditate on it (John 15:1-17)—and through faith-fueled prayers of thanksgiving and praise, and holy worship (Psalms 29:2; Psalms 95:6; Philippians 2:9-11; Psalms 99:5; Revelation 4:11). By our faith in Jesus Christ and the Holy Spirit Who dwell in us, we can activate God's

Kingdom Power within us, and take dominion over challenges like racism and its negative effects.

The limitations that racism attempts to place on you are illegal, because God never places limitations on the creative abilities of any man or woman. Men and women create and implement such limitations on themselves and others. If God meant to limit men and women, He would never have placed them in such a great universe of which the earth is only a small part. He meant for us to discover and subdue the earth on both individual and corporate levels. If God meant to limit our creative energy, He would never have allowed us to explore this universe as we wish, and in many cases, even to cause destructions in the very universe, especially the Earth we live in, that He created for our good.

*Racism cannot be a valid excuse for your lack of creativity.*

If God Who is our Creator has not placed any limitations on our creative abilities, then no man or woman should attempt to place any such limitations on us. So, a blind man becomes one of the greatest musicians of our times. So, an autistic child stares at an intricate city skyline for a short while and sometime later, recreates the same skyline as a pencil drawing with the same intricate details. So, a quadriplegic paints the most awesome pictures with a pencil in his or her mouth—a task that would have been expected of one with functioning hands and legs. And so many other similar cases that we rightly label as miracles—all of which show that even in seemingly handicapped situations, the creative energy and abilities of any man or woman remain undiminished. God has given us individually and corporately, dominion over the wicked activities of the foul spirit of racism. God's grace to us, that is, Jesus Christ within each of us, is sufficient to give us complete victory over racism or any other adversity (2 Corinthians 12:9; Revelation 12:11).

*Racism does not have power over you; rather you have the authority and power of Christ over it.*

Therefore, racism cannot be a valid excuse for your lack of creativity or accepting mediocrity or failure as your destiny. Don't allow the wicked tradition of racism in the world to dictate or dominate your heart and mind; rather let God's Holy Word and Holy Spirit direct your heart, mind and thinking. God has given you creative power—so use it positively to do great things in His Holy Name, and don't allow racism to be your excuse for failure. Don't let the vile spirit of racism and its willing hosts around you dictate or dominate your thinking and mindset; rather, let God's Holy Word soak your heart and His Holy Spirit empower your mind to rule over the wicked tradition of racism. Always remember that He, Jesus Christ, in you is greater that the vile spirit of racism, its willing human hosts and its foul outgrowth that manifests as racist activities directed against your life (1 John 4:4). Yes, believe and declare that through Christ, you are victorious over racism (1 John 5:4).

**Chapter Quiz**

1. True or false: You have authority and dominion over the evil spirit of racism. Explain your answer.

______________________________________________

2. True or false: You are more than a conqueror through Jesus Christ over the loathsome spirit of racism. Explain your answer.

______________________________________________

3. In what ways can you activate God's spiritual authority in and over your life?

______________________________________________

4. True or false: Racism and the wicked spirit of racism have placed limitations on your creative abilities, your future and success. Explain your answer.

______________________________________________

5. True or false: God understands that racism is your bona fide excuse for receiving or allowing permanent failure or lack of success in your life. Explain your answer.

______________________________________________

6. True or false: God's Holy Word declares that God will back you against the foul spirit of racism as long as you

continue to complain about racism and racists without taking positive, constructive spiritual steps against them, and without having to work hard towards achieving success in your life. Explain your answer.

---

∞∞∞∞∞∞ ♦ ♦ ♦ ♦ ♦ ∞∞∞∞∞∞

**Reflections:**

---

---

---

---

∞∞∞∞∞∞ ♦ ♦ ♦ ♦ ♦ ∞∞∞∞∞∞

# CHAPTER 20: False Security in Worldly Attachment

Most of us have been taught or conditioned to have more of a worldly attachment than a godly connection with the only One divine, God through our Lord and Savior, Jesus Christ. For many of us, our physical environment dictates the state of our being, and if we happen to have accumulated worldly materials we tend to have a false sense of security. This is false knowledge because the truth is that we came into this world with nothing and we also leave with nothing (Matthew 6:19-21; Proverbs 11:4). Let's not forget that material things can only attend to the needs of our physical body, but not our soul and spirit. We should not become attached to superficial things that cannot, in any way, connect us to our Maker. God instructed Moses and Israelites, and Jesus Christ taught humanity, that material things are not enough to sustain us (Deuteronomy 8:3; Matthew 4:4; 1 Timothy

6:17). What brings true meaning to our lives is first our utmost love for God, our relationship and spiritual walk with Him through Jesus Christ and His Holy Spirit who dwells within us; and also our knowledge and obedience of God's Holy Word and its holy power in us through Jesus Christ and His Holy Spirit. Then, as one of God's earthly vessels, our love for humanity, our realization of God's purpose for our lives, its fulfillment and the positive spiritual impact we have on others—fuel within us real meaning of our lives.

Before we encounter challenges that surpass our human strengths, the actions of some of us seem to suggest that we believe the illusion that short-lived material things can give peace to our inner chaos. But at some point in our life when we experience injustice, oppression, loss of a loved one or dear friend, or other traumatic circumstances, we quickly discover that our wealth, success or other earthly gains cannot shelter our soul from pain, hurt, anxiety or other negative experiences. Our worldly connections cannot protect us from subtle racist experiences. In many instances, due to racial bias, innocent people have been followed around in stores having been stereotyped as potential thieves, in some cases shot fatally or wounded or accused wrongly of crimes, and wrongly convicted and sentenced to death and executed.

*Material things do not define a person's true worth, cannot give us true joy here on earth or eternal salvation.*

Attachment to material things is not pleasing to God. Material things do not define a person's true worth. Although material things can contribute to life's comfort and temporary happiness, they cannot give us true joy here on earth or eternal salvation. There are many definitions of happiness. I like to define happiness as a temporary state of feeling good about something or one's life; a state of being that is based on an external reason. Happiness is usually triggered by something we perceive to be positive; but one's state of happiness can be easily disturbed by something else, usually something we see or perceive as negative. On the other hand, true joy is an internal state of positive being that can also exude happiness on the outside, but is usually unperturbed by any external change. From a Christian perspective, authentic joy is Christ-rooted within our soul; a constant expression of our Holy Spirit-filled nature, our new person in Jesus Christ. This is why the Bible tells us that the joy of the Lord is our strength and the Lord is our strength (Nehemiah 8:10; Exodus 15:2; Psalms 28:7; Proverbs 18:2,10; Psalms 46:1). Basically, we cannot have true joy without *truly* receiving Jesus Christ in us. Money may make you happy temporarily but it cannot give you true joy. You can acquire a lot of money and material wealth and still have a huge void in you that they cannot fill.

*Do you feel secure in your worldly possessions?*

Money and affluence are good, but should not be worshipped or ranked above human life. Money can increase your buying power but may not necessarily give you true and sustained joy and contentment. A very successful and wealthy person as the world defines it that may seem happy outwardly, could at the same time lack authentic joy in their heart, and may be going through bouts of intermittent depression with feelings of hopelessness and unworthiness. This person though very wealthy has other challenges that money is not able to fix. God is the only One Who can fix all things; therefore our relationship with Him should be ranked above all other things.

An English lawyer and philosopher, Francis Bacon, Sr., (1561-1626) once said that "money is a good servant but a bad master." I agree with this statement because as a child of the Most High God, if you make money your servant you will use it to bless your family and loved ones, support God's true ministries and churches, spread the good news of the Gospel of Jesus Christ, and help many people in your community, state, country, and around the world. On the contrary, if you make money your master, you may strive to make money at any cost and by any means necessary, legal or illegal, ethical or unethical, moral or immoral, and you may use money to control or destroy others, rig elections by suppressing legitimate votes, support unjust laws, self-indulge, brag, and so on.

*Our worldly connections cannot protect us from subtle racist experiences.*

Many of us often confront this reality that our material possessions have not earned us and may never earn us true respect or regard from our fellow humans because of their negative response to our racial make-up. Sometimes, we experience people clutching tightly to their purses and briefcases, or running out of an elevator, as we enter for fear that we might attack or rob them of their possessions. Someone, let's call her "Rubie" once shared a story with me: she was at London Heathrow airport's Terminal 5 waiting to board a flight and decided to walk around the terminal like so many other travelers. She stopped at a well known retail shop to look at women's handbags. Let's call the shop "H." Rubie said that from the time she entered Shop "H" she was followed around and watched by one of the shop attendants. Finally, Rubie decided to purchase a handbag but not before she approached the shop attendant and asked her why she was following her around the shop. The attendant immediately denied that she was following Rubie even when it was obvious that she was. It is not surprising that the shop attendant denied that she was following Rubie because racism is a secret sin that most people deny practicing. Most people deny being prejudiced against any race or ethnic group and will never admit having a racist attitude.

*God's purpose for every single one of us is to become spiritual empowered for great success in our lives.*

A very wealthy individual "Gerald" once talked about their experience in an elevator. I call it the "elevator racism experience." As "Gerald" recalled the experience, when the door of the elevator opened, and he entered, he could see some of the individuals clutching tightly to their purses and briefcases. Those who had wrongly judged "Gerald" had no idea who he was and that he was far wealthier than all of them and was a respectable citizen in that society; they judged him solely based on his race and skin color. His humanity was not important to those in the elevator who stereotyped him to be a criminal; all that mattered to them was his race and skin color—to them he was just a potential thief getting ready to strike. Some people justify such racist attitudes by insisting that the perpetrators are simply fearful for the lives.

When we experience, hear of or see incidences like the elevator experience or Rubie's experience at London Heathrow airport Shop H, our hearts are wounded because we feel that we have been stereotyped based on our race and judged wrongly. We also realize that our level of education and professional achievements, wealth, succes, individual societal status, fine clothes or polished appearance, do not protect us from those sorts of negative racist experiences. In general, human respect for one another is usually based on race, money, education or possessions and other superficial reasons due to individual or collectively flawed judgments. However, the spirit of racism even

*Most people deny being prejudiced or racist against any race or ethnic group.*

seems to cancel the general norm that is the basis used to respect our fellow human beings.

Yet, God has asked us to respect one another simply based on our humanity—we are all human beings created in the excellent Image of One God—our God Who is the Triune God—God the Father, God the Son Jesus Christ and God the Holy Spirit. This is a very simple basis of respect for all humans that most people don't seem to care about; rather people tend to base their respect for other humans on what society considers the "right" or "preferred" race and ethnicity along with economic status, good education, wealth, possessions and so on. This is a flawed premise on which to base respect because they are tangibles that are temporary. Individually and collectively, we should fight racism because it is a viscious attack on our God-given freedom, humanity and dignity.

*Racism can cause a person to bury his or her God-given talents if he or she internalized its negative effects.*

Racism could cause a person to bury his or her God-given talents if he or she internalized its negative effects, especially, the lack of regard for his or her humanity by racists. If you allowed yourself to feel devalued by racism, it could defeat your mind and life and this is not God's holy plan for your life. A famous quote by Eleanor Roosevelt says that "No one can make you feel inferior without your consent." This is very true because

God has not authorized anyone to make you feel inferior, only you can allow it.

When a person feels devalued, he or she also receives a victim mentality and begins to believe that he or she lacks the ability and power to achieve anything worthwhile in life. In some cases, a person who feels devalued due to his or her experiences with racism may begin to assume a whole new false identity, and operate solely based on a defiled "photocopy" of him or her—one which their immediate environment or the world designed for them. This is one of the negative spin-off or lingering effects of racism which could also cause a person to begin to develop self-rejection, self-dislike, self-loathing or self-hate. Deep within such an individual is his or her true and excellent blueprint from God which remains buried in him or her. This person lives in a state of spiritual ignorance (Hosea 4:6) and does not know who he or she is in Jesus Christ. This person is operating based on a defiled copy and not the true blueprint of who he or she truly is in Jesus Christ. It is unlikely that such individuals recognize their blueprint because they lack a true godly spiritual connection and likely, function solely from a worldly perspective.

*Racism can cause a person to bury his or her God-given talents if he or she internalized its negative effects.*

Such a perspective cannot adequately equip anyone to deal victoriously with racism; rather it allows his or her soul to become a slave to racism. Lack of authentic spiritual knowledge veils his or her heart and mind with its negative cloud. Over time, consciously or unconsciously, such individuals, some of whom may be born-again children of God and His heirs and co-heirs with Jesus Christ, lose godly direction for their true purpose, and feel spiritually powerless to deal with racism. And yet, God's holy purpose for them and every single one of us is to become spiritually empowered for great success in our lives (Jeremiah 29:11).

How can you activate the holy power of Jeremiah 29:11 in your life? Through daily relationship and true holy intimacy with God—prayer, thanksgiving, praise, worship and spiritual fasting—and trusting God always! The devil battles your life daily in the spirit realm and these battles manifest as challenges and obstacles in your physical environment. He plans to use evil attacks upon your life to derail you from what God has destined for you, from blessings that God has released into your life (Daniel 10:12). Racism is only one of many evil intrigues that the devil stages and manifests against your life through other humans. You should be spiritually alert always because the devil continually stages evil spiritual battles against your life.

*Prayer is your spiritual weapon for activating the power of God's Holy Word in your life.*

Faith-fueled prayer, praise and worship are your spiritual weapons for activating the power of God's Holy Word in your life. Prayers can successfully change the course of your life for the better (1 Chronicles 4:9-10). Prayer is the spiritual tool for you to take your stand in the victory of Jesus Christ over any form of evil (Esther 3-7; 2 Chronicles 20). The power of prayers will turn the evil meant by racists into something good and prosperous in your life (Romans 8:28).

Once in my life, my racist managers gave me the worst job to do in the department because they intended to "slow down" my career by giving me mundane roles and responsibilities that no one else wanted. But God turned it around for my good—one year later it turned out that the skills I acquired while performing the "bad" job was what was needed in another company for a much higher position. The company hired me and my new position and salary became two levels higher than my previous position. You see, what my racist offenders meant for my destruction, God turned around for my good (Romans 8:28).

*Stand firmly on Jesus Christ and racism will never succeed in destroying you.*

A successful and sustained spiritual connection with God is the most important resting-place for our spiritual and physical well-being. Our authentic spiritual foundation needs to be built on the solid Rock of Jesus Christ Who is God's Kingdom Power within those of us who are Christian born-again believers. When you stand firmly on Jesus Christ, racism may bombard you with its fiery darts, but will never succeed in destroying you (Matthew7:24-27).

Now is the time to delete any negative mindset that fosters self-dislike, self-rejection, self-loathing or self hate, and claim the victory of Jesus Christ for your life (1 John 5:4). Now is the time to begin to declare: "I am loved by God Almighty, in the awesome Name of my Lord and Savior, Jesus Christ; and no spirit that is contrary to God's Holy Spirit will ever dwell in me. In the mighty Name of Jesus Christ, I cancel any negative mindset and declare myself free of the the foul spirit of self-dislike, self-rejection, self-loathing or self. I claim the victory that God has released to me through Christ, Amen.

> *Our authentic spiritual foundation needs to be built on the solid Rock of Jesus Christ.*

**Chapter Quiz**

1. True or false: Our worldly possessions can protect us here on earth and provide us the key to eternal salvation. Explain your answer.

---

2. True or false: God measures our true worth by our race, ethnic, nationality, material possessions, proper educa-

tion, status in society or any other tangible wealth that we may have accumulated in the world. Explain your answer.

---

3. True or false: Our true spiritual connection to God through Jesus Christ is the most important resting-place for our spiritual and physical well-being. Explain your answer.

---

4. Your true spiritual foundation needs to be built on who and what, and maintained how?

---

ooooooooooo ♦ ♦ ♦ ♦ ♦ ooooooooooo

**Reflections:**

---

---

---

---

ooooooooooo ♦ ♦ ♦ ♦ ♦ ooooooooooo

# CHAPTER 21: A Negative Mind Fosters Spirit of Self-Hate

Have you allowed the loathsome spirit of racism to deposit self-hate within your soul? The foul spirit of racism deposits self-hate in both the perpetrator and the target of racism. Racists exhibit self-hate by hating others; they try to intimidate those they hate; they verbally insult them and may act violently against them. Their self-hate stems from internalized self-loathing, self-dislike and self-rejection which they project outwardly as hate for others. Those targeted by racists may also develop self-hate as well as hate for others, especially their racist offenders.

Self-hate is usually hidden at the sub-conscious level, but manifests at the conscious level in negative and self-condemning thoughts, words and actions and perception of self. Self-hate can manifest itself in many different and subtle ways, especially in a person who receives the deceptive spirit of rejection from racists. The person who receives the spirit of rejection may dislike him or herself, as well as others who may share similar racial or ethnic identifiers. Such an individual experiencing self-hate may make a conscious effort to stay away from others with similar racial identifiers, while making a concerted effort to look like or mingle with those considered by society as the "preferred race." An individual expressing self-hate at their sub-conscious or conscious state may feel rejected by society, primarily by his or her daily experiences with racism. By negative reinforcement, that is, continuing to receive and internalize the negative perceptions about him, her or others with similar racial identifiers, this individual ultimately develops chronic feelings of self-loathing, self-dislike or self-rejection that silently transform into self-hate. Subconsciously, by distancing him or her from others of the same race and by associating with those endorsed by society to be the "preferred race", he or she thinks that society will become more accepting of him or her. Such a person may also allow him or herself to be used by the vile spirit of racism and its racist human hosts as a tool against others, including those with similar racial identifiers. This is a subconscious self-deprecating process, a self-limiting and destructive course that blurs one's view of their true identity and nature in Jesus Christ.

> *When you have feelings of self-hate within you, you lack authentic spiritual knowledge of self.*

Yet the true reality is that such individuals should have godly self-love in them because they are so fearfully and wonderfully made in God's excellent Image (Genesis 1:26-27; Psalms 139:14); God loves you so much without boundaries or limitations (Jeremiah 1:5; Romans 8:35-39). He validated and enriched you through Jesus Christ (John 3:16; 2 Corinthians 1:22). Therefore, when you have feelings of self-hate within you, you have no real spiritual knowledge of who you are in Jesus Christ; and you lack true spiritual knowledge of your divine Source—God Himself, who is love and in whose Image you were created. To harbor self-hate is to perish due to lack of true spiritual knowledge (Hosea 4:6).

Another form of manifestation of self-hate is a silent wish to be one of society's "preferred race;" rather than what you really are. It is a desire to be accepted by other "majority" or those who define the power structure and the benefits within a society. A feeling that another is actually more significant and better than you because they are of a certain race and have economic and political dominance, and as such, given the choice, you would prefer to be the other rather than yourself. This sort of feeling is a signal of a major internal spiritual crisis, which stems from a lack of true knowledge of God, lack of wholeness of one's spirit, and clearly, a lack of true knowledge of one's authentic identity and nature in Jesus Christ. True knowledge from God, our Creator, is that no individual, race or

*Do you see yourself as God sees you, and as His Holy Word declares: that you are a new creation in Jesus Christ? (2 Corinthians 5:17; Galatians 2:20).*

ethnic group is better than the other, in which case, no one is superior or inferior to another.

Self-hate can also result in self-limitation. When you are bound by self-hate, you become bound by self-limitations through the negative power of your mind. Through this negative force and energy, your own thoughts become dominated by "I can't", instead of "I can." To limit or doubt yourself is to limit or doubt God's awesome power within and through you. You cannot receive from God when your mind is in a state of doubt; it is either you believe and trust God or you don't (James 1:6-8). God's power cannot work and explode through you to do great things when you are bound by limitations. To limit yourself is to limit God's potentials within you (Proverbs 23:7). God Himself cannot be limited by anyone, situation or challenge. However, we, on the other hand, by our unbelief, lack of faith, and self-limitation set in our minds, can limit within us the manifestion of God's awesome power that transforms us into a positive spiritual "fire ball," positioning us to stand in the victory that Jesus Christ obtained for us (1 John 5:4).

*Do you see yourself as God sees you?*

Do you see yourself through the view of true knowledge of God's Word? Do you see yourself through God's holy purpose for which He created you? Or do you see yourself through the eyes of prejudiced and racist men and women who see you as unworthy, inferior or unequal to others? Do you see yourself as God sees you, and as His Holy Word declares: that you are a new creation in Jesus Christ? (2 Corinthians 5:17; Galatians 2:20) Do you spend quality time reading God's Holy Word and meditating on it to renew your mind? (Ephesians 4:21-24; Romans 12:2) You alone can answer these questions, and through your answers you can know if you have true spiritual knowledge in Jesus Christ or not. Knowledge of God and His Holy Word through Jesus Christ gives you the only authentic key to true self-knowledge. With true self-knowledge from God's Holy Word, self-hatred or rejection of self is no longer an option that you should entertain or leave a place for in your heart, mind, thoughts, emotions, will, resolve or actions.

To release the awesome power of God within you, you must unveil and remove the thick white cloud of self limitation that has kept you bound. So check yourself whenever feelings of self-dislike, self-loathing, self-distaste, self-hate or self-limitations start to creep-up in your mind; invite the Holy Spirit of God to help you clear and clean your mind with God's Word and His holy revelation power. In the Name of Jesus Christ, God's revelation will bring His restoration to your heart, thoughts, emotions, will, resolve or actions, through a process of daily renewal of your mind (Ephesians 4:21-24; Romans 12:2). He, Jesus Christ, Who is in you, is greater than he that is in the world (1 John 4:4). Through Him, allow God to transform you from having "victim mentality" to

*Self-hate is usually hidden at the sub-conscious level.*

"spiritual warrior and victor mindset" (Romans 8:37). Believe this now and always that you are a victor over racism and not its victim!

## Chapter Quiz

1. What is your own understanding of self-hate?

______________________________

2. Describe at least two ways that a racist exhibits self-hate.

______________________________

3. Describe at least two ways that one who is the target of racism can exhibit self-hate.

______________________________

4. Describe some of the effects of negative reinforcement that the foul spirit of racism uses against you through its willing racist human hosts.

______________________________

5. True or false: To limit or doubt yourself is to limit or doubt God's awesome power within and through you. Explain your answer.

______________________________

∞∞∞∞∞∞♦ ♦ ♦ ♦ ♦∞∞∞∞∞∞

**Reflections:**

______________________________

______________________________

______________________________

∞∞∞∞∞∞∞∞∞∞∞∞ ♦ ♦ ♦ ♦ ♦ ∞∞∞∞∞∞∞∞∞∞∞∞

# CHAPTER 22: From "Victim" to "Victor" of Racism

There are things we have to do to be able to move from victim to victor mentality. We have to ask God to give us His fresh breath (Genesis 2:7) so that we will become a new living being—a new person in Jesus Christ Whom we have accepted as our Lord and Savior (2 Corinthians 5:17; Galatians 2:20). We have to continually renew our mind with God's Holy Word (Romans 12:2; Ephesians 4:23-24). We have to believe, receive and apply God's Holy Word in our lives. We have to ask God for a fresh anointing by the power of His Holy Spirit to cleanse our wrong thoughts and beliefs about who we are. We must participate in this change process by reading and meditating on God's Holy Word for continual renewing of our mind (Romans 12:2; Ephesians 4:23-24). We have to be open to receiving and operating in God's divine favor, His grace that is more than sufficient for us, to oppose the "victim mentality" and replace it with the "victor mentality" that Jesus Christ has given us (2 Corinthians

12:9; Romans 8:37). This is the right, godly, spiritual and mental attitude to deal with racism because thoughts of being a victim can pollute our heart, weaken our inner person and disorganize our mind and thinking and these are signals of a crisis within our soul. The "victim mentality" can dismantle or disorganize the powerful force of a conqueror within us—power that Jesus Christ already gave us (Romans 8:37). The holy power of God within us through Christ is what will defeat any form of racism that is aimed at any one of us. God is the only real strength and power that transforms us into unquenchable and rechargeable "batteries" so that we remain undefeated and undestroyed by evils such as racism. Revelation knowledge of God's Holy Word through Jesus Christ and His Holy Spirit gives us authentic spiritual knowledge, which is the key to the conqueror within us. Without true spiritual knowledge from God's Holy Word, we lack true self-knowledge (Hosea 4:6), and we may continue to see ourselves as a "victim" of racism or other negative circumstances.

*God is the strength and power that transforms us into unquenchable and rechargeable "batteries."*

God has not authorized any child of His, who has *truly* accepted Jesus Christ as his or her Lord and Savior, and Redeemer of the world, become squashed by racism or claim the victim mentality (Isaiah 54:15,17). You have God's power thoughts from His Holy Word in you. Power thoughts are positive thoughts that renew and empower you for victorious living based on God's Word. You have to believe this and act on your faith in daily spiritual prayer warfare against racism. Fully knowing and understanding who you are is an essential ingredient for your victory over racism. This is because you have the victorious power of Jesus Christ in you—the spiritual power of God within you Who has already obtained permanent triumph over hidden or blatant racism. Therefore, even when it seems like you are outnumbered and overpowered in your physical surroundings, know that you are surrounded by God's invisible and invicible army and victory is yours to claim (2 Kings 6:16-17). Even if you fell or made mistakes in your daily battles against racism, through Christ God has gained victory for you because you love, acknowledge and trust Him (Psalms 91:14-15), and obey Him (Joshua 1:7-9). Believe now that God will always protect and rescue you from those who plan to defeat and destroy you; He, God, Who is the Alpha and Omega—the Beginning and the End, will honor you before your enemies and He will be with you wherever you go—if you trust Him and hold onto His Holy Word (Joshua 1:7-9; Psalms 23:5).

*Your enemies will become God's enemies and He will oppose those who oppose you (Exodus 23:22).*

God will position you for victory as He takes you from being a victim to a victor over racism. He will begin to sharpen the skills and talents you know you have, and bring out hidden ones that you never knew that you had; He will purge your mind of the negative junk from your experiences with racism, and fill you up like a holy jar with His anointing oil—the power of Jesus Christ (the Living Word of God) through the Holy Spirit. Like God did for Jabez, may He use the pain you have experienced from your racist offenders, the rejection you experienced from those who mocked you, the wicked words of racists who said that you were insignificant and not good enough because of your race, ethnicity or nationality, to bless and anoint you, enlarge your territory, keep you from evil, and make you a blessing to many, and not an instrument of pain to anyone (1 Chronicles 4:9-10)

If you let God, He will use the racial barriers raised by your racist attackers to make ladders of opportunities and hedges of protection for you (Romans 8:28). He will demolish the vile spirit of Haman that comes against you in the form of racism (Esther 7:6, 8-10). He will remove racists from your career paths and replace them with those whom He has selected and appointed to do right by you in accordance with His will and purpose for you in that environment. If you stayed close to God and obeyed His Holy Word, your enemies will become God's enemies and He will oppose those who oppose you (Exodus 23:22); and there will be no way any weapon they have fashioned against you will ever prevail (Isaiah 54:17). Through Jesus Christ, God placed in you His Holy

*Ask God for a fresh anointing by the power of His Holy Spirit to cleanse your wrong thoughts and beliefs.*

Spirit—His Stamp of Ownership in you (2 Corinthians 1:21-22). The power of God will be released in your life like an endless fountain of His glory; and through Jesus Christ He has given you victory over racism.

Now, watch and see how God will deliver you from the evil spirit of Haman and save you from the gallows that racists built for you (Esther 7). Watch and see how God will do great and mighty things for you with quiet splendor! Just believe God and in Him through Jesus Christ!

**Chapter Quiz**

1. How does having a victim mentality contradict Romans 8:37?

___

2. How does having a victim mentality contradict Luke 10:18-19?

___

3. True or false: God's Holy Word, the Bible, encourages you to have a victim mentality because that's where your victory lies. Explain your answer and cite one Scripture passage to support your answer.

___

4. True or false: God's Holy Word, the Bible, encourages you to have a victor mentality because that's where your

victory lies. Explain your answer and cite one Scripture passage to support your answer.

---

5. Romans 8:28: Do you believe that God can use the racial barriers raised by your racist attackers to make ladders of opportunities and hedges of protection for you? Explain your answer.

---

6. Do you believe that God can use racial barriers to create stepping stones for a victorious life for you? Explain your answer.

---

7. If your answer to # 5 and #6 is "yes", what power thoughts must you apply daily for you to change how you see racism?

---

∞∞∞∞∞∞ ♦ ♦ ♦ ♦ ♦ ∞∞∞∞∞∞

**Reflections:**

---

---

---

---

∞∞∞∞∞∞ ♦ ♦ ♦ ♦ ♦ ∞∞∞∞∞∞

# CHAPTER 23: God's Stamp of Validation and Ownership

If you have received Jesus Christ as your personal Lord and Savior, then you are born again (John 3:6-7, Romans 10:9-10) and have received God's Stamp of Validation and Ownership sealed by His Holy Spirit. God's Stamp of Validation on you costs you absolutely nothing because Jesus Christ has already paid the cost on your behalf—and God has placed His Stamp of Ownership on you by giving you His Holy Spirit Who dwells within you (2 Corinthians 1:20-22; Ephesians 1:13-14). The cost of God's Stamp of Validation on you, paid by the precious Blood of Jesus Christ, has invaluable eternal worth (1 Corinthians 6:19-20). This Holy Stamp is not seen by human eyes; it is received by faith in Jesus Christ. It is a spiritual Stamp that can only be perceived by a spiritual mind (1 Corinthians 2:6-10-15). The precondition required for you to receive and apply this Stamp of Validation is by faith: to believe that Jesus Christ died for your sins and was raised from the dead by God, and to receive Him as your personal Lord and Savior (John 3:16; Romans 10:9-10), and then receive God's Holy Spirit to abide in you (John 14:16-24). You have to believe in your heart that God's Stamp of Validation and Ownership of you—the Holy Spirit has been sealed in and on you through the precious Blood of Jesus Christ.

It is God Who reveals to us who we *truly* are in Christ, what we are, and our invaluable worth and purpose to Him first, and then to others in the world. It is also God Who reveals to us that once He validates us through Jesus Christ, no demon, human or circumstance can erase His Holy Spirit-sealed Stamp of Ownership off us—to deem us worthless, inferior, lower, unable, weak, defeated, or a victim of any circumstance. Why? How? Through Christ, God has transformed you into more than a conqueror of the vile spirit of racism, its evil fruit of racism and its willing human hosts who are racists (Romans 8:37). The power of God hidden in His Holy Word, the Sword of the Spirit, drawn by His Holy Spirit within us by faith, removes from our way any evil accuser or attacker, including our racist offenders being backed by the foul spirt of racism. God has cancelled all charges leveled against us by Satan through any means including racism. He has disarmed principalities and powers that have stood against us and made a

*God's Stamp of Validation has been sealed in and on you by the precious Blood of Jesus Christ.*

public disgrace of them, giving us the final victory through Jesus Christ (Colossians 2:14-15)

No man or woman has been given the right to control your mind, thoughts or actions. No man or woman has been authorized by God to attack you and if they did, surely, they would fail (Isaiah 54:15). If you abide in secret place of the Most High God you will come under His awesome Shadow—His holy protection (Psalms 91:1-2). Your spirit, soul and body belong to God, your Creator—He, God, owns you and if you let Him, He will provide you guidance through His Holy Spirit Who dwells within you through Jesus Christ. Nurture your spirit for it is the core of your being. The power of your spirit controls your soul—that is, your heart, mind, thoughts, emotions, will and resolve, and also your words, actions and entire being. True knowledge of God by His Holy Word, gives you authentic spiritual understanding, equips your own spirit and soul with divine power and wisdom, and unravels your true identity and nature in Jesus Christ to you. Now, once you truly know yourself, then you can harness the power of God's Holy Word through Jesus Christ, and His Holy Spirit Who dwells within you.

*No man or woman has been given the right to control your mind, thoughts or actions.*

Don't be fooled by the prejudiced and racist person who attempts to convince you that you are nobody and insignificant, less than human or unequal to them or others. Don't be fooled by the untruth, for they speak the lies of the devil who is the father of all lies (John 8:44). In reality, you are significant—you are a victor over racism and not a victim of racism—and you are not inferior or superior to anyone. You are a special and unique individual, have always been and always will be. You are an intelligent and gifted child of the Most High God. The evil spirit of racism has lied to you and veiled your mind (2 Corinthians 4:4). All lies are from the devil (John 8:44). Thrash all lies! Thrash all racist lies!

*The power of God's holy light suffocates the darkness of racism.*

To help you unveil your mind to discern and recognize any and all partial truth and lies: read and meditate on the Holy Word of God (Joshua 1:7-9); continually renew your mind with God's Holy Word by reading and dwelling in it (Romans 12:2; Ephesians 4:23-24); pray without ceasing (1 Thessalonians 5:1); praise and worship God in spirit and truth (John 4:24); and reach out to *true* women and men of God to learn more about the glory and power of God. Once revelation power of God's Holy Word through His Holy Spirit has removed the veil from your eyes (2 Corinthians 3:18), no demon, human or circumstance can ever fool you with their lies. Then authentic spiritual knowledge by revelation knowledge of the Holy Spirit of God will spring forth like an oasis in a desert and become the unceasing, sustaining and restoring fresh spring in your life (John 7:38; John 4:5-15).

God's Holy Stamp of Validation and Ownership on you through Jesus Christ lets you know through authentic spiritual knowledge from His Holy Word and Holy Spirit that you are worthy and able, whole and complete in Jesus Christ, and an overcomer and conqueror of your life's challenges through Him. True spiritual knowledge lets you know that if only you believed God and His Word, you will witness His glory in your life (John 11:40). You are a child of an awesome God and you have His brilliant light, His rays of victory within your spirit and soul. God is light and wherever His light is there can never be darkness (1 John 1:5). The power of His holy light suffocates the darkness of racism. It's up to you to claim and activate His victory within you through Jesus Christ and allow the power of Christ's victory to translate first into spiritual victory and then into material success. This becomes your applause of your true spiritual identity of God Kingdom Power within you through Jesus Christ.

*All lies are from the devil (John 8:44). Thrash all lies! Thrash all racist lies!*

**Chapter Quiz**

1. As a believer in Jesus Christ, in what way has God validated you?

______________________________________________

2. What do you need to do to activate God's validation in you through Jesus Christ?

---

3. Explain the power of God's Holy Stamp of Validation and Ownership in you over the spirit of racism.

---

4. True or false: Your racist accuser or offender is superior to you. Explain your answer.

---

5. True or false: Your racist offender is inferior to you. Explain your answer.

---

6. True or false: You are superior to your racist offender. Explain your answer.

---

7. True or false: You are inferior to your racist offender. Explain your answer.

---

8. True or false: Your racist offender is neither superior nor inferior to you. Explain your answer.

---

9. True or false: You are neither superior nor inferior to your racist offender. Explain your answer.

---

∞∞∞∞∞∞∞∞ ♦ ♦ ♦ ♦ ♦ ∞∞∞∞∞∞∞∞

**Reflections:**

________________________________________

________________________________________

________________________________________

________________________________________

∞∞∞∞∞∞∞∞ ♦ ♦ ♦ ♦ ♦ ∞∞∞∞∞∞∞∞

# CHAPTER 24: Applaud Your True Spiritual Identity

Your racial and ethnic make-up is exactly as God wants you to be in His excellent Image. Your skin color is exactly how God intended you to look and you do not have to tan your pale skin or bleach your dark skin or make any apologies, feel ashamed or feel unworthy for being as your were created.

What is your race, ethnicity or nationality? Whatever it is, you are created in God's excellent Image. Yes, you are beautiful in the eyes of God your Maker. You are born equal to every person. You are born and created rich with unique gifts, talents and abilities. You are neither superior nor inferior to any person. God's grace to us, Jesus Christ is His divine favor in your life and is enough for your spiritual and material success, because He has already blessed you with many talents and potentials. He is the only One through Whom God gives you true, holy and heavenly power to get wealth (Deuteronomy 8:18). You have many talents and at least one of these talents, if channeled properly, effectively, efficiently and guided by God's Holy Spirit will make you highly successful despite racism and its many evils. You are elegant in the eyes of all of God's worthy creations. You are a special being with a unique purpose in life. The power of God inside of you is greater and bigger than any negative challenge that is outside of you (1 John 4:4). Therefore, the power of God inside of you is greater than racism and His grace is sufficient for you to overcome it (2 Corinthians 12:9).

God meticulously created you with His own Hands and directed your conception and nine months of gestation (Jeremiah 1:5; Psalms 139:13). Even if you were born prematurely, God still directed it. He watched you minute-by-minute during each day and night until you became "fully-grown" in your mother's womb and was ready to be born and presented to the world. So, your unique creation and life is designed to be a blessing to the world. Your race or ethnicity, whatever it may be, is designed to add diversity to the world. Creation and nature embraced and welcomed you into the world. Therefore, no man or woman has the right to use racism to make you uncomfortable in this world that Jesus Christ has already defeated on your behalf (John 16:33). He, Jesus Christ, has overcome this world for you; and because by faith you have received Him as your Lord and

*Your unique creation and life is designed to be a blessing to the world.*

Savior, you too have overcome the world (1 John 5:4-5)—you have overcome racism in the world.

Every human, man or woman, irrespective of what their skin color, racial makeup or ethnicity may be, has the intrinsic and innate ability to dream great dreams and achieve the greatness of his or her dreams. God has a unique purpose for you; He has only thoughts of good and not of evil for you; and He has designated a beautiful journey for you (Jeremiah 29:11). He has given you the gift to first capture this journey in your dreams, then as you go through life, to continue to visualize this journey as it is in your dreams. Then by staying the course of your dreams by faith in Jesus Christ, through God's inspiration, and by working hard to achieve your dreams through His divine favor, your dreams will become reality. God gave you the power to dream as your first baby steps to claiming your life's purpose and journey.

*God has a unique purpose for you, and He has designated a beautiful journey for you (Jeremiah 29:11).*

In Ephesians 1:18-23, Apostle Paul presents to us quite vividly the awesome power of God in us who are believers in Jesus Christ. Undoubtely, we have the victorious power of Christ in us! So, if you knew who you were in Jesus Christ, the psychological effects of racism designed to break you should instead, sail over you as though they were made of oil and you of water. The evil effects of racism should be repelled off you on the outside, while your inner person remains untouched; bubbling with joyous expectation of the fulfillment of the excellent purpose for which God made you (Jeremiah 29:11). You must be deeply rooted in Jesus Christ. You must be and remain like a giant fruit tree planted by the streams of a gushing fresh spring and which will yield good fruit in season (Psalms 1:3). On the outside of a giant fruit tree are multiple concentric rings of age: small, medium and large sizes of rings. It may have scars of wounds from many assaults of mankind and other elements of nature. Still on the outside, in between some of the scars and rings of age, may be more cuts and bruises from recent assaults by mankind and inclement weather effects. Nonetheless, the giant fruit tree has large, healthy and deep roots firmly planted below the ground. So, as you cut through the bark of the trunk of the giant fruit tree into its insides, you are amazed to find that it remains fresh, supple, without scars, and completely whole. This is simply because the tree was prepared for the assault from mankind and other elements of nature. It protected its inner core even as its outside was assaulted with bruises and what seemed like deep wounds.

*Fine focus your faith, work hard and achieve the greatness of your dreams to fulfill God's purpose for your life.*

Are you like the giant fruit tree? Are you deeply planted by the rivers of living water, Jesus Christ? (Psalms 1:1-3; John 4:13-15) Are you sure that in the face of any adversity, including the fiery darts of racism, that you will not wither and give up? (2

Corinthians 4:8-11) Are you ready to receive God's Holy Spirit anointing so that whatever you do will prosper in the Name of Jesus Christ? It is a 'wise' tree that knows that its core is the essence of its life and existence. So, it holds on to the power vested inside it by God Who is its Maker, and it refuses to die even when all of the external elements of assault have engineered plans to ensure its death.

There is some semblance to your soul when it is powered by your spirit and empowered by God's Holy Word and Holy Spirit Who dwells within you through Jesus Christ. You may be wounded on the outside by many assaults; painful past and present experiences with racism, but if you are rooted in Christ, the power of the Holy Spirit of God Who dwells within your spirit, if you recognized and allowed it to work for you, would protect your inner core, your spirit, and shield your soul from toxic damage. Your spirit, now empowered by God through Christ and the Holy Spirit, could subdue and overcome the effects of any such assault on your soul, leaving the cuts, bruises and scars only on the outside, while your inside, like the giant fruit tree, would remain completely intact and whole. Then, by the awesome power of God through Christ and the Holy Spirit, your heart and mind would be free from any and all assaults of racism that would be rendered completely useless and harmless

*You are a unique person carrying God's great and unique purpose.*

against your life. Now, you are able to fine focus your faith, work hard and achieve the greatness of your dreams to fulfill God's purpose for your life. Then, you would become more than a conqueror of racism and other challenges through Jesus Christ (Romans 8:37).

So, now you know that you have always been and always will be that special child of God, your Maker. Now, you know that His creation has embraced you, and He, God, has a special place and role for you in this world. Now, you know that you are a unique person carrying God's great and unique purpose. You must live your life to the fullest and become the awesome person that God has planned you to be. You must do great exploits for God in the Name of our Lord and Savior Jesus Christ. Don't let racism derail you and mess up God's wonderful and excellent plan for you (Jeremiah 29:11). Don't allow yourself to be downtrodden by racism! Don't disappoint God! Don't disappoint yourself!

*Don't let racism derail you and mess up God's wonderful and excellent plan for you (Jeremiah 29:11).*

∞∞∞∞∞∞♦♦♦♦♦∞∞∞∞∞∞

## Chapter Quiz

1. True or false: God made a mistake when He created you to be of a specific race or ethnicity. So you must strive to change your physical appearance in order to

look like individuals of a "preferred" race, ethnicity or nationality. Explain your answer.

---

2. True or false: The power that God has given to you to succeed is under the control of your racist oppressor or offender; so you must submit to them and not to God. Explain your answer.

---

3. True or false: The negative power of your own mind has more power than racism to destroy you. Explain your answer.

---

4. Jeremiah 29:11: How can you "stand" on this Scripture when you encounter racism?

---

∞∞∞∞∞∞ ♦ ♦ ♦ ♦ ♦ ∞∞∞∞∞∞

**Reflections:**

---

---

---

---

∞∞∞∞∞∞ ♦ ♦ ♦ ♦ ♦ ∞∞∞∞∞∞

# CHAPTER 25: Are You Downtrodden by Racism?

If you allowed yourself to be downtrodden by racism, you would fail to be a conqueror of it, which Jesus Christ has already made you (Romans 8:37). This also means that you are not walking boldly in the authority (Psalms 91:13), power (2 Corinthians 13:4) and strength (Philippians 4:13; 2 Corinthians 12:9) that Christ has given to you to overcome challenges, obstacles and trials like racism. God has given us His grace—Jesus Christ, Who is sufficient (2 Corinthians 12:9) for us to gain victory and triumph over our circumstances.

God's grace is His divine favor, Jesus Christ, Who went ahead of us to clear the paths of racism or any other evil that was designed to obstruct us. Christ has cancelled all charges against us (Colossians 2:14-15). He, Christ, God's divine favor to you, opens doors of opportunities for you, presents to you ladders which lead to your success, and instructs others, including strangers, to assist you in your endeavor. Therefore, exercise the spiritual authority that you have as a child of God, heir of God and joint heir with Jesus Christ, and receive through the precious Blood of Christ, God's divine favor for your life. As a child of God, seed of Abraham, joint heir with Jesus Christ, you have unlimited access to God through Christ Who is His divine and unmerited favor. You have also received God's Holy Spirit through Christ. So, now you have access to all that God has in store for you; you are loaded with strategies, plans, ideas, road maps, open doors and opportunities, and all that you need to survive, overcome and triumph over racism.

*Exercise the spiritual authority that you have as a child of God, heir of God and joint heir of Jesus Christ.*

Open up your spirit to God's illuminating light, His glorious rays of victory. Let His holy light radiate within you true spiritual knowledge. Let this illuminating and radiant light of the Holy Spirit within you turn off all thoughts of your being downtrodden by racism and quench your negative perceptions of any form of defeat by racism. These misguided thoughts do nothing for you, but weaken your heart and mind and dissipate or "scatter" within you the power of Jesus Christ and the Holy Spirit within you given to you by God.

Discard the grasshopper mentality (Numbers 13:30-33) that you have obtained from your experiences with racism and begin to see yourself as the spiritual giant that you are against the foul spirit of racism. Through Jesus Christ, tap into God's grace to receive constant flow of His spiritual power in your life. With this, you can defeat any racial attitude that is directed against you (Psalms 18:29; 2 Samuel 22:30).

Through Jesus Christ, God will give you wisdom and understanding to grow in the knowledge of His Holy Word. He will flood your heart and mind with His brilliant Light of knowledge and understanding so that you will know the wonderful future that He has in store for you. This godly knowledge and understanding will give you divine wisdom of the greatness of God's power in your life (Ephesians 1:18-26). God's Holy Spirit will reveal to you that God has given you, through Jesus Christ, authority over evil domination (Luke 10:18-19), including racism, and you will come to receive the restoration power of this revelation by your measure of faith.

*You are created in God's excellent image for a unique purpose.*

You will come to understand that the same awesome Holy Power of God, His Holy Spirit, Which raised Jesus Christ from the dead and seated Him in heavenly places (Ephesians 2:4-7), has also raised you above racism. God gave Jesus Christ all authority in Heaven and on Earth (Matthew 28:18); He has put all things under the Feet of Christ [including racism], and made Him Head over His body [the church] of which you are a part, a member (Ephesians 1:22). Thus, Christ has gained complete victory for you over racism and every other form of evil (1 Corinthians 15:57; 1 John 2:14; Revelation 12:11).

True spiritual knowledge lets you know that to feel unworthy or to let another person convince you that you are unworthy or inferior means that God made a mistake in creating you. And this is an illusion and a lie because the truth is that through Jesus Christ, you are a very worthy person before God, and humans or circumstances do not determine your worth. God determines your worth and He has already deemed you worthy through Jesus Christ and He put His Stamp of Ownership on you by giving you the Holy Spirit (Ephesians 1:14). Authentic spiritual knowledge empowers your mind positively based on the absolute truth of God's Holy Word, and frees you from the lies of the devil. True spiritual knowledge rejects the lies of the devil packaged in racism (John 8:44).

*You are born rich with unique gifts, talents and abilities.*

Our inheritance in Jesus Christ has been guaranteed to us through the Holy Spirit (Ephesians 1:14). You are a citizen of God's Heavenly Kingdom (Philippians 3:20), and with all who have accepted Jesus Christ, you are a fellow citizen with them (Ephesians 2:18-19). So now, be assured that you are indeed a worthy person. You are created in God's excellent Image for a unique purpose. You are not inferior or superior to any man or woman. You are born equal and are equal to any man or woman in this world. You are born rich with unique gifts, talents and abilities. To everyone including you, God has given at least one talent or gift that can make them or yourself a success. Even those whom we wrongly ascribe the name "Street Bums", have the same potentials as you and I. But they have let go of God's Holy Word and promises for their lives. Should they reclaim the truth of God's Word and its promises for their lives through Jesus Christ, they would be whole again and soon on track with the purpose for which God created them. By their faith and acceptance of Jesus Christ, they would reconnect with God and take back their rightful place of victory both here on Earth and in Heaven.

*God could take you from "grass to grace" or from "indignity to dignity", if you allowed Him to work with you.*

Have you not heard about stories of how individuals made a "come back" from "grass to grace" or from "indignity to dignity"? Are such people extraordinary people who overcame adversities, setbacks, injustices, oppressions or defeats? No they are not! These are ordinary people like you and I who reclaimed the truth and power of God's Holy Word and its promises in their lives, and allowed their spirit, once again, to be illuminated and awakened by the awesome power of God's Holy Spirit Who lives in them.

Joseph's story in the Bible is one of faith, resilience, and manifestation of the power of the truth of God's Holy Word and promises in a believer's life (Genesis 37,39,40-46). Evil did not overcome Joseph—good had the final victory (Romans 8:28). Joseph's story went from experiencing great love of his earthly father Jacob to him being thrown into a pit by his brothers; then to being sold into slavery due to the jealousy and wickedness of his own brothers; and yet again from the pit and slavery to being a servant in a palace in Egypt, and then to prison due to a wicked false accusation, and finally from prison to being the second in command in the whole of Egypt.

There are so many other people like Joseph who have gone from grace to Grace, and from disgrace to Grace. Every one of them, claimed back God's glorious Light; His illuminating rays of victory within them. These individuals opened up to God's power and might, and to the possibilities of achieving the great heights that He had already made possible for them and for every one of us. Then, finally they acknowledged to God that they were tired of being buried in and under the "grass" (Psalms 34:18-20,22) and they were ready to rise to the mountaintop of victory through His Grace. God heard their cry in prayer, thanksgiving and worship, and raised them far above their circumstances and the wicked plot and schemes of their offenders (Psalms 30: 11-12; 31:21-24, 33:18-19, 34:15-22, 118:22-23). God will do the same for you when you cry out "Ab-

*Through Jesus Christ, tap into God's grace for constant flow of His spiritual power in your life.*

ba Father" to Him for help (Romans 8:14-17) and you will triumph over your daily experiences with racism.

Yes, God will hear your genuine cry for help (Psalms 142, 144) and release His new breath in you (Genesis 2:7), His awesome spiritual anointing on your spirit and soul, and infuse you with true spiritual knowledge and self-knowledge. God will empower you for spiritual warfare (Psalms 144:1-2). Then, suddenly, racist situations that once seemed insurmountable will become surmountable for you. You will no longer see such situations as obstructions rather you will view them as building blocks and stepping-stones to God's higher levels of triumph in your life. Human assaults such as racism or thoughts of defeat will no longer bind your heart and mind. In time, you will become completely whole, guided first into spiritual victory, and then to material success. Then, racism will become nothing but a barking, toothless bull to you.

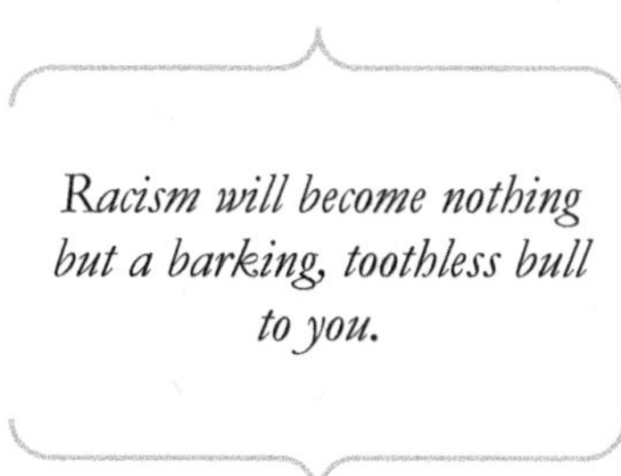
*Racism will become nothing but a barking, toothless bull to you.*

Are you tired of the evil schemes of racism dragging your spirit down and burying you under mounds of its oppression and injustice? If you are, now (I mean this very moment) is the time for you to cry out "Abba Father" to Almighty God (Romans 8:14-17; Psalms 140, 142) for His divine power and glory to illuminate you with true spiritual knowledge, understanding and wisdom to tackle and extinguish the evil forces of racism victoriously along with your fear of them, and give you His divine triumph over racism through Jesus Christ.

**Chapter Quiz**

1. Describe some of the ways that you can refuse to allow yourself to be downtrodden by racism.

---

2. True or false: If you allowed yourself to be downtrodden by racism, you fail to be a conqueror of it, which Jesus Christ has already made you. Explain your answer.

---

3. John 8:44: How can your knowledge of this Scripture equip you to reject the lies of the devil which he tries to deliver to you through racists in the form of racism?

---

4. Can racism or racists raise or lower your true worthiness? Through who has God made you worthy?

---

ꝏꝏꝏꝏꝏ♦ ♦ ♦ ♦ ♦ꝏꝏꝏꝏꝏ

**Reflections:**

---

---

---

∞∞∞∞∞∞ ♦ ♦ ♦ ♦ ♦ ∞∞∞∞∞∞

# CHAPTER 26: Fear is a Weapon of Defeat

Fear of racism and its potential destructive effect on you is a spirit of negative control. This control has been engineered by no other than the evil one, the devil, to keep you in bondage outside of God's Kingdom light and holiness. You did not receive a spirit of bondage to fear, worries, anxiety or hopelessness, but you have been given a spirit of love, power and a sound mind (2 Timothy 1:7). Apostle Paul declares in Romans 8:15 (NKJV): "For you did not receive the spirit of bondage again to fear, but you received the Spirit of adoption by whom we cry out, "Abba, Father." Racism tries to plant the seed of fear in you through hidden or blatant intimidation by racists. Racism nurtures and grows the unfruitful spirit of fear in your heart. The spirit of fear is a wicked weapon of spiritual attack and emotional and psychological terrorism which causes self-defeat and self-destruction and is an obstacle to claiming victory in your life.

Fear is one of our natural responses to physical or emotional threats of danger to our person. It is an emotion that arises from an expectation of release of danger that could be of potential harm to us. Every human being feels fear at one point or another in his or her life. Even Abraham, the Father of all nations, did experience fear on some occasions, and God calmed his fears by reminding Him that He, God would shield him [Abraham] from danger and gave him a great reward (Genesis 15:1). For some of us, we cannot imagine a life without fear of something because our lives have always been an embodiment of fear of one thing or another. The world around us injects fear into our hearts and minds, and we respond to such fear with worries and anxieties that cause us to lose our inner peace.

Fear comes against us in so many ways. Sometimes, it is fear of the wickedness of powerful and racist people who control material things in our workplace, schools and other environments that cause so many of us to turn the other way when we see injustice being done to us or others. We simply explain our way through the injustice of racism as the way things have been and are likely to remain. Consciously and subconsciously we teach our children to become spiritually complacent about racism and as they grow up, they too subconsciously accept the lower levels into which racism forces them and the limited levels of achievement that racists in society tell them they are only capable of achieving. So many people who

*The emotion of fear is a spiritual blindfold.*

are targets of racism are at the same time bound by the spirit of fear.

As a child of God, you must never allow fear of anything to take root within your heart and mind except the fear [reverence, utmost respect and worship] of God Almighty. You should not accept any unjust or oppressive action against you based on your carnal fear rather than choosing God's path of justice and equity. If anything, the fear of God should propel you to fight the good fight of faith spiritually (1 Timothy 6:12), and fight for justice and equity constructively in the natural realm, in accordance to His Holy Word as led by God's Holy Spirit, through positive just and lawful actions, to tackle the injustices of racism. A spiritual fight of faith that is sustained with the power of God's Holy Word is greater than fruitless energy-consuming carnal battles against evils like racism. If you trust God, He will open up His paths of justice and provide you with strategies to triumph over racism that you face at your individual level. The emotion of fear is a spiritual blindfold. It causes us to focus on our challenges, obstacles or setbacks rather than on God who always works out all things in accordance with His purpose for us.

*A spiritual fight of faith that is sustained with the power of God's Holy Word is greater than evils like racism.*

Sometimes, when we experience situations that cause us discomfort, anger or fear, our immediate response is to ask God to take it away, and He may very well do what we ask at that point. On the other hand, God may want us to go through the experience so as to witness His glory in His timed future when what we once thought was a negative situation and perhaps was, is transformed into a building block for victory in our life, and a glorious testimony for many others to witness (Romans 8:28; Daniel 3:25-30). Remember the story about Shadrach, Meshach, and Abed-Nego who refused to worship the image of gold made by Nebuchadnezzar (Daniel 3). They had the choice to worship the image of gold or continue to worship the only true God and be thrown into a burning fiery furnace—and they chose the latter option. The Son of God showed up in the burning fiery furnace where Shadrach, Meshach, and Abed-Nego were thrown into: "…Lo, I see four men loose, walking in the midst of the fire, and they have no hurt; and the form of the fourth is like the Son of God." (Daniel 3:25). God will show up in your circumstance when your faith and trust in Him defies your human logic and circumstances.

*It is the fear factor that binds the mind of the oppressed or those who have been made subject to racist power.*

A friend of mine "Sue" was unjustly fired from her job. Sue believed that her manager was racist and she prayed for two weeks after she was dismissed from her job. Then, she received a phone call from a lawyer friend of hers whom she had not heard from for a while—she told him how she was dismissed unjustly from her job. He decided to take on her case and wrote her employer a stern letter and asked for a settlement for his client (Sue). Following multiple negotiations, the employer agreed and paid Sue one-year salary as the settlement. You see, Sue trusted God to deliver justice on her behalf, and He did.

One of the sources of real fear that we feel is our daily experience with racism in the workplace or elsewhere. In our physical realm, racism and its negative effects have the potential to dominate our existence with fear of the power that sustains such actions. So, we sometimes fear the consequences of the negative power of those in authority over us who are evil, wicked and racist, and who direct negative actions against us. For the most part, our daily experiences with racism are very real and are by no means a figment of our imagination. Ironically, fear also fuels the power that sustains the practice of racism against others. The fear of losing or sharing power with others drives individuals to want to dominate, restrict and deprive others of opportunities that would ordinarily allow them to advance towards reaching their highest potentials some day.

> *The real victory over fear is our spiritual courage that resists and dispels it.*

Prejudiced and racist individuals react from their inner fears by fostering negative and harmful actions against those they perceive want to take or share their power structure or take some material privileges they believe belongs to them. It is the fear factor that sustains racist actions by some individuals who have carnal powers and who choose to use such powers to oppress others who are racially different. It is also the fear factor that binds the mind of the oppressed or those who have been made subject to that power. People become fearful of their oppressors and over many years of being conditioned with fear, they succumb to the lies that they are less or inferior and that their careers and life's success are in the hands of their oppressors. Yet, the only truth is that every child of God has his or her life in the Hands of God and not in the hands of any mortal human being.

*When we fear evil like racism we ascribe greater power to it in our mind.*

The authority, power and goodness of God in us through Jesus Christ will always overcome evil. A child of the Most High God should never allow his or her life to be bound by fear of evil that any mortal or spiritual being is capable of doing to their physical body (Luke 12:4; Matthew 10:28). When we walk in perfect faith, believing in the limitless power of God's glory and grace in our lives, mountains are moved from our way in the Name of Jesus Christ (Mathew 17:20-21; John 11:40). However, when we fear evil like the negative carnal power of a prejudiced and racist person in the workplace, in our minds, we ascribe greater power to such a person than to God, the Creator of that person and Who alone has the only real authority and power. When we fear the evil that a prejudiced and racist person can do to us in the workplace or elsewhere, then we accept the lie that God's authority and power are limited and that evil will overcome

His goodness, might and justice. In essence, what you are saying to God is that His power and grace are insufficient to protect you from evil and thus, you cannot trust to place your career and life in His holy Hands. This kind of wrong thinking contradicts God's Holy Word which tells us that His grace is sufficient for us and His strength is made perfect in our weakness (2 Corinthians 12:9).

To confront real or imagined fear, you need spiritual courage which comes from knowing and believing God's Holy Word (Joshua 1:7-9). To have spiritual courage, you must believe that the authority and power of God in your life are above any other that is in the world (1 John 4:4). To sustain your belief in God, you must study and meditate daily on the Holy Word of God and from this, build unwavering faith in the limitless power of God's Holy Word and its promises. Undoubting faith in God and His Word then becomes your source of spiritual courage (Joshua 1:7-9). With spiritual courage you can dwarf and level mountains of fear. Spiritual courage becomes your daily weapon of defeat of fear; the enemy of your soul. So, whenever fear comes knocking at your door, your spiritual courage armored with the ammunition of God's Holy Word and your belief and undoubting faith in God through Jesus Christ, become a permanent spiritual guard door that resists and dispels the spirit of fear.

*Racism tries to plant the seed of fear in you.*

As born again Christian believers, the real victory over fear is never the complete absence of fear in our lives, but the permanent presence of our spiritual courage, which constantly resists and dispels fear leaving no room for it to have prolonged or permanent habitation within us.

**Chapter Quiz**

1. Describe some of the ways that racism can attack your heart and mind if you are on the receiving end of it.

---

2. The emotion of fear is a spiritual blindfold. Explain what this means to you.

---

3. Describe some of the ways that the foul spirit of racism pollutes your heart and mind if you are the one perpetrating racism against another person.

---

4. Describe some of the ways that the odious spirit of racism can place a stranglehold on your heart and mind if you are the one being attacked by perpetrators of racism.

---

5. Describe in what ways spiritual courage can become your daily weapon to conquer the spirit of fear that racism attempts to impose on your heart and mind.

---

∞∞∞∞∞∞∞∞∞∞ ♦ ♦ ♦ ♦ ♦ ∞∞∞∞∞∞∞∞∞∞

**Reflections:**

______________________________________________

______________________________________________

______________________________________________

______________________________________________

∞∞∞∞∞∞∞∞∞∞∞ ♦ ♦ ♦ ♦ ♦ ∞∞∞∞∞∞∞∞∞∞∞

# CHAPTER 27: Fear Cripples Your Faith

Racism fuels fear and intimidation, and fear is the devil's weapon, which is designed to cripple your faith and hold you under carnal bondage. In 1 John 4:18 (NKJV) God tells us: "There is no fear in love; but perfect love casts out fear, because fear involves torment. But he who fears has not been made perfect in love." God is love—He is perfect love. Fear will make you lose sight of the awesome and wholesome power of God's love for you. It is a love that is so deep and boundless that nothing could ever separate you from it (Romans 8:35-39).

Fear is not of God, but of the devil, the prince of darkness and the ruler of all wickedness in this world. God, the universal Creator of this Earth, the Alpha and Omega, the Beginning and the End, the First and the Last (Revelation 1:8), is greater than the devil. Vicious lies, such as racist lies, are one of many weapons of the devil, the enemy to your soul. Racism and other challenges and obstacles, are conquered by your faith in the power of the Blood of the Lamb, our Savior Jesus Christ, our Lord and Redeemer—and we who are Chrisitian born again believers have received the victory of Jesus Christ (I John 5:4).

Human beings, regardless of race, ethnicity or nationality, are all creations of God and so the natural power of all humans is subject to the supernatural power of God (Revelation 12:11a). The power of God overcomes the evil that is planned against any child of His who has submitted his or her life to Him and who has undoubting faith in the limitless power and grace of God through Jesus Christ. God has promised those who love Him that He will rescue and deliver us; He will protect us because we acknowledge His holy Name; He will answer us when we call upon His Name; He will be with us when we are in trouble; He will honor us and bless us with long life (Psalms 91:14-15).

*Faith in God's Word over any situation does the exact opposite of what fear does.*

When you fear humans who are creations of God you fail to reverence the protective, limitless and boundless power of God, the Maker of all humans. Meditate on this for a moment and see what an offense such fear is to God. The truth is that being a child of God, He will protect you and guard you from evil (Psalms 91:14). So, fear only God by worshiping Him and reverencing His power and glory, and do not allow your fear of man, woman or any circumstance to dominate your life.

To master control of fear is not to destroy it, but to hold every fearful thought (including racism) captive with the Holy Word and promises of God (2 Corinthians 10:3-6). This means that knowledge of God's Word and promises is spiritual ammunition against fear. Drenching your heart with the Holy Word and promises of God dispels fear in your mind, thereby replacing it with faith that God's higher supernatural power quenches all evil and unfavorable actions, which trigger your fear. No fearful thought that is bound or held captive by the Word and promises of God by undoubting faith will ever become victorious in your life (2 Corinthians 10:3-6). This is God's unshakable and unchangeable promise to us. So you must not fear any man, woman, circumstance or challenge. Therefore, resist, rebuke and renounce racism—and never fear it!

*You have to claim your rightful and victorious position against racism.*

Your fear of any situation and your conditioning to fear can lead you to believe all that the perpetrators of racism dictate to you. In addition, negative spin-offs or lingering effects of racism can build strongholds in your heart, mind and life. Fear diminishes our faith and transforms it into a double-minded kind of faith that does not move God to act on our behalf. Fear smothers the power of our spiritual warfare because God responds to our faith and not to our fears; God does not respond to a double-minded nature (James 1:6-8).

Should God respond to your individual need to overcome racism when you lack the faith to believe that He has absolute power to demolish any form of racism that you may experience? When you face daily challenges like racism in the workplace, present your situation and report your offenders to God in prayer with undoubting faith in Jesus Christ. Where fear is dominating your life, you must ask God in prayer to first remove the fear so that your faith will begin to take over and give you access to God's promises for you through Jesus Christ. It is through sustained and undoubting faith that God grants us the desires of our heart. Fear breeds feelings of frustration and accomplishes nothing for you. It exaggerates the problem in your mind to the extent that it cripples you by taking your mind captive; making you to believe that you are powerless, helpless and hopeless. This is why we must pull down every stranglehold, cast down arguments and every high thing that elevates itself against the knowledge of God, and hold every thought captive to the obedience of Jesus Christ (2 Corinthians 10:3-6).

*The Power of God overcomes the evil that is planned against any child of His.*

Faith in God's Word over any situation does the exact opposite of what fear does. Faith affirms in your heart God's love for you. Faith speaks the truth of the power of God's Word against evil situations. It builds your own spiritual courage and takes captive every negative thought (2 Corinthians 10:5). You have to claim your rightful and victorious position of Jesus Christ over racism and its evils. Racism is one of the devil's machinery that is used to control your heart and mind. You are a child of God—a seed of Abraham and a child of God's promises. You are a child of God who has the victory of Jesus Christ through His redeeming Blood (1 John 5:4). Therefore, banish your fear of racism and claim your victory over it through Jesus Christ.

**Chapter Quiz**

1. True or false: Racism fuels fear and fear is the devil's weapon designed to cripple your faith and hold you under carnal bondage. Explain your answer.

______________________________

2. In what ways can you counteract the spirit of fear when it attempts to settle in your heart and mind?

______________________________

3. True or false: When your fears oppose your faith, you can become anxious, confused or unfocused. Explain your answer.

______________________________

4. In what ways can fear of racism cripple your mind and your creativity?

______________________________

5. True or false: When your faith opposes your fears, you are able to deal victoriously with any Goliath—huge intimidating challenges—you are able to see yourself as a godly giant and not as a grasshopper—and you are able to spiritually position yourself to triumph over your fears. Explain your answer

______________________________________________

∞∞∞∞∞∞ ♦ ♦ ♦ ♦ ♦ ∞∞∞∞∞∞

**Reflections:**

______________________________________________

______________________________________________

______________________________________________

______________________________________________

∞∞∞∞∞∞ ♦ ♦ ♦ ♦ ♦ ∞∞∞∞∞∞

# CHAPTER 28: Banish Your Fear of Racism

A child of God who has developed a daily close relationship with God in prayer, thanksgiving and worship understands through His Holy Word that He is our provider, shield and armor in all battles (Psalms 23, 27, 35, 37, 91, 121). You are a child of the Most High God—you are God's holy and awesome purpose wrapped in flesh. You possess the victory of Jesus Christ over the world (John 16:33; 1 John 5:4).

Are you a perpetrator of or racism or a target of racism? Are you ruled by the spirit of fear of individuals of other races? Has your fear opened up your heart to receive the spirit of racial hostility? Whether you are the perpetrator of racism or one on the receiving end of it, you need to banish the spirit of fear in you. If you were racist and fostered racist activities against others, perhaps you were bound by the spirit of fear of other races; fear that they would take over what you deemed to be yours; fear that they would partake of God's blessings to your family, community, county, district, borough, state or country as a whole. If you were on the receiving end of racism, you may have been bound by the spirit of fear of racists; fear that racists may unjustly imprison, or kill you or your loved ones and even get way with nurder; fear that racists may deprive you of your job or prevent you from getting one; block your promotion at work or bar you from living in what they deem to be their rightful neighborhoods; wrongly accuse and convict you of a crime that you did not commit, and possibly have you or your son or daughter executed for a crime they did not commit, and so on.

*Grow your faith in God's Holy Word and smother any fear of racism.*

Fear is neither the right answer to racism nor the right solution. Your spiritual strategy should be to grow your faith in God's Holy Word and smother any fear of racism. Your individual goal should be to resist, defy and conquer any potential negative effects of racism on you. Your goal should be to focus on drawing from God's holy and awesome spiritual power to gain complete spiritual and physical victory over any form of blatant or hidden racism that may be directed towards you.

You should channel your sustained hard work through the daily guidance of the power of God's Holy Spirit who dwells within you to His ordained success for your career and life (Jeremiah 29:11). Through God's grace, power and glory within you through Jesus Christ, racism will not have the power and authority to taint, stifle, diffuse, control, distort or destroy your dreams. Racism cannot stop God's holy purpose from appearing in your life unless you grant the vile spirit of racism permission and access into your heart and mind and welcome it in your life. Submit your life completely to God and let Him be the sole authority and power in and over your life.

If you loved, believed and trusted in God, He would fight for you and defeat all carnal and spiritual battles for you through Christ Who has won the ultimate spiritual warfare for you (Psalms 35, 37, 92, 120, 124; Exodus 14:14; Deuteronomy 1:30; 2 Chronicles 20:17). Yes, Christ has already won the battle for you over all forms of evil (including racism), wickedness, oppression and injustice. He, Christ, has overcome the world for you (John 16:33). Knowing and believing this is having pure and undefiled faith in the awesome, limitless and boundless power of God in your life. This kind of faith defeats your fear which is a constant enemy of your spirit and soul. A child of God ascribes to the greatest power of God rather than to any living human, as God is the Creator of all things including human beings. Mankind, which is God's creation, can NEVER become greater than God who is the Creator and Maker of all things.

*Fear blinds your spiritual wisdom and fills your mind with lies and distortions.*

Fear could drive you to become racist and could also drive you to believe that you are a victim of racism. When you fear any man, you limit God's power within and through you. It is not an act of faith, but an act of fear to believe that the power of any man to do evil against you is greater than the authority and power of God in you through Jesus Christ to overcome that evil with good in your life. This is a fallacy of fear, for faith knows better and faith is confirmed by the Holy Word of God that we can all achieve great things and are more than conquerors through Jesus Christ, and that no evil is greater than the awesome power and glory of God in our lives (1 John 4:4; Romans 8:37; Matthew 19:26; John 11:40).

*God created you and only He has the power to dictate your life in accordance with His will and purpose for your life.*

The only fear that is well placed is fear of our Creator, God, which is fear that is out of our genuine love and reverence for Him—and His boundless love, mercy, faithfulness, grace and kindness for all of humanity. Accompanying such fear and reverence of God is His peace and protection from any form of evil (Isaiah 26:3, 12; 19:20-21; Psalms 20:7, 37:5-6, 55:22, 91:14). Faith and trust in God give rise to spiritual courage and wisdom and banishes all carnal fears.

Fear blinds your spiritual wisdom and fills your mind with lies and distortions about what the evil power of any racist human or the foul spirit of racism can accomplish in your life. For example, only fear could convince you that your life, career and success lie in the hands of another mortal human—perhaps, a racist boss or other authority above you? How could this fear be real when no human can dictate his or her own birth and existence or knows the hour of his or her death? How then could you allow fear to dominate your mind with falsehood and convince you that your life, career and success lie in the hands of another human? If your life were truly in the hands of another human and if it were up to him or her, perhaps, you would never have existed in the first place. The truth is that God created you and only He and you have the power to determine your life's success in accordance with His will and purpose for your life. Only God has ultimate supernatural power and dominion over your life and career—and your success is in His holy Hands and yours.

*God is the pure and holy One who judges and hands out pure and impartial justice.*

Jeremiah 29:11 tells you that God has the best plan for your life. To claim the power of the promises of God's Holy Word and His awesome rays of victory within you, fear must be replaced by faith—faith will in turn generate hope—hope will give rise to patience and will sustain your daily journey into the present and future that will unfold God's miracles daily in your life. Your undoubting faith in the limitless and boundless spiritual power of God will break down all racial barriers, challenges and obstacles, and give you complete victory over them. God has the power to protect you from racism. He has the power to remove racist elements from your path. He alone has the authority to absolve your racist attackers and offenders of their sinful actions if they repented and turned from their racist ways (2 Chronicles 7:14) or to bring them to impartial justice if they failed to repent (Romans 2:5-6). God is the pure and holy One who judges and hands out pure and impartial justice giving equal time for all to repent and change from their wicked ways. God is patient with all of us because it is His wish that we repent of our sins by the precious Blood of Jesus Christ, and turn from our evil ways and escape His wrath of justice for the disobedient, unrepentant heart (2 Chronicles 7:14; 2 Peter 3:9; Matthew 18:12-14).

*God will not fail you!*

If you allow God, He will hold your hand as you experience racism, and replace your fear of racism with anointed faith, hope and trust in what He can accomplish in your life (Psalms 56:1-4). He will deliver you from your racist offenders and give you triumph over their carnal plans (Psalms 37:9-15). The Sword of the Spirit, which is the Holy Word of God, travels with greater than lightning speed and will dismantle any racist plans, which are being directed against you. The Sword of the Spirit will not relent until every racist offender that has attacked you [God's anointed vessel] is defeated and brought to His justice (Hebrews 4:12-13). Be encouraged by God's Holy Word when you are experiencing racism and you seem overwhelmed, overpowered and outnumbered in the natural. God's Word is not void and the truth of His Word endures forever (Isaiah 55:11). It is filled with power and might, and is a life-giver and life restorer. For as you pass through the rough waters of racism, your racist attackers will not overrun you (Psalms 23:5). God is saying to you: "Fear not, for I *am* with you; Be not dismayed, for I *am* your God. I will strengthen you, yes, I will help you, I will uphold you with My righteous right hand.' "Behold, all those who were incensed against you shall be ashamed and disgraced; They shall be as nothing, and those who strive with you shall perish. You shall seek them and not find them—those who contended with you. Those who war against you shall be as nothing, as a nonexistent thing. For I, the LORD your God, will hold your right hand, saying to you, 'Fear not, I will help you.'" (Isaiah 41:10-13 KJV) The Power of God's Holy Word will give you divine protection (Psalms 31:23-24, 33:18, 32:6-7; Isaiah 26:3-6). Bank on this protection, and have absolute faith and trust in it (Psalms 27:13-14) because it never fails and stands forever (Isaiah 40:8; 1 Peter 1:25).

*You are God's holy and awesome purpose wrapped in flesh.*

When you confront racism and its evils, continue to do what is right in accordance with God's Holy Word. Walk in obedience of God's Word (Ephesians 4:1; James 4:7) by the leading of His Holy Spirit within you and offer forgiveness to your racist offenders (Mark 11:25). After you have done what is right as God has asked you to, stand firm on His Word until His deliverance manifests in your physical surroundings (Hebrews 10:35). God will not fail you—He has NEVER failed anyone who put his or her trust in Him (Psalms 9:9-10, 125:1; Romans 10:11). You have the victory Jesus Christ over the odious spirit of racism (1 John 5:4). Do you believe this?

**Chapter Quiz**

1. Describe some of the ways that the foul spirit of racism can attack your heart and mind and turn you into a racist weapon against another person.

---

2. Who has defeated the foul spirit of racism on your behalf and how?

---

3. Why does the evil spirit of racism seek to replace your faith with fear?

---

4. True or false: When you fear any man, situation or circumstance, you limit God's power within and through you. Explain your answer.

---

∞∞∞∞∞∞∞∞∞∞∞ ♦ ♦ ♦ ♦ ♦ ∞∞∞∞∞∞∞∞∞∞∞

## Reflections:

________________________________________

________________________________________

________________________________________

________________________________________

∞∞∞∞∞∞∞∞∞∞∞ ♦ ♦ ♦ ♦ ♦ ∞∞∞∞∞∞∞∞∞∞∞

# CHAPTER 29: Lay Down Your Hurt and Pain

In prayer with thanksgiving, bring your case of racism before God and place it at the feet if Jesus Christ (Philippians 4:6). God has given Christ power over all things except God Himself (Hebrews 2:8; Ephesians 1:22; 1 Corinthians 15:27). You need to lay down all of your hurt and pain from your experiences with racism at the Feet of Jesus Christ (Psalms 55:22). Let Him take all of the emotional distress that racism has ever caused you (Matthew 11:28-29). If the hurt and pain from your experiences with racism are weighing down your soul and making forgiveness difficult, ask God for His grace to forgive your racist offenders. Present your case to God and He will surely shower more grace upon you to help you deal with your hurtful experiences with racism: "The Lord is near to those who are discouraged; he saves those who have lost all hope." (Psalms 34:18; 103:6)

If the pain and hurt you feel are making it difficut for you to forgive, acknowledge this before God and tell him that your spirit is willing to forgive by His grace, but your flesh is being an obstacle to your spirit. Know that God already sees your heart and He wants you to honestly acknowledge the burden of your unforgiveness before Him. He also knows that He has given you one option, which is to forgive your offenders—God has commanded us to do so. For it is through forgiveness through Jesus Christ that we obtain the promises and blessings of God. Once you forgive those who have offended and hurt you, their negative plans will NEVER prevail against you (Isaiah 54:17). Forgiveness protects you from the spirit of anger, bitternessand vengeance the poluutes the soil of the heart.

To gain God's rays of victory over any situation, you must believe that God can and will take care of any and all situations for you. If there are any thoughts of anger, unforgiveness and bitterness, banish them and replace them with thoughts of faith, hope in the glory and power of God, and forgiveness through Christ. Know that God has dominion over the whole earth and universe and all that is seen and unseen (Daniel 7:14). The racist situation that you may be facing is under God's dominion and if you have sustained faith, it will be exterminated and extinguished before your eyes to the glory of His holy Name. No man, woman or demon can have power over you when you have undoubting faith and have submitted your life to Jesus Christ, and to the awesome power and glory of God!

*Let Christ take all of the emotional distress that racism has ever caused you.*

When your fear is banished by the power of God's Holy Word and His Spirit Who dwell within you, it is replaced by undoubting faith in the power of God that can do all things. To release fully the power of the Holy Spirit of God to help you activate your faith for spiritual breakthroughs in your life, you must lay down your hurt and pain and offer a spirit of forgiveness (Mark 11:25). When you offer forgiveness to individuals who are prejudiced and racist, you cancel the effects of their negative words and actions that are directed towards you, and release yourself from the pain and hurt. When you forgive, God also forgives you your own sins (Matthew 6:12) and blesses you with greater divine empowering, inspiration, opportunities and possibilities. Your divine reward will also become a daily spiritual bind of the negative actions and words of prejudiced and racist individuals.

*Banish any thoughts of anger, unforgiveness and bitterness.*

## Chapter Quiz

1. Why must you forgive your racist offenders?

---

2. Why must you lay down your hurt and pain from your experiences with racism?

---

3. True or false: God rewards a spirit and soul that is centered on daily forgiveness with greater inspiration, opportunities and possibilities. Explain your answer.

___

4. True or false: When you offer forgiveness to individuals who are prejudiced and racist, you cancel the effects of their negative words and actions. Explain your answer.

___

∞∞∞∞∞∞ ♦ ♦ ♦ ♦ ♦ ∞∞∞∞∞∞

**Reflections:**

___

___

___

___

∞∞∞∞∞∞ ♦ ♦ ♦ ♦ ♦ ∞∞∞∞∞∞

# CHAPTER 30: Breaking the Yoke of Racism

Anyone or group of people can be prejudiced, regardless of race, ethnicity or nationality. Racism that you may encounter today has its roots from centuries past and is still practiced in many countries and regions in the world. The foul spirit of racism is a generational spirit, passed down from one racist generation to another. History has forever documented the unimaginable racial acts of indignities, injustice, oppression, rapes and murders that have taken place during every century of human existence. Throughout the history of humanity to date, individuals with carnal power believed that their lives were worth more than the lives of others whom they oppressed by subjecting them to all kinds of indignities. During every century of oppression, the oppressors believed in their innate superiority, and as such, that they had the right and authority to dehumanize other human beings and usually, they acted on that false belief.

Racism originates from misconceptions, untruth and lies about superiority of one race, ethnic group or nationality over another, and gives birth to oppression and injustices in various forms. Such individual false beliefs become cultural and social beliefs and practices that are passed down from one generation to another, and lead to negative strongholds in the minds of those who declare themselves superior, as well as in others who accept the falsehood of their inferiority. Racism also has an evil spiritual dimension to it. It originated from the pit of hell, orchestrated by the devil who is the father of all lies (John 8:44) who sows "tares" among the "wheat" (Matthew 13:24-30). The devil is the father of the vile spirit of racism who perpetrates and perpetuates racism through its willing human hosts.

Collectively, individual beliefs and strongholds of superiority and inferiority have become everyday's cultural strongholds that are intricately woven into the fabric of society as institutionalized racial prejudices and discrimination. Today, what we see as the effects of racism on so many individuals is a manifestation of the physical chains of the past transformed into psychological [mental] chains that hold their minds captive.

*As a "slave' to racism, you are living in disobedience to God's Holy Word.*

Human souls in carnal captivity by racist lies become defeated persons who accept mediocrity or failure as their rightful place and settle for less or nothing in their daily lives. And yet, by the precious Blood of Jesus Christ that freed us all who believe in Him, God has delivered every "slave" or a descendant of a "slave" from negative spiritual, mental or physical bondage (John 8:32,36). By this freedom, we are no longer slaves to any evil doings [including racism], but through Jesus Christ, we have become "slaves" unto God and His righteousness (Romans 6:16-18). The word "slave" here means that you are now a "bond servant" of God (and not of man) who is subject only to God and His Word through Christ—His virtue, morality, justice, integrity, truth, impartiality, uprightness, decency, honesty, and all of His goodness. Whenever you allow yourself to succumb to racism and its lies, you remain a "slave" to the evil spirit of racism and the racist human being who uses racism against you. As a "slave' to racism, you are living in disobedience to God's Holy Word and blocking His promises from manifesting in your life. If you allowed racists or racism to define your limitations, as well as the heights that you can achieve, you would have allowed yourself to become a "slave" to racism and not to God and His righteousness through Jesus Christ. If you allowed the effects of racism to erode into your soul and take captive your heart and mind, then you would have given unauthorized access to the foul spirit of racism and this is contrary to God's Word and His promises for your life.

*Every child of God should have an empowered and not a defeated spirit.*

Just as it is a sin against God to accept the evil spirit of racism within you and to perpetrate racism against anyone, likewise, it is also a sin against God to allow yourself to succumb to this foul spirit and accept the label of being a "victim" of racism. This would be contrary to God's Word, which says that you are more than a conqueror ["victor"] through Jesus Christ (Romans 8:37). If you are an instrument being used by the evil spirit of racism or see yourself to be a "victim" of this foul spirit, either as a perpetrator of racism or a target of it, reach out now to the liberty by which Christ has set you free so that you do not continue being entangled [knotted, intertwined] with the yoke of the burden of racism (Galatians 5:1).

Jesus Christ has set you free from the record of the charges of racism against you (Colossians 2:14-15), and you have become subject only to God and His righteousness (Romans 6:16-18), and racism will never be able to defile you, a temple of God's Holy Spirit Who dwells in you (1 Corinthians 6:19-20). Yes, through Jesus Christ, God redeemed every one of us and made us free when we accepted Him as our Lord and Savior and the Redeemer of the world (John 3:16; Romans 10:9-10; Isaiah 61:1-3), and we became worthy to be called sons and daughters of God (2 Corinthians 6:18; Romans 8:14,17). Therefore, there is never a time when any child of God should live with a defeated spirit. We have to live by faith so that we can partake of the promises of God who already declared both spiritual and material success in our lives. Every child

*Anyone or group of people can be prejudiced, regardless of race, ethnicity or nationality.*

of God should have an empowered and not a defeated spirit. Every child of God has His awesome rays of victory within him or her waiting to be claimed in accordance with God's promises, purpose and will for his or her life (Jeremiah 29:11). Having been justified and sanctified in the Name of Jesus Christ (1 Corinthians 6:11), every child of God belongs to His mountaintop of victory where through Christ, His holy love and light—His rays of victory shine without ceasing, through pain and sorrow, dry and fruitful seasons and even through death and eternity(Romans 8:35-39). Through Jesus Christ God has already taken us into triumph over our adversities in the world (John 16:33). Believe and receive this spiritual truth in the awesome Name of our Lord and Savior Jesus Christ!

*Through Jesus Christ, we are no longer slaves to any evil doings, including racism.*

**Chapter Quiz**

1. What and who is the true source of the foul spirit of racism and its unfruitful product racism?

2. True or false: A racist oppressor believes in his or her innate superiority. Explain your answer.

---

3. True or false: The evil spirit of racism is also a generational spirit. Explain your answer.

---

4. True or false: If you allowed racists or racism to define your limitations, you would have allowed yourself to become a "slave" to the vile spirit of racism and its nasty fruit of racism. Explain your answer.

---

5. True or false: Jesus Christ has set and made you free from the sin of racism and you have become subject only to God and His righteousness. Explain your answer.

---

ထထထထထထ ♦ ♦ ♦ ♦ ♦ ထထထထထထ

**Reflections:**

---

---

---

---

ထထထထထထ ♦ ♦ ♦ ♦ ♦ ထထထထထထ

# CHAPTER 31: God's Rays of Victory Within You

Child of the Most High God, I pray you now believe that Jesus Christ in you is evidence of God's validation of your worthiness? He, Christ, is the only Mediator (1Timothy 2:5) to God, the Eternal Rock of Ages, within Whom He is One with the Holy Spirit. Through Christ, God's divine and powerful rays of victory shine brilliantly within you (Habakkuk 3:4).

When you draw nearer to God, He too will draw nearer to you (James 4:8a). If you seek God with all your heart, you will find Him (Deuteronomy 4:29; Jeremiah 29:13; Matthew 7:7). If you love God, He will deliver you from all evil and adversities; He will elevate and promote if you truly come to know His Name (Psalms 91:14). If you acknowledge the Name of the Triune God, He will reveal Himself to you (Jeremiah 29:13); He will also reveal to you His unique and excellent purpose and plan for your life (Jeremiah 29:11). If you call unto God, He will answer you—He will be with you in the face of troubles and difficulties—He will rescue and honor you (Psalms 91:15). Yes, if you call unto God, He will show you great and mighty things that you do not know (Jeremiah 33:3). If you make your request known to God by faith He will answer you (John 16:23-24).

God's Holy Word and His rays of victory are for your life's triumph and not defeat in your life. Now, shake off the dust of defeat by racism from the soles of your feet. Soak your heart and mind in the Holy Word of God, and begin to learn the real and only truth about who you are. This will come through a gradual process of revelation by His Holy Spirit who dwells within you. Let the holy truth of God's Word flood you with His spiritual knowledge, understanding and wisdom, free your soul from captivity, and unshackle your mind from mental slavery and oppression (Isaiah 61:1). Your mind will never again be fooled by lies about your worthiness or would you ever again rely on being validated by others. Whatever you do, do it to honor God and not man (Colossians 3:23). God has validated you through Jesus Christ. This validation is complete and enough for you, because His holy Light—His rays of victory, will now radiate permanently in your spirit.

*Let the holy truth of God's Word free your soul from captivity, and unshackle your mind from mental slavery and oppression (Isaiah 61:1).*

Now, you know that before He created you, He knew you, loved and cherished you (Jeremiah 1:5); then He created you, you were still precious (Genesis 1:26-27; Psalms 139:13-14); and then He conceived you through your mother's womb and you were born after a nine month gestational period, and you are still loved and cherished by Him as you were from the very beginning even before your conception (Jeremiah 1:5). Even if you were a premature baby He [God] still loved and cherished you. By the precious Blood of Jesus Christ, our Lord and Savior, you became righteous and worthy and have received His free gift of eternal salvation (John 3:16; Romans 5:19, 10:9-10; 1 Corinthians 1:30; 2 Corinthians 5:21). Therefore, who is the man or woman—racist or otherwise—to deem you unworthy if God created you and made you worthy through Jesus Christ? Selah! [Pause and think about this]

*God's Holy Word and His rays of victory are for your life's triumph and not defeat in your life.*

Today, the practices of racism have for the most part become silent, covert or subversive. These racist practices are now designed to silently attack your heart and mind. By the very nature of these practices, they can enslave and pollute your heart, control your psyche, and imprison your mind. Outwardly, your body may be unshackled, but inwardly, your mind could be shackled with chains of lies about who you are, what you can achieve and your worthiness to society. These invisible shackles are iron-heavy and can weigh down on your entire soul to the extent that they can fill your mind with negative thoughts and emotions, and derail you from your dreams and ambitions.

Therefore, you need to guard your heart with God's Holy Word against the lies and deceit of the foul spirit of racism. "Above all else, guard your heart, for everything you do flows from it." (Proverbs 4:23)

In the Book of Exodus, we see how the Israelites were enslaved for four hundred years when they suffered at the hands of the Egyptians and their Pharaohs. The physical bodies and minds of the Egyptian slaves were in shackles of defeat and oppression; later God freed them from physical and mental bondage, but many still remained in mental bondage when they were in the wilderness. The Trans-Atlantic slave trade was no different. Africans were enslaved for about four hundred years at the hands of Europeans, Spanish, Portuguese, Arabs, Americans and others who willingly participated in the indignity of brutal human trafficking and slavery, and who committed abominable acts of wickedness and murdered millions of the Africans forced into slavery. Again, both the physical bodies and minds of those enslaved were in shackles of defeat and oppression. Although God later freed their forefathers and their descendants from physical and mental bondage, still many remain in mental bondage to this day.

*Your mind could be shackled with chains of lies about who you are, what you can achieve and your worthiness to society.*

Today, although physical slavery may not be a common occurrence, it still exists in various forms. There are also many who may not be physical slaves but their minds remain in shackles of defeat and oppression. And yet through Jesus Christ, Al-Almighty God already freed all humanity from both physical and mental bondage, and from the power of evil and sin (Romans 6:14; John 8:32,36; Isaiah 61:1-3). Now, it is up to you to accept His gift of freedom in your heart and mind, and become the new creation that Jesus Christ has already made you (Galatians 2:20)—and renew your mind daily with God's Word (Romans 12:2; Ephesians 4:23-24).

The Word of God makes it clear that it was never His design for mankind to be under the bondage of physical or mental slavery. God has set all of us free from evil bondage through Jesus Christ (Isaiah 61:1; Colossians 3:11; Galatians 3:27-29; Galatians 5:1; John 8:32,36). Through Christ, your spirit has been renewed making you a new person in Him (2 Corinthians 5:17; Galatians 2:20). This new person that you are is no longer subject to the lies and distortions of racism, but only to God's truth, righteousness and holiness.

*Allow God to take the burden of the yoke of racism from you.*

It was never God's design for any child of His to live with a defeated mind. If you are one of those who have mental shackles from their experiences with racism, it needs to and must come off you today—yes, this very moment! The shackles that racism imposes on the mind should not be on anyone let alone weighing down a child of the Most High God. Allow God to remove the burden of the yoke of racism from you (Isaiah 10:27). Believe and receive the truth that Jesus Christ has set you free from the evil shackles of racism and that you are free indeed (John 8:32,36). God's brilliant Light, His rays of victory, are always there to help you break free from the negative spirit of racism. The truth and power of God's Word, if you receive and accept it in your heart as the truth, it will *surely* set you free forever from the burden of racism (John 8:32,36).

**Chapter Quiz**

1. If you wanted God to reveal Himself to you what must you do?

___

2. If you wanted God to reveal your real self to you what must you do?

___

3. How does God's Holy Word free your soul from the mental captivity of racism?

___

4. True or false: God has freed you from the lies and distortions of racism. Explain your answer.

___

∞∞∞∞∞∞∞∞∞∞∞∞ ♦ ♦ ♦ ♦ ♦ ∞∞∞∞∞∞∞∞∞∞∞∞

## Reflections:

_______________________________________________

_______________________________________________

_______________________________________________

_______________________________________________

∞∞∞∞∞∞∞∞∞∞∞∞ ♦ ♦ ♦ ♦ ♦ ∞∞∞∞∞∞∞∞∞∞∞∞

# CHAPTER 32: Spiritual Truth You Must Know

How do you recognize that you are mentally enslaved by your experiences with racism? How do you know that you have mental shackles on your mind? The fiery darts of racism are numerous and their negative effects on one's mind can be identified by any thoughts created by the lies of racism that do not allow the true knowledge of God's Word to soak your heart and mind—thoughts that are opposed to God's holy spiritual truth and purpose for your life. God's spiritual truth has destroyed the burden of the yoke of racism—know these truths and bind them to your heart ALWAYS! Here they are:

- All humans are created in the excellent Image of God (Genesis 1:27) and are on the same level of humanity. Therefore, all human beings are equal in God's eyes, in humanity and dignity.

- No race is superior or inferior to another. Whoever thinks he is better than another person is in self-deceit (Galatians 6:3).
- God loves you more than anyone can ever love you, and through Jesus Christ, nothing can ever separate you from His love (Romans 8:35-39).
- God loves you so much that He gave His only Son Jesus Christ to die for your sins so that by His precious Blood you will have eternal salvation and not persish, if you believe in Him (John 3:16; Romans 10:9-10)
- Wholeness of the spirit, soul and body is a free gift of God, which is there for you to claim as yours (3 John 1:2).
- Your worthiness is validated by God through Jesus Christ and your ownership guaranteed by the promise, gift and deposit of the Holy Spirit (Ephesians 1:13-14).
- True spiritual knowledge cultivates your self-regard, self-acceptance and self-appreciation. God's desire and plan is for your soul (mind, emotions, thoughts, will and resolve) to flourish based on His Holy Word which is the only authentication of His Holy truth. You can only achieve and obtain godly self-regard, self-

*How do you recognize that you are mentally enslaved by your experiences with racism?*

acceptance and self-appreciation through authentic spiritual knowledge. Your old carnal "self" has been transformed into your new and true identity and nature in Jesus Christ—in Him and Him alone (Psalms 118:8).

- Only God (and you) can set the limits of your career and life's success (Deuteronomy 8:18, 28:1-14; Jeremiah 29:11).
- It is God, not humans, who gives you power to get wealth (Deuteronomy 8:18). Racists and racism cannot take this power away from you unless you submit your heart and mind to the vile spirit of racism that is behind them.
- You are not a slave or bondservant to any man or woman—racist or otherwise. You should be a bondservant only to God and His righteousness (Romans 6:18). Only to God, His Holy Spirit and the redeeming power of our Lord and Savior Jesus Christ should you allow access to "enslave" your heart and mind with God's divine Holy Word—not to any sin—and certainly not to racism. Therefore, you should know God's Holy Word by reading and meditating on it and receiving its revelation power through God's Holy Spirit Who dwells in you. If you do not know God's Word and His Holy

*You are not a slave or bondservant to any man or woman—racist or other.*

Spirit through Jesus Christ, the devil will lie to you; he will manipulate you either directly or through racists and others with deceptive lies.

- The power of God's Holy Spirit and Jesus Christ in you is greater than any evil, obstacle, challenge or adversity in your life or in the world around you (1 John 4:4). Certainly, you must believe that He (Christ) Who is in you is far greater than the foul spirit of racism.
- You are more than a conqueror through Jesus Christ who loves you (Romans 8:37).
- God's design for your life is first everlasting salvation; that is, victory for your spirit and soul (John 3:16; Romans 10:9-10); and good health, wealth and success, that is, abundant life here on Earth (3 John 2; Jeremiah 29:11; John 10:10b).
- Walk worthy and live a life of integrity (Ephesians 4:1). You have to walk in daily obedience and reverence to the God's Holy Word, His Son Jesus Christ and His Holy Spirit within you.
- The power of holy worship, in truth and in spirit (John 4:24), will destroy any form of evil being orchestrated against you, including the foul spirit of racism.
- God's power within and around you, His child, is far greater than the negative power of the carnal world that

directs any fiery darts of the odious spirit of racism (1 John 4:4).

- Racist attacks against you are without God's backing and will fail (Isaiah 54:15).
- You are God's workmanship and He created you in Jesus Christ for good works which He planned for you long ago (Ephesians 2:10). Your life was planned by God to be a success before you were conceived or born (Jeremiah 29:11); God created and made you rich in Christ—and He put the greatness and power of Christ in you.
- Any negative thought of your person or others is not of God, but of the devil and must be held captive and demolished by the Word and promises of God (2 Corinthians 10:3-6).
- God has not given you a spirit of fear but of power, love and a sound mind (2 Timothy 1:7)
- You have the power and authority of Jesus Christ in you to trample on the scorpion and serpent spirit of racism that orchestrates racism and the activities of racists against you (Luke 10:18-19).
- You have the victory of Jesus Christ in you (1 John 5:4).

ꝏꝏꝏꝏꝏꝏ♦ ♦ ♦ ♦ ♦ꝏꝏꝏꝏꝏꝏ

## Chapter Quiz

1. List at least four spiritual truths that you can apply to gain daily victory over racism.

___

2. In what ways does God's spiritual truth destroy the burden of the yoke of racism?

___

3. True or false: Racist attacks against you are without God's backing and will fail. Explain your answer.

___

4. True or false: Any negative thought of your person or others is not of God, but of the devil, and by faith, must be held captive and demolished by the Holy Word and promises of God. Explain your answer.

___

ꝏꝏꝏꝏꝏꝏ♦ ♦ ♦ ♦ ♦ꝏꝏꝏꝏꝏꝏ

## Reflections:

___

___

___

___

ꝏꝏꝏꝏꝏꝏ♦ ♦ ♦ ♦ ♦ꝏꝏꝏꝏꝏꝏ

# CHAPTER 33: Release from Mental Slavery

The vile spirit of racism wants to dominate your mind, thoughts, emotions, will, resolve, actions, attitude, personality and behavior, so as to negatively impact your ability, hopes, dreams, and aspirations. The fiery darts of racism are the devil's design through other humans to hold your soul captive under evil control and oppression. This is what your experiences with racism could and would do to you if you allowed them. Total spiritual release and freedom from the spirit of mental slavery by your experiences with racism require the grace of God and the power of His Holy Word.

God's Holy Word has the power to give you spiritual freedom, which will translate first into mental freedom from the shackles of racism (John 8:32). A prisoner who completes his or her prison term is set free by the State, but is not made free in their mind. Therefore, if a prisoner is set free physically, but his or her mind is not renewed with God's Holy Word, they are likely to commit another crime, be convicted and sent back to prison. On the other hand, if he or she is set free physically, and their mind is renewed and made free by God's Word, the devil will not lure them back into the same actions that took them to prison in the first place.

Have you allowed God's Holy Word to continually renew your mind? Through Jesus Christ, God's Word has the power to permanently unchain once and for all the shackles of mental slavery caused by racism (John 8:36). God's rays of victory within you sounds a trumpet of triumph, which channels your gifts, talents, potentials as directed by His Holy Spirit into paths of spiritual and material success. Alas! The brilliance of God's chandelier within you illuminates your spirit and soul with His radiating beams of peace, faith, joy, hope, patience, mercy, faithfulness, forgiveness and righteousness, and love for all humanity. Now you know that you are one of God's mighty works and racism cannot hold your mind captive. Selah! Pause and think of this!

*Whatever the enemy, the devil, stole from you through racists, it is time for you to claim all back.*

By your daily faith fueled meditations on God's Word, worship and prayer, and giving thanks to Him, He will surely give you complete release and freedom from the mental slavery of racism. This is the first step towards rebuilding within the new you all that was destroyed by the injustices, oppression and negative beliefs from your experiences with racism. Whatever the enemy, the devil, stole from you through your human enemies who perpetrate different forms of racial oppression and injustice against you, it is time for you to claim everything back through spiritual warfare (1 Samuel 30:1-8,18-19; Ephesians 6:10-18). Yes, it is time for you to let God renew your strength by the resurrection Who is Jesus Christ (John 11:25). God's resurrection power that raised Christ from the dead is in you; the power of His Holy Spirit that is so great that it can bring to life all that the devil has tried to kill in you through the vile spirit of racism (John 11:25; John 10:10; Romans 4:17). God's empowering by His Holy Word will enable you to speak to the dry bones in your life and bring them back to life (Ezekiel 37:1-14). Before you continue reading please take a moment now to say this prayer and meditate on it:

*Let God remind you that He will reward all of your efforts and accomplishments.*

*"Where there was daily weakness, Father Lord God, please give me daily strength. Through Jesus Christ, I can declare that I am strong even when I am weak (2 Corinthians 12:10). When and where any negative thoughts begin to creep into my mind, let Your Holy Spirit help me to quickly change the course of my thoughts and begin to activate within me only positive thoughts—power thoughts that are based on Your Holy Word—Your Spiritual truth (Philippians 4:8-9; Psalms 51:10). Let Your Holy Spirit, awesome Lord God, flood my thoughts with Your absolute truth*

*about my spiritual and physical well-being, success and abundance on Earth and everlasting glory in Heaven, in Jesus' Name, Amen."*

When anyone tells you that you are mediocre or less than able, let God flood your heart and mind with the real truth that you are a high achiever by His grace and power and that you are more than able to achieve great success in your life with Holy Spirit-directed hard work. When and where you are told that you can't or won't succeed, let God tell you daily that you can and that you are more than able through Jesus Christ. When all is said and done, let no one convince you that you are not valuable for you are truly valuable and worthy by the precious Blood of Jesus Christ, which He shed for you and I and all of humanity on the Holy Cross of Calvary. When and where anyone tells you that you are less likely to succeed let God reveal the only truth to you that through Jesus Christ, God already made you a success. Therefore, your only true divine option is to be faithful in whatever God has called you to be and success will follow. Let God Who called you more than a conqueror through Christ, reveal the real winner in you to you!

*Let God's Holy Spirit remind you to lay down your burden at the holy Feet of His Lamb, Jesus Christ.*

When at your workplace or any other environment where your efforts and accomplishments are ignored, never rewarded or you are not promoted when you should be, let God remind you that He has acknowledged all of your efforts and accomplishments, and that it is He who gives real promotion and growth in all areas of your life (Psalms 75:6-7). In due season you shall surely bear good fruit because you are deeply and firmly planted on the Rock, Jesus Christ, in Whom God's gushing fresh spring never dries up (Psalms 1:1-3; Matthew 16:18). Let God remind you that He will reward all of your efforts and accomplishments, and that He will promote you to a higher level than that which your workplace denied you (Psalms 75:6-7). When any thoughts of unworthiness begin to creep into your mind let the Holy Spirit of God remind you of God's Stamp of Validation and Ownership on and in you through Jesus Christ (Ephesians 1:13-14). When you become weary and you need encouragement let the Holy Spirit of God fill your heart and mind with God's empowering and encouraging Word: He, God, loves you very much and nothing can ever separate you from His divine love through Jesus Christ (Romans 8:35-39) and He will never leave nor forsake you (Hebrews 13:5). Let His Holy Spirit remind you to lay down your burden at the holy Feet of His Lamb, Jesus Christ, our Lord and Savior, the Redeemer of the world (Psalms 68:19; Matthew 11:28,30).

*Let God's Holy Spirit remind you of His Stamp of Validation and Ownership on and in you through Christ.*

On a daily basis, let God begin to rebuild your view or perspective of your authentic spiritual image, identity and nature within the new you who is rooted in Jesus Christ. Allow God's

Holy Spirit to lead you to all truth (John 16:13) through revelation knowledge of God's Holy Word. Let the lies of the enemy, the devil, through your human enemies, including racists, become like dust that you brush off you. Let the absolute truth of God's Holy Word, which is God speaking to you, be your shield and buckler (Psalms 91:4). Let revelation knowledge of His Holy Word by His Holy Spirit Who dwells within you, become your main guiding lamp to your feet and light to your path (Psalms 119:105). Let God's glorious Holy Light, His beaming rays of victory, shine always through and around you daily through Jesus Christ.

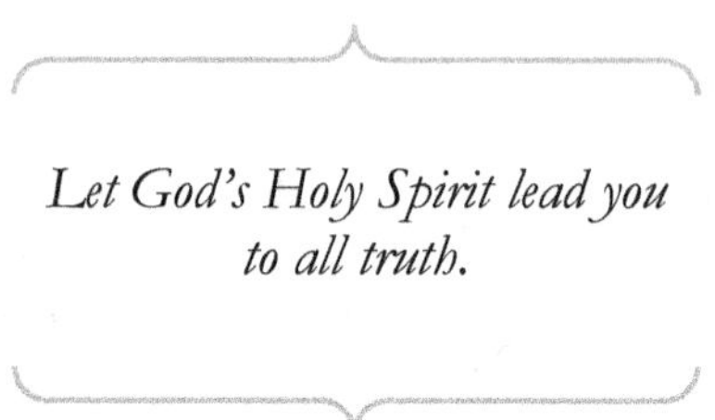

*Let God's Holy Spirit lead you to all truth.*

**Chapter Quiz**

1. Do you understand the meaning of the "fiery darts of racism"? Please explain.

___

2. How does believing any racist lie keep your mind in psychological chains of mental slavery?

___

3. What does Deuteronomy 8:18 say about who gives real power to get wealth?

___

4. What does Psalms 75:6-7 say about who gives real promotion and increase?

___

5. True or false: Racists are your real masters and you cannot be promoted or become successful in life unless they approve of you and promote you? Explain your answer.

___

6. Describe ways that you can resist the spirit of unworthiness and weariness, which racism tries to impose on you?

___

∞∞∞∞∞∞∞◆ ◆ ◆ ◆ ◆∞∞∞∞∞∞∞

**Reflections:**

___

___

___

___

∞∞∞∞∞∞∞◆ ◆ ◆ ◆ ◆∞∞∞∞∞∞∞

# CHAPTER 34: The Greatest Builder of True Self-image

God created you and I in His excellent Image (Genesis 1:26-27, 5:1) as He did the first Adam and Eve (Genesis 2:7). By disobedience to God, Adam and Eve fell in sin, and through them the curse came upon mankind and we became estranged and separated from God (Genesis 3:6-7; 3:14-19; Romans 5:11-19; Colossians 1:21). But God has given every one of us the chance to be reconciled to Him. He did this by giving us a second Adam, His only Son Jesus Christ for the redemption of mankind (John 3:16).

Jesus Christ shed His Blood on the Cross of Calvary for the salvation of mankind and lifted the curse from us (Romans 6:18; 6:22-23). God loved and washed us from our sins in the precious Blood of Jesus Christ (Revelation 1:5b), justified and sanctified us though Him and by His Holy Spirit (1 Corinthians 6:11). It is Christ, and not any man or woman, Who reconciled us to God (2 Corinthians 5:18-19, Colossians 1:20).

So, if you believed in your heart and professed with your mouth that Jesus Christ died for you and God raised Him from the dead, then you are saved through Him (Christ) (Romans 10:9-10). Having been saved though Jesus Christ in you, you have become a new creation and old things have passed away (2 Corinthians 5:17). Your old self has been crucified with Jesus Christ who now lives in you, and you live by faith in Him Who loves you and who gave Himself up for you (Galatians 2:20). This is the foundation of your true spiritual identity and nature, which is solidly built in and on Jesus Christ. God designed you and me to have a Christ-rooted nature, a godly spiritual and self-image. You are a spirit that is expressed through a soul and encased in a physical body—and the expression of your true spiritual nature in Jesus Christ is your godly nature.

> *God is the original Maker of your true spiritual image.*

Are you a natural, carnal or spiritual being? A natural person has not accepted Jesus Christ as their Lord and Savior and is completely of the world. A natural man relies on his or her human abilities and nature. A carnal person is a "believing unbeliever." What does this mean? A carnal person may have accepted Jesus Christ as their Savior, but he or she has not made Him his or her Lord. A carnal person lives and operates solely based on wordly directions and the needs of their flesh (Romans 8:5,8). A spiritual person lives and operates based on God's Holy Word and is directed by God's Holy Spirit. A spiritual person is not controlled by the needs of their flesh because his or her mind is set on spiritual matters and is renewed daily by God's Holy Word; he or she lives by faith and worships God in spirit and in truth (John 4:24). A spiritual person may slip sometimes and get carried away by the needs of their flesh, but they are quick to hear the voice of God's Holy Spirit and the Holy Word of God stored within his or her heart that directs them back to being spiritually minded.

In simple terms, your natural or carnal self is your overall perception of what and who you are in the physical realm or environment. It is also how you see your own individual world in the context of the world around you. If a racist or other person calls you "inferior," your natural or carnal mind receives it, but your spiritual mind rejects it and calls it foolishness. Why? You know you are made in the excellent Image of God—and you are not inferior to anyone because God's Word confirms that you are equal to all persons, in humanity and dignity (Genesis 1:26-27).

*Does your own spiritual image dominate your natural image?*

Your spiritual image is your identity and nature in Jesus Christ (Galatians 2:20, 2 Corinthians 5:17; John 1:12). Your spiritual nature in Christ manifests through your renewed mind (Romans 12:2; Ephesians 4:23-24). So, when your Christ-rooted spiritual nature dominates your natural or carnal image, you have a godly self-image.

Does your own spiritual image (Romans 8:5-11; 8: 14-16; 12:2; 1 Corinthians 2:12) dominate your natural or carnal image? Do you allow your natural or carnal image to dominate your daily existence (1 Corinthians 3:3)? Do you see yourself based on your natural image, or do you see yourself primarily from your true spiritual image in Jesus Christ? Does the world around you define for you who you are or does God's Holy Word define for you who you are in Jesus Christ through your faith? How does the foundation of your Christ-rooted nature manifest in your daily life?

*God's plan for your life is excellent (Jeremiah 29:11).*

To have a godly image means to see yourself primarily through who you *truly* are in Jesus Christ; to have faith in who and what you are Him; to be at peace with whom and what you are in Him; to have a sense of purpose, direction and confidence that you can and will succeed in life through Him (Philippians 4:13; Romans 8:37). You trust God on His great purpose for your life. Your healthy sense of purpose stems from your understanding and belief that God's plan for your life is excellent (Jeremiah 29:11). Therefore, you know and believe that you can and will succeed in your life's endeavors when God is your primary focus through Christ, and as you work hard daily to achieve your goals.

When you have a godly image, you view "self" from the perspective of your spiritual identity and nature in Christ, and not from a natural or carnal selfish perspective. So, your godly self-esteem, which encompasses a positive self-respect, self-regard, self-acceptance, self-confidence, self-love (not self-indulgence) and self-esteem (not arrogance), and your expression of your self-competence, self-efficacy and self-efficiency, are based on your faith in Christ. You must believe that you can do all things through Jesus Christ (Philippians 4:13), and you are more than a conqueror through Him (Romans 8:37). God has made you a winner through Christ—believe it!

The good news is that God is the original Maker of your true spiritual image; He is the original Designer of your true person and He can remold you from any negative "out-of-shape" back to your true positive "in-shape," if you believe and receive His Holy Word (Jeremiah 18:1-6). Rejoice, therefore, for through Jesus Christ, you have a God Who can help you reclaim in your heart and mind, your positive true image by the restorative power of His Holy Word and revelation knowledge of His Holy Spirit Who dwells within you.

*God is the original Designer of your true person.*

All you need to do is to call unto God (Jeremiah 33:3) and cry out "Abba Father" to Him (Galatians 4:6-7; Romans 8:14-16); ask Him for help through Jesus Christ, and you shall receive it from Him (Matthew 7:7, 21:22; Luke 11:9; John 16:24). In the Name of Jesus Christ, God will answer you and show you great and mighty things that you do not know (Jeremiah 33:3). He will give you His divine and winning strategies to apply against the vile spirit of racism, its willing hosts and their wicked racist activities being orchestrated against your life. His divine and winning strategies will empower you to rule over racism and make your racist enemies your footstool (Psalms 110:1-2).

**Chapter Quiz**

1. What is the difference between your natural, carnal and spiritual self-image?

---

2. True or false: Your natural or carnal image is greater than your spiritual self-image in Jesus Christ? Explain your answer.

---

3. True or false: When racism distorts your natural or carnal image in your mind, this means that it has also distorted your true spiritual identity and nature in Jesus Christ. Explain your answer.

---

4. Who is the original Maker of your true spiritual image?

---

5. True or false: Your true spiritual image, identity and nature in Jesus Christ should dominate your natural or carnal image amd nature? Explan your answer.

---

∞∞∞∞∞∞∞∞∞∞∞ ♦ ♦ ♦ ♦ ♦ ∞∞∞∞∞∞∞∞∞∞∞

## Reflections:

___

___

___

___

∞∞∞∞∞∞∞∞∞∞∞ ♦ ♦ ♦ ♦ ♦ ∞∞∞∞∞∞∞∞∞∞∞

# CHAPTER 35: Acquiring True Self-image

True self-respect and self-regard arise from authentic spiritual knowledge, understanding and wisdom of God's Holy Word. True self-respect and self-regard originates from authentic knowledge of who you are in Jesus Christ, in partnership with God's Holy Spirit Who reveals the wonderful things that God has freely given to you (1 Corinthians 2:12). Low self-respect or self-regard expresses itself as feelings of low: self-worth, self-acceptance, self-appreciation, self-confidence, self-competence, self-efficacy or self-efficiency, and arises from lack of true spiritual knowledge (Hosea 4:6). Low or lack of self-respect is tied to your view or perception of and belief in your self-worth.

Most often when you have low self-respect or regard, you see yourself through the limitations that others place on you and their negative judgment of your person. In this case, you allow the world and circumstances around you to rule your soul instead of allowing your own spirit to rule your soul and surroundings.

Low or lack of self-respect or self-regard places limitations on most areas of your life and may hinder your performance and accomplishments. When this is the case, you cannot see your authentic godly image, and true identity and nature, which is Jesus Christ in you.

By soaking your heart and mind in the Holy Word of God, which is the all knowing truth, you develop a positive view of your authentic identity and nature in Jesus Christ that the world cannot tamper with. Such truthful perspective is having a healthy and positive sense of our self-worth, self-acceptance, self-confidence, self-competence, self-efficacy and self-efficiency. When you have a positive view of your authentic self, you can reject the limitations that others and circumstances attempt to place on you and refuse to bow down to negative situations. You submit yourself to God and to Him alone; resist the devil when he comes in various forms including racism, and he will flee from you (James 4:7). With true spiritual knowledge, you know that you can tackle the daily challenges and obstacles that you encounter, because Jesus Christ lives in you (Galatians 2:20); you are more than a conqueror through Him [Christ] Who loves you (Romans 8:37), and through Him Who strengthens you, you can do all things (Philippians 4:13). When you understand and believe that your true self-worth is solid, unshakable and un-

*Godly self-acceptance cultivates godly self-respect and self-regard, and vice versa.*

changeable in Jesus Christ, you will acquire godly self-acceptance. Accept yourself as a beautiful child of the Most High God who has been justified, validated and sanctified through Christ, and received the Holy Spirit. When you do, you have Christ-rooted self-worth that is unchangeable by the world. Then, you develop godly self-respect and self-regard. Godly self-acceptance cultivates godly self-respect and self-regard, and vice versa.

Self-acceptance is how comfortable you are with what and who you are, regardless of your flaws and imperfections that you are aware of. It is not based on your own performance, but on God's acceptance of you through Jesus Christ (Ephesians 2:10; Jeremiah 31:3; Jeremiah 1:4-7; Isaiah 43:7). There is a burden that comes with the performance-based self-acceptance and God has already destroyed the yoke of any such burden (Isaiah 10:27). Performance-based self-acceptance is the kind of self-acceptance the world teaches, and it is not godly self-acceptance through the cleansing Blood of Jesus Christ. Worldly self-acceptance places the condition of your acceptance on your material achievements, and on other external and tangible factors.

*He, Christ has deemed you worthy and no person is qualified to define you otherwise.*

Our self-image, that is, our mental picture of ourselves, is created by facets of what we have learned about who we are, either from our personal experiences or perceptions, or by us receiving and accepting judgment of others, positive or negative.

Over many years your own mental picture of yourself is created by how you see your persona, who and what you believe you are; what kind of person you believe you are or that others think you are; how much you like and accept yourself or you perceive others like or accept you; how you respect and regard yourself; and how others esteem you or the status you believe you have, or you have accepted from others based on their judgment of you.

Based on the world's definition of self-image, many individuals value themselves based on their race, skin color, external beauty, education, skills, job title, position, wealth and societal status. Therefore, their natural or carnal self-image and their material possessions, not their spiritual self-image (that is who they are in Jesus Christ), become the shaky foundation of their external, carnal self-image. Their self-image is built on a false foundation which is their riches and their human connections (Psalms 62:10; Psalms 146:3). Thereby, their self-acceptance is neither permanent nor built on a solid foundation (Matthew 7:24). Their self-confidence is high when they have material things, *feel* beautiful and are well connected to individuals in "high places;" and low when they lack such things and *feel* ugly. The key work here is "feel." Our external, carnal image relies on our feelings which are unreliable in many instances. Our authentic spiritual image relies on the truth of God's

*Godly self-confidence is not arrogance of the flesh (Romans 12:3).*

Holy Word—that we are truly made worthy through Christ. Therefore, self-acceptance rooted in Jesus Christ, that is, true godly self-acceptance, is based on God's holy truth, and not our feelings, and has the foundation of peace about who we are in Him (1Corinthians 3:11 Isaiah 26:3, 12; Philippians 4:7).

Jesus Christ is within you and has set a true and solid Foundation for your intrinsic value and worth which is not based on external opinions or situations. Basically, you live by the absolute holy truth that through Jesus Christ God has deemed you worthy, and no person is qualified to define you otherwise. Through Jesus Christ, you are "blessed with every spiritual blessing in the heavenly places" (Ephesians 1:3), and the same Holy Spirit power of God that raised Christ from the dead lives in you (Ephesians 1:15-23). What contrary power around you could be greater than this! Selah! (Pause and think of this!)

*Our authentic spiritual image relies on the truth of God's Holy Word.*

Self-acceptance is an important foundation of your self-love (not arrogance or carnal pride) and love of others, and also cultivates self-respect and respect and acceptance of others (1 Corinthians 13:13, Psalms 139:13-14). Self-love does not mean superficial love of self or self-indulgent love of your carnal nature; it means spiritual love of who you are in Jesus Christ which cultivates your love of others. Self-acceptance stems from Christ-rooted spiritual knowledge and wisdom (Proverbs 1:7, 9:10;

Psalms 111:10; Corinthians 8:2-3) and cancels self-dislike, self-distortion, or self-hate. True self-acceptance gives you a positive and healthy sense and view of who and what you are based on how God sees you through Jesus Christ. He, Christ, is the authentic foundation of your self-worth, self-confidence, self-competence, self-efficacy and self-efficacy. (Galatians 2:20, 6:1-5; Romans 12:3; 2 Corinthians 5:17)

As a born again Christian believer, your godly self-confidence is not arrogance of the flesh (Romans 12:3)—it is the confidence that you have in your potential abilities in Jesus Christ. The feeling that you can accomplish what you set out to do because of who you are in Christ, a competent child (son or daughter) of the Most High God (Hebrews 10:35; Romans 8:37; Philippians 4:13). As an ambassador of God (2 Corinthians 5:20), you become fully confident in your God-given abilities in Jesus Christ.

*As an ambassador of God (2 Corinthians 5:20), you become fully confident in your God-given abilities in Jesus Christ.*

When you allow Christ to take over your entire being, the manifestations of your authentic Christ-rooted nature become your daily applause of God's Kingdom power and glory within and through you. No evil spirit, including the vile spirit of racism can successfully come against God's Kingdom power and glory within. Receive and believe this holy truth that racism can never change!

ooooooooooooo ♦ ♦ ♦ ♦ ♦ ooooooooooooo

## Chapter Quiz

1. What do you understand to be true spiritual self-knowledge and how does it differ from natural or carnal self-knowledge?

---

2. In what ways can racism negatively affect your self-respect, self-regard, self-worth, self-acceptance, self-appreciation, self-confidence, self-competence, self-efficacy and self-efficiency?

---

3. How can you apply God's Holy Word to prevent racism's negative effects, or fight back spiritually to reverse them?

---

4. Who has set the true foundation for your intrinsic value and worth?

---

5. What is your understanding of godly self-respect?

---

6. What is your understanding of godly self-regard?

---

7. What is your understanding of godly self-worth?

---

8. What is your understanding of godly self-acceptance?

---

9. What is your understanding of godly self-appreciation?

10. What is your understanding of godly self-confidence?

11. What is your understanding of godly self-competence?

12. What is your understanding of godly self-efficacy?

13. What is your understanding of godly self-efficiency?

14. Are you spiritually, natural or carnally-minded?

15. Do you have a spiritual, natural or carnal self-image?

∞∞∞∞∞∞ ♦ ♦ ♦ ♦ ♦ ∞∞∞∞∞∞

**Reflections:**

∞∞∞∞∞∞ ♦ ♦ ♦ ♦ ♦ ∞∞∞∞∞∞

# CHAPTER 36: The Refiner and Purifier of Your True Self-image

"For God so loved the world that he gave his only begotten Son, that whosoever believeth in him should not perish, but have everlasting life." (John 3:16 KJV) The offer and sacrifice of our Lord and Savior, Jesus Christ, is God's holy expression of first, His love, and then His amazing grace, mercy, kindness and faithfulness to all of humanity. Christ paid the cost for our eternal salvation and yet offered it to us at no charge! There is no return on investment that can match this one. Whilst we were still sinners, in exchange for the huge and evil investment made by us (that is our sins), we received eternal salvation through Chist who died for us. We invested in disobedience and sin, yet on our behalf, Christ paid the price for our sins (Isaiah 53; Hebrews 8:12; Isaiah 43:25-26; Romans 3:24-26; 1 Corinthians 15:22,45-47). All that is required of us is to receive Him as our Lord and Savior and repent of our sins to receive eternal salvation (Romans 10:9-10).

Once we become saved through Jesus Christ, we (our spirit) are cleansed by His precious Blood and we have full access to God's divine grace and His Kingdom Power. In God's eyes, old things in our lives become washed away and we are made brand new in Jesus Christ and God forgets our sins (2 Corinthians 5:17; Hebrews 8:12). Christ is the only Mediator between God and humanity and He has reconciled us to God (Malachi 3:2-3; 1 Timothy 2:5; 2 Corinthians 5:18,20). God wants us to draw nearer to Him; and as we do so, He too draws nearer to us (James 4:8). Then, our souls begin to go through a refining and purification process. God the Father is the Refiner and Purifier of our souls through Him [Jesus Christ]. Like a goldsmith or silversmith who places their metal over hot flames to burn away impurities, God uses the unsavory circumstances in our lives to purge us of anything He disapproves.

*Through Jesus Christ, allow God to burn away the impurities that you have allowed racism to deposit on your soul.*

Our experiences with certain situations can sometimes cause toxic impurities to settle on our hearts, minds, thoughts, emotions, will and resolve. Our daily experiences with racism cause the impurities of its spin-offs or lingering effects to settle in our soul. Such impurities can cause us to become angry, hateful, vengeful, embittered and unhappy, and negatively impacts our self-respect, self-regard, self-acceptance, self-confidence, self-competence, self-efficacy and self-efficiency. When this happens, our hearts and minds become burdened with negativity and we see ourselves as victims of racism rather than victors over it. God does not want you to perceive yourself as a victim of racism or any challenge that you face, because He has already made you a victor through Jesus Christ Who loves you (Romans 8:37).

Let God burn away the impurities of the negative effects of racism that have settled on your soul and encrusted in your heart and mind. When your experiences with racism cause deep-rooted anger and create an embittered spirit within you, let God burn away such impurities with the power of His Word, love and grace through Jesus Christ. How is this possible? By you receiving God's Holy Word in your heart, believing it and applying it in your daily living. When you do what God's Word says you should do, you receive His promises. Let God give you daily victory by the precious Blood of Jesus Christ Who has overcome all evil machinations for you. It is crucial to keep your heart and mind open to God's refining and purifying process, this will help you to rebuild a new mindset and give you the true view of your authentic self-image, which is Christ-rooted and based on your true spiritual image, identity and nature in Him.

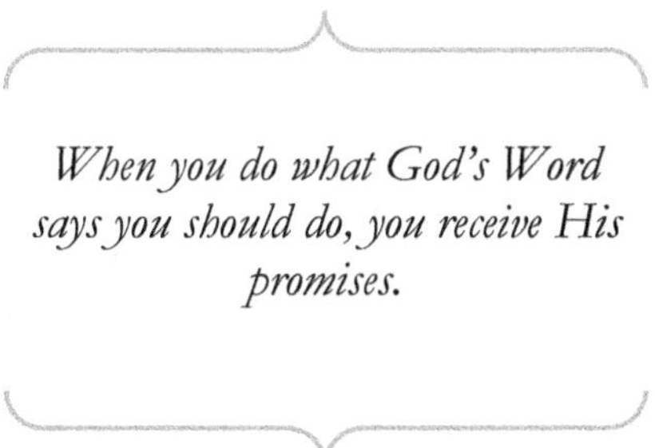


Are you uncomfortable with the skin that God created you in? If you are, this signals a deep spiritual crisis within you. Do you wish to be of another ethnicity, race or nationality? If you do, this feeling did not originate from God but from the devil who is the father of all lies (John 8:44). This signals a lack of true spiritual knowledge (Hosea 4:6). God wants you to be comfortable with the skin that He created you in. He wants you to be happy and grateful that He made you to be of your specific ethnicity, race or nationality. Receive God's Holy Word and Holy Spirit in you to help you to restore in your heart and mind your godly self-esteem: your self-worth, self-respect, self-regard, self-acceptance, self-confidence, self-efficacy and self-efficiency, and rebuild your healthy and true positive mental picture of you.

*Through Jesus Christ, allow God to burn away the impurities that you have allowed racism to deposit on your soul.*

The Webster dictionary defines self-esteem as "confidence and satisfaction in oneself." From the standpoint of a believer in Jesus Christ, I redefine self-esteem as the "confidence and satisfaction in oneself through Jesus Christ." It is one's belief in oneself because of the power of Jesus Christ Who dwells within us; the same power, the Holy Spirit, that raised Christ from the dead, works within and through us, to the glory of God's Name (Ephesians 1:15-23). Thus, your true self-esteem should be based on you knowing your authentic self-worth in Jesus Christ, which is the value that you place on yourself because of the power of Christ in you, who you are in Him, and the Holy Spirit Who also dwells within you. Your true worth in Christ is eternally invaluable and can never be devalued or compromised by anyone or anything.

A healthy self-esteem in Jesus Christ encompasses your positive self-regard, self-respect, self-acceptance, self-dignity, self-integrity, self-competence, self-efficacy and self-efficiency. The word "self" does not refer to your carnal self, but your renewed nature in Jesus Christ (Galatians 2:20). A positive self-esteem stems from authentic spiritual knowledge about whom and what you are, and maintains your belief that you can tackle challenges and obstacles you may encounter. Why? Because Jesus Christ Who lives in you is greater that he that is in the world (1 John 4:4); and so you are more than a conqueror through Him, Christ, Who loves you (Romans 8:37)—and through Him Christ Who strengthens you, you can do all things (Philippians 4:13). This is God's holy truth that the vile spirit of racism can never change!

*Jesus Christ has delivered you from the evil power of racists and the foul spirit behind them, and cancelled all their charges against you.*

Jesus Christ has delivered you from the evil power of racists and the foul spirit behind them, and cancelled all their charges against you (Colossians 2:13-14). Through Christ, God has delivered you from the power of the darkness of racism and all other evil domination into the Kingdom of Light (Colossians 1:12-14). Through Christ, you have received the holy light of

God's glory that smothers the darkness of racism around you! Believe this holy truth! Receive it! It's your to claim!

**Chapter Quiz**

1. True or false: God is the Refiner and Purifier of your true self-image? Explain your answer.

---

2. In what ways can God use your unsavory experience with racism to purge you of the negative things that He disapproves of in your character?

---

3. Why does God need to refine and purify your soul?

---

4. True or false: True self-confidence in Jesus Christ lies in your carnal self and not in your spiritual nature? Explain your answer.

---

5. True or false: True self-confidence in Jesus Christ lies in your spiritual nature and not in your carnal self? Explain your answer.

---

6. True or false: Can God use the evil, wicked and oppressive activities of racists around you to transform you into a spiritual "weapon" against racism and make you more a victor over racism? Explain your answer.

____________________________________________

∞∞∞∞∞∞∞∞∞∞∞ ♦ ♦ ♦ ♦ ♦ ∞∞∞∞∞∞∞∞∞∞∞

**Reflections:**

____________________________________________

____________________________________________

____________________________________________

____________________________________________

∞∞∞∞∞∞∞∞∞∞∞ ♦ ♦ ♦ ♦ ♦ ∞∞∞∞∞∞∞∞∞∞∞

# CHAPTER 37: True Self-Worth is Christ-rooted

True self-worth is rooted in Jesus Christ, the Living Word of God. He, Christ, is our Lord and Savior, our solid Foundation in God that does not shake or move based on success or failure, praise or criticism (Matthew 7:24-25). Understanding that you are truly worthy in Christ is a necessary foundation for self-acceptance and self-appreciation. Then you begin to cultivate authentic self respect and self-regard which position you to develop true self-confidence, that is, spiritual confidence based on God's Holy Word. Authentic self-confidence drives self-competence that fuels self-efficacy and self-efficiency—all of which are necessary for a healthy self-esteem and overall positive perception of your self-image—banishing any insecurity that plagues your soul. How do you define "self-esteem" and "self-image, and what is the difference between them?"

"Self-esteem is your overall opinion of yourself — how you honestly feel about and value yourself. Self-esteem involves judging your worth as a person. People with healthy self-esteem feel good about themselves and believe they are worthwhile. People with low self-esteem, on the other hand, put little value on their opinions and ideas and constantly think that they are not "good enough."[1]

*Your true self-respect is tied to your true self-worth—it is the belief that you have in your inherent value of self-worthiness in Jesus Christ.*

Therefore, self-image is "the perception that one has of oneself, including an assessment of qualities and personal worth."[2] The National Association for Self-Esteem defines self-esteem as "the experience of being capable of meeting life's challenges and being worthy of happiness." [3] "Self-esteem is based on subjective feelings that change according to the current environment; self-image is one's view of self, and beliefs about self, based on life experiences"[4] You see, to have a healthy self-esteem, you need to like yourself and also have a positive and authentic view of your self: worth, regard, respect and integrity.

"Self-image may consist of three types: self-image resulting from how the individual sees himself or herself; self-image resulting from how others see the individual; and self-image resulting from how the individual perceives others see him or her."[5]. "Self-image is the personal view we have of ourselves. It is our mental image or self-portrait. Self-image is an internal dictionary that describes the characteristics of the self, including intelligent, beautiful, ugly, talented, selfish and kind. These char-characteristics form a collective representation of our assets and liabilities as we see them."[6] If your self-esteem and self-image were rooted in Christ, you would have a positive view of yourself and it won't matter to you what others (including racists) think of you. So it is better to have Christ-rooted self-esteem and self-image which is your new person in Him, than to retain your old carnal person that is defined and dictated by the world and racism that exists in it.

Racists who show lack of respect or regard for others also lack true self-respect or regard. They lack inner confidence and assurance about their authentic person in Jesus Christ. They are spiritually ignorant (Hosea 4:6), carnally arrogant (Galatians 6:3), and their souls are ruled by fear of others of a different race or ethnicity. So, they exhibit a false superiority complex as a way to mask the immense fear, insecurity and inferiority complexes that plague their souls.

> *When you lack authentic spiritual understanding, you question your self-worth and abilities.*

The person who is the target of racism may also lack true self: acceptance, respect, regard, appreciation and confidence, because he or she receives the lies of the odious spirit of racism and its willing human hosts (racists), develops a deep inferiority complex, and allows feelings of insecurity to plague his or her soul. It is believed that carnal confidence is not inherited but learned and developed. Therefore, rather than having carnal self-confidence that can be easily swayed by negative words, actions or circumstances, it is better to develop Christ-rooted self-confidence, that is, spiritual confidence. The latter is based on God's Holy Word which cannot be shaken by external opinions, circumstances or perceptions (Matthew 7:24). Sometimes, our carnal or wordly self-confidence has already been bruised by our negative experiences from the past, elements of racism in our society or the negative words or actions of racists and other persons whom we encounter in our daily lives. The truth is that regardless of our prior negative experiences that may have hampered our carnal confidence, God's Holy Word can renew our minds (Romans 12:2; Ephesians 4:23-24) and rebuild our spiritual confidence.

*Your godly self-confidence overcomes the negative power of failure and prepares and leads you to greater success.*

If you receive and believe God's Holy Word, read and meditate on it daily, it ultimately gives you Christ-rooted confidence that is positive and healthy, and it builds true confidence in your abilities through Him. Then, the world around you and its external issues of life cannot and will not impact negatively on your Christ-rooted confidence. Remember that your new spiritual nature in Jesus Christ is no longer your old carnal self (Galatians 2:20).

Your self: competence, efficacy and efficiency are driven by your self-confidence. Your Christ-rooted confidence is your belief in your abilities through Jesus Christ, empowered by the Holy Word and Holy Spirit. It is the assurance you have that when you stand and live by God's Word, His promises to you through Christ will back your honest hard work. It is the deep-rooted belief that if you did your very best to accomplish what you have set out to achieve, you would be successful, because God is on your side (Romans 8:31) and has already blessed the work of your hands (Deuteronomy 2:7,28:12). Your godly confidence also exhibits a healthy mental balance that allows you not to crumble under the weight of temporary failure or setback—because it is managed by your Christ-rooted heart and mindset. So, even if you failed to be successful at one thing, that one or more failures should not dictate negatively your godly self: worth, acceptance, appreciation, respect, respect and integrity, and impact upon your overall perception of your godly self: confidence, competence, efficacy and efficiency Why?

> *Our self: acceptance, appreciation, respect, regard or inner self validation should not be dependent on the external opinions of other individuals.*

Firstly, because you know that you are a child of the Most High God, redeemed by the precious Blood of Jesus Christ and no failure can change your true spiritual value and worth in Him. Secondly, because any failure that you may experience today or have already experienced may be the foundation for greater success tomorrow, if you take it to God in prayer in the Name of our Lord and Savior, Jesus Christ, for His divine instructions and directions. Thirdly, failure can empower you rather than discourage you, if your faith is Christ-rooted and you truly believe the promises of God's Holy Word—one of which is that He has excellent plans for your life (Jeremiah 29:11). So, rather than allow failure to discourage or defeat you, you should learn from it and whatever mistakes you made that led to it, and at the same time, you should also continue to pursue your goals and heart's desires in a Christ-rooted and Holy Spirit-led and constructive manner.

*Let failure be your teacher and not your destroyer!*

Your godly confidence overcomes the negative power of failure and prepares and leads you to greater success. Your godly confidence continues to drive your competence, efficacy and efficiency, regardless of any failures, because your hope and trust is in God—for your excellent future and it remains unchanged (Jeremiah 29:11; Deuteronomy 8:18). Simply put, you come to believe that your downtime caused by temporary failure is really your preparation time for your uptime and greater success because you are focused on Jeremiah 29:11. Let failure be your teacher and not your destroyer! Let your experiences with racism empower you for greater success rather than discourage you and set you up for failure. Let your Christ-rooted self-worth determine your self-acceptance and self-appreciation, cultivate your spiritual self-confidence, and drive your true competence, efficacy and efficiency in Him.

Your true efficacy is driven by your Christ-rooted confidence in your mental abilities and talents that God has given you as an individual. God has empowered you by His Holy Spirit through Jesus Christ, to develop and sharpen your specific skills, and your capability to apply such skills. The word "efficacy" means the power or capacity to produce a desired effect[7,8]. From a Christian, Bible-based perspective, it is your belief in your ability and competence through Jesus Christ, empowered by God's Holy Spirit to accomplish a target task. Your positive perception of your competence impacts your efficiency and efficacy; and your positive view of your true efficiency also drives your efficacy.

*A healthy spiritual state in Jesus Christ dictates your healthy mental state.*

Self efficiency refers to your perceived ability and motivation on how to proficiently complete a task successfully. If you believe that you are efficient through Jesus Christ (Philippians 4:13; Romans 8:37), you have a "can do" mindset and attitude towards a specific assignment or challenge in life. As a believer in Christ, your belief in your self-efficiency is not carnal or prideful; it is based on your empowering by the Holy Spirit through Christ (Romans 8:37; Philippians 4:13). If you don't value your true self-worth in Christ or like who you are in Him, you cannot have authentic self: respect, regard, acceptance or appreciation. Therefore, you are likely to also lack or have low self: confidence, competence, efficacy or efficiency. In fact, your true self- respect and regard is tied to your perception of your true self-worth. It is the belief that you have as a Christian in your inherent priceless value of your worthiness in Jesus Christ. Your respect and value of who you are in Christ is based on the truth that you have been justified and validated by the precious Blood of Jesus Christ. Through Christ Who you believed, God put his stamp of ownership on you by giving you the Holy Spirit he had promised. The Holy Spirit is the guarantee that we shall receive what God has promised his people—we who are believers in Christ, and this assures us that God will give those who are his the inheritance that He has promised (Ephesians 1:13-14; 2 Corinthians 1:20-22).

*Our self-respect, self-regard or self-validation should not be elated or hampered by the positive or negative opinions of others.*

If we believe that we are unworthy, we live and operate in spiritual ignorance (Hosea 4:6). If we believe we are unworthy we would most likely have low: self-respect, self-regard, self-acceptance and self-appreciation, and we would also likely have low: self-confidence, self-competence, self-efficacy and self-efficiency in what we could accomplish. We would also have a "can't do" mindset and attitude towards a specific assignment or challenge in life. However, if we believe that we are worthy in Jesus Christ, we think and act as individuals who have invaluable worth in Him. If we believe we are worthy in Christ, we would acknowledge that we deserve the respect and love of others, but we would affirm the truth that our self-worthiness is not dependent on their respect and love, or validation by them, but on God's only truth about who we *truly* are in Christ. In other words, our self-respect, self-regard or inner self validation should depend on Christ, and not be dependent on the external opinions of other individuals. Our true self-respect, self-regards, self-appreciation or self-validation should not be elated or hampered by the positive or negative opinions of others—and good or bad treatment meted out to us by others should not determine if and how we value ourselves.

*True self-efficacy is your self-efficiency fueled by your Christ-rooted self-confidence in your mental abilities and capabilities, skill and talents.*

Through Jesus Christ, your sense of self-worthiness should be dependent only on authentic spiritual knowledge from God, His Holy Word, through revelation knowledge of His Holy Spirit Who dwells within you. Basically, your true self-worthiness is rooted in Jesus Christ Who lives in you, and in authentic spiritual knowledge in God's Holy Word. This means that you know that God loves you beyond measure (Romans 8:35-39)—and because you too love God He will deliver you from any and all evil plots, schemes, intrigues and machinations of racists fueled by the foul spirit of racism (Psalms 91:14-15). You also know that all things will surely work together for your good and the good of other true believers because we are all called according to God's holy purpose (Romans 8:28).

Without Christ-rooted self: respect, regard or appreciation, your positive perception of your self: confidence and competence diminishes and reflects negatively on your self-efficacy and self-efficiency—and so would your discernment of your overall self-esteem and self-image. Your self- respect and regard plays a critical role in how you perceive yourself—that is your self-esteem and self-image. Your self-acceptance and self-appreciation form a positive foundation for your self respect and self-regard. Your view of your self-respect, self-regard, self-esteem and self-integrity affect your perception of your self-confidence. Your self-confidence drives your self-competence, self-efficacy and self-efficiency.

*When you abide daily in God's Holy Word, He, not humans, will dictate your mindset.*

When you have a poor or negative perception of who you are, you are likely to also have low self-appreciation and lack self-regard and self-respect. A negative perception of your self-image could also place limitations on your performance and accomplishments. Your achievements are unlikely to exceed your low or negative self-image. However, even if your achievements and accomplishments did exceed your low or negative self-image, deep down within your soul, they would never give you true self-regard or self-respect that is Jesus Christ-rooted.

One's perception of their self-image can be very different from how the world sees them. A person who has attained worldly success and who has outward beauty, glamour and intelligence may have a poor perception of their own self-image; while someone who does not have as much worldly success and who has faced greater life's challenges and difficulties, may have a positive self-image. From a Christian perspective, we who are Christian believers know that "…Man shall not live by bread alone, but by every word that proceeds from the mouth of God (Matthew 4:4, Deuteronomy 8:3)." So we need to dwell in God's Holy Word, and our hearts and minds need to feed on it daily, for us to be filled with the truth, and be able to function properly—to be truly alive, well and whole in Jesus Christ.

*Have you allowed racists to dictate and shape your mind-set and direct your daily thoughts and emotions?*

Our experiences with racism, if we let them, can distort our thinking and outlook on things and our horizon, giving us a negative view of ourselves, contrary to the truth of who we are in Jesus Christ. If we do not reject such negative view, we could begin to believe the lies of the vile spirit of racism repeated to us through its willing human hosts who attack us with their vile words and actions. A negative self-image often stems from low: self-respect, self-regard, self-acceptance and self-appreciation, and self-confidence, and you end up with a distorted, untrue view of yourself and others. This is a self-destructive cycle that is usually a result of negative images, thoughts and feelings that you accept daily from the lies of the devil about you, through your own mindset and thoughts, and other human instruments in your society that he uses against you.

When you lack authentic spiritual understanding, you question your self-worth and abilities, then you have low self-esteem because you lack or have low self: respect, regard, acceptance and appreciation, and you perceive yourself to have low self: confidence, competence, efficacy and efficiency. When you have low or lack self-confidence, you are not able to believe that you are more than a conqueror through Jesus Christ Who loves you (Romans 8:37). You acquire the grasshopper mentality, and feel, act, and live like a victim and not a victor over your life's challenges (Numbers 13:30-33). Your dreams become fuzzy and you bury your talents, gifts and abilities (Matthew 25:24-26); and you no longer use your power of visualization to first capture your dreams in the mind, let alone work towards achieving them. In time you become passive in your efforts to reach for your goals and achieve heights that you are capable of, because you longer believe that you are empowered in and through Jesus Christ to accomplish great things in your life. Please know the truth that it is God's holy purpose for you to acquire and main-

*Your healthy spiritual mind in Jesus Christ is powered by God's Holy Word.*

tain a victor mentality and not a victim, grasshopper mentality (Numbers 13:30-33).

Many people have allowed racists to dictate and shape their mindset and direct their daily thoughts and emotions. They have allowed racism to rule them as their master and dictate the limits of their accomplishments. They have received and internalized the lies of racism from the devil through his human instruments (racists) who perpetrate it. In most cases, a person's negative self-image can result from internalizing negative words, actions and false images of who they are as defined by others and external situations. Know that this was never and still is not God's design for your life.

*You should bring every wicked and racist thought into captivity to the obedience of Jesus Christ.*

Having a godly self-image fueled by Christ-rooted self: acceptance and appreciation, respect, regard, esteem, integrity, worth and confidence, cancels the effect of the negative thoughts, words and actions of others or circumstances around you. If you believe and receive God's Holy Word as the truth, it will be your shield and buckler (Psalms 91:4) and protect your heart and mind from the lies of the odious spirit of racism, and will make you free from the stranglehold of racism (John 8:32,36). Then the negativity of the world around you will have no effect on your authentic spiritual image. It will have no effect on your heart, mind, thoughts, emotions, will and resolve, as well as your attitude, actions, behavior, character or personality.

Your healthy spiritual mind in Jesus Christ is powered by God's Holy Word, dictates your optimistic mindset, and is critical for your positive self-esteem and healthy self-image. A healthy spiritual mind in Christ gives you a true and good view of your self: worth, respect and regard in Him. This then activates your self: acceptance, appreciation, confidence, competence, efficacy and efficiency—your ability to tackle daily challenges with the belief that you can win because of the awesome power of Jesus Christ and the Holy Spirit in you. The times when you don't win due to your own mistakes, those of others, deliberate or inadvertent challenges, or simply because of the trials of life that build our faith as believing Christians, your spiritual confidence still plows ahead in the right direction with the belief that though you may not win everything, you can and will win greater things and achieve greater heights according to God's excellent promises for your life (Jeremiah 29:11)—and you never have the option of quiting because in Jesus Christ you are a winner and not a loser!

*You can become a modern day Jabez (1 Chronicles 4:10).*

Having *true* self-respect and self-regard stems from you knowing who you are in Jesus Christ and allowing God's Holy Word to rule your mind. God's Holy Word can renew your mind and change the distorted view that you have of who you are. You are truly worthy in Christ and absolutely nothing can change this holy truth! The awesome power of God's Word can change the negative course set up for you by the devil—to a divine victorious path. You can become a modern day Jabez with God's victorious power bubbling inside of you daily, clearing your paths of the roadblocks set up by the foul spirit of racism, and releasing God's awesome glory in your life, as you pray the powerful prayer of Jabez in 1 Chronicles 4:10(NKJV): "And Jabez called on the God of Israel saying, "Oh, that You would bless me indeed, and enlarge my territory, that Your hand would be with me, and that You would keep *me* from evil, that I may not cause pain!" So God granted him what he requested."

*God's Holy Spirit will lead you to all truth and cancel every lie of the devil that tries to take root in your mind.*

When you abide daily in God's Holy Word, He, not humans, will dictate your mindset through the revelation knowledge of His Holy Spirit Who dwells in you. God's Holy Spirit will lead you to all truth (John 16:13) and cancel every lie of the devil that tries to take root in your mind. So, you should be pulling down strongholds, casting down arguments and every lie of racism that exalts itself against the knowledge of God, bringing every wicked and racist thought into captivity to the obedience of Jesus Christ (2 Corinthians 10:3-6). God is the Source, Foundation, original Architect and Builder of your true self-image, your true spiritual nature, which is rooted in His Son, Jesus Christ, Who is your Savior and Redeemer.

Jesus Christ gave you access to God's awesome power and His Holy Spirit—and you have received His glorious power! Maintaining a Christ-rooted nature requires faith as well as conscious belief, will and effort. You have to believe in God's Holy Word, dwell in it, live and act on it, and stand on it always (Joshua 1:7-9; John 7:38; Hebrews 10:35-38). You cannot allow yourself to go back to your old and unproductive ways and this includes allowing racism to dictate your mindset (Galatians 5:1). You have to receive and live by true spiritual knowledge based on God's Holy Word which renews your mind daily (Romans 12:2; Ephesians 4:23-24). Having the knowledge that Jesus Christ is in you, you cannot let racism or anything other than God's Holy Word enslave your mind; you cannot and should not allow racists to distort your thinking pattern or mindset; you cannot allow any weaknesses or sins of the flesh to rule and overcome you because Jesus Christ has already delivered you from the yoke of every bondage (Galatians 5:1; Romans 6:6-7). Jesus Christ has also delivered you from the yoke of the bondage of racism.

*You cannot and should not allow racists to distort your thinking pattern or mindset.*

Your self-acceptance and appreciation, self-respect, self-regard, self-worth, self-esteem, self-confidence, self-competence, self-efficacy and self-efficiency, as the world defines them, are not Christ-rooted; they fluctuate depending on your present circumstance and experience. On the contrary, when who you are is built on the Solid Foundation, Jesus Christ, the Rock, you move from being carnal to spiritual (Romans 8:6; 1 Corinthians 2:14), and you become Christ-rooted—in God's unchangeable Holy Word, which is God Himself Who never changes (Malachi 3:6; John 1:1) or fails (Matthew 24:35; Isaiah 55:11; Joshua 23:14).

You are a modern day Jabez (1 Chronicles 4:10) and you are rooted in Jesus Christ (Colossians 2:5-8; Ephesians 3:15-21). Allow God to expand your horizon, and bless you exceedingly, abundantly, above and beyond anything that you could have ever asked for or imagined (Ephesians 3:20-21). Your self: worth, acceptance, appreciation, respect, regard, esteem, confidence, competence, efficacy and efficiency, if rooted in Jesus Christ, will be able to withstand the fiery darts of the devil—against the storms and challenges of life—and the evil attacks of the foul spirit of racism.

*Christ paid the cost for our eternal salvation and yet offered it to us at no charge!*

**Chapter Quiz**

1. What and why do you need to have Christ-rooted self-respect and self-regard?

2. What and why do you need to have Christ-rooted self-confidence and not carnal arrogance?

_______________________________________________

3. What is the difference between Christ-rooted self-confidence (spiritual confidence), carnal confidence and carnal arrogance?

_______________________________________________

4. Your true self-worth is based on whom? How and why must you guard it?

_______________________________________________

5. Why must you always reject all negativity from the foul spirit of racism?

_______________________________________________

6. What is the true foundation of your authentic spiritual image?

_______________________________________________

∞∞∞∞∞∞ ♦ ♦ ♦ ♦ ♦ ∞∞∞∞∞∞

**Reflections:**

_______________________________________________

_______________________________________________

_______________________________________________

_______________________________________________

∞∞∞∞∞∞ ♦ ♦ ♦ ♦ ♦ ∞∞∞∞∞∞

---

Chapter References:

1. https://my.belmont.edu/mybelmont/student_life/counseling/pdf/self_esteem_mayo_clinic.pdf
2. http://www.thefreedictionary.com/self-image
3. http://www.self-esteem-nase.org/
4. http://www.uwa.edu/Self_Esteem.aspx
5. http://en.wikipedia.org/wiki/Self-image
6. http://my.clevelandclinic.org/healthy_living/mental_health/hic_fostering_a_positive_self-image.aspx
7. thefreedictionary.org
8. thefreedictionary.com

# CHAPTER 38: Attaining Spiritual Victory Over Racism

The truth is that spiritual victory over racism is possible and it is your individual spiritual victory that will also birth material success into physical existence. First, you must believe and be armed with the Holy Word of God and receive its revelation knowledge from His Holy Spirit Who dwells within you and its restoration power. Then, knowledge of your true spiritual identity in Jesus Christ will be revealed to you. You will come to know and believe that God is the only One who can define your worth and He has already defined you absolutely worthy through Jesus Christ, and no other is qualified to redefine your true worth. Knowing this, you must stand on God's Holy Word and allow its awesome power to work in your heart, mind, thoughts, emotions, will and resolve, for you to gain daily victory over racism.

Let God, through Jesus Christ and His Holy Spirit in you, complete the awesome work that He already started in you (Philippians 1:6). Do not give room within you for temporary or permanent habitation of the foul spirit of racism and any of its negative effects, but rather, soak your entire being in God's Holy Word and His righteousness through our Lord and Savior Jesus Christ. Let your daily affirmation of God's Holy Word through Jesus Christ fortify your spirit and soul, thereby empowering you to achieve daily victory over racism and the odious spirit behind it.

**Your Daily Affirmation Against Racism:**

I affirm that in and through Jesus Christ, the powerful radiance of God's Kingdom Power glows within and through me daily. His rays of victory empower me daily through Jesus Christ and by the guidance of His Holy Spirit Who lives in me. I see the manifestations of God's glory and power in my life; daily, clearing my paths of any roadblocks, obstacles and challenges placed by racism. I declare daily, that I am more than a conqueror of any form of racism through Jesus Christ. I affirm boldly that I am empowered by God's Holy Word and possess the courage of the Holy Spirit of God within me. I am under God's divine guidance. I reaffirm that His guidance, through the paths of my journey, will take my hard and sustained labor to great heights of success de-

*God is the only One who can define my true worth and He has already defined me absolutely worthy through Jesus Christ.*

spite racism that I may face daily. I know that I am able, I can, and I have won the ultimate spiritual, mental and physical war over the vile spirit of racism. Thank You, Lord God, for your limitless power within me through Jesus Christ, Amen.

∞∞∞∞∞∞♦ ♦ ♦ ♦ ♦∞∞∞∞∞∞

**Chapter Quiz**

1. Why and how must you strive to attain daily spiritual victory over the loathsome spirit of racism?

---

2. How does God's Holy Word empower you to gain spiritual and material victory over the obnoxious spirit of racism and its abhorrent outgrowth of racism?

---

3. Why is your daily spiritual affirmation over the foul spirit of racism and racism crucial?

---

4. Since God has deemed you worthy through Jesus Christ, can the vile spirit of racism or racism make you unworthy in any manner?

---

∞∞∞∞∞∞♦ ♦ ♦ ♦ ♦∞∞∞∞∞∞

**Reflections:**

---

---

---

---

ooooooooooooo ♦ ♦ ♦ ♦ ♦ ooooooooooooo

# CHAPTER 39: Power of God's Holy Spirit in You

"The conscious mind includes everything that we are aware of. This is the aspect of our mental processing that we can think and talk about rationally. The unconscious mind is a reservoir of feelings, thoughts, urges, and memories that is outside of our conscious awareness. Most of the contents of the unconscious are unacceptable or unpleasant, such as feelings of pain, anxiety, or conflict."[2]

Our natural conscious mind is our state of awareness and rational thinking while our natural subconscious mind exists and operates beneath or beyond conscious awareness[1]. Our conscious mind is the first guard gate into our subconscious mind. However, our conscious mind also draws information from the memory bank of our subconscious mind. Yet, although our subconscious mind is below the active awareness of our conscious mind, it dominates a larger percentage of our mind, while our conscious mind dictates only a small fraction of the total makeup of our mind. When we doze off on board a passenger train, it is our subconscious mind that wakes us up when we get to our target station. It is our subconscious mind that makes it possible for us to drive while we think about the errands we need to run and other business and family issues we need to deal with. Our subconscious mind makes it possible for us to coordinate the movement of our feet and hands while driving a car with either a manual or automatic gear system. I am not recommending that you become an absentminded driver as this can be dangerous. I am simply trying to illustrate the power of our subconscious mind.

*Our conscious mind is the first guard gate into our subconscious mind.*

Our conscious mind has limited access to information that we gather from our environment, while our subconscious mind has limitless access to the same information. Our minds can gather more "junk", either positive or negative information, at the subconscious level. Therefore, on a daily basis, we need God's Holy Word to renew our minds (Romans 12:2; Ephesians 4:23-24) and His Holy Spirit to help us guide and guard our thoughts with power thoughts that are Word-based and Holy Spirit-directed. Also, we need God's Holy Word to soak both our conscious and subconscious mind, and His Holy Spirit to help us to continuously cleanse our subconscious mind of untruth and toxic debris, and direct us to all truth (John 16:13).

Our subconscious mind stores both good and bad information. It lacks the ability to effectively select, sort or filter only positive information; so, it's a memory bank for both positive and negative information. Therefore, with negative information, our subconscious mind could also become a destructive weapon against our soul. Our subconscious mind can become our enemy as it continues to collect and recollect "junk," falsehoods and untruths about who we are. Our natural mind (conscious and unconscious) can project failure, defeat and inadequacy within us, while our spiritual mind (empowered by God's Holy Word and His Holy Spirit) can reverse these thoughts with power thoughts, that is, positive thinking and encouragement from the Holy Word of God (1 Corinthians 2:12; Ezekiel 36:27; John 16:13; Proverbs 1:23).

*The Holy Spirit of God Who dwells within us, inspires, guides, reveals ideas and plans and gives us directions.*

The Holy Spirit of God gives our inner person a brand new, clean and positive perspective, which is how we should see things. From the outside, He retrains our conscious mind on how to better recognize and allow only positive information to take up residence in our subconscious mind. Christ-rooted positive thoughts and ideas will also flood our subconscious mind on a continual basis and our conscious mind will begin to act consistently based on them as we let God's Holy Word and His Holy Spirit work and move in our lives.

As Christian believers, while we may be able to practice positive thinking to some degree solely on our own, we cannot sustain it at both our conscious and subconscious mind levels without the power of God's Holy Word and the assistance of the Holy Spirit of God. This is simply because the natural surveillance ability of our conscious mind has limitations. Also, the negativity that we accumulate in our subconscious mind can later dominate our conscious mind. For example, our subconscious mind can convince us that what is a lie is actually truth, but God's Holy Word and His Holy Spirit, Who knows all truth, can reverse our mindset by providing us with the real truth (John 16:13; Romans 12:2).

*God's Power within us births divinely-inspired ideas for us.*

There are many individuals who have received the vile spirit of racism and believe its lie that their race or ethnic group is superior to others. This lie which they have received in their conscious mind, has also settled in their subconscious as the "truth." Based on this lie, such individuals project their race or ethnic group to be better and more intelligent than others. They disrespect and disregard the humanity of individuals of other races, and make no apologies about their racist remarks and discriminatory actions. Many of these individuals may also claim that they are born again believers and will never admit to themselves or others that they are actually instruments of the vile spirit of racism, a product of the kingdom of darkness.

Our ability to maximize our full potential in order to fulfill our life's ambitions lies in the supernatural power of our subconscious mind, which we receive only through the Holy Spirit of God. The supernatural zone of our subconscious mind is also sustained by the Holy Spirit of God, Who dwells within us. The Holy Spirit of God is the Person and power Who guides both our conscious and subconscious mind to focus on and tap into only positive thinking. Some may argue that humans can maximize the power of their subconscious mind without God's Holy Spirit. Here, the word "maximize" refers to being able to completely exploit the power of one's mind to its utmost capacity with little or no untapped reserve. I believe that no human has the ability to maximize to the fullest the power of either their subconscious or conscious mind. In addition, I believe that no person can maximize the positive supernatural power of their subconscious or conscious mind without the empowering of the Holy Spirit through Jesus Christ.

*God's Holy Spirit trains our conscious and subconscious mind.*

As born-again believers in Jesus Christ, His righteousness is imputed to us by God. Also, we become baptized by His Holy Spirit. We receive anointing power of God through the Holy Spirit in the Name of Jesus Christ. The Holy Spirit dwells within us, and if we listen to Him and obey Him, He leads us to all truth

(John 16:13), and helps us to begin to live a life of holiness in Christ. Under the guidance of the Holy Spirit, our subconscious mind inspires, guides, reveals ideas and plans and gives us directions that will help us achieve our goals, ambitions and ultimate purpose in life. The power of the Holy Spirit within our subconscious state triggers our creative energy and thoughts, and finally, directs our creativity through our conscious, intelligent thinking into the righteous paths of Christ holiness and Christ-rooted success (1 John 2:27; Romans 8:14-17; John 16:13).

*The Holy Spirit of God directs us into the right path of Christ's holiness and Christ-rooted success.*

The power of God's Holy Spirit within our subconscious mind births divinely-inspired ideas which are higher than ordinary ideas. All you need in your lifetime is to receive and successfully implement one God-idea and you will reap a great harvest. For our subconscious mind to gain and retain positive spiritual renewal and empowerment by the Holy Spirit of God, we must first receive Jesus Christ in our hearts as our Lord and Savior, and be willing to submit our inward and outward person completely to God through Him. We must be willing to submit our conscious mind to God and His Holy Word, and to give up our will and embrace only God's will and purpose for us through Christ (Matthew 6:10, 26:39; Luke 22:42).

We must love God above all things, read, believe and receive His Word in our hearts and meditate on it daily (Jeremiah 1:7-9). We need to seek, know and understand God's holy purpose for our lives in our hearts (Jeremiah 29:11); and to live daily in obedience to His Holy Word, if we are to reap His blessings (Deuteronomy 28:1-14). This does not mean that we can reach a state of perfection while still in our mortal bodies; but we have the righteousness of Jesus Christ in us to keep us on His path of holiness with the help of the Holy Spirit.

Once our spirit submits completely and without doubt or hesitation to the Holy Spirit of God, then our subconscious and conscious mind will also submit. This means that our spirit man and intermediate soul would no longer be in conflict with the Holy Spirit of God. Our inner spirit, empowered by God's Holy Spirit, and our soul empowered by His Word, become the permanent "guard gate" to our conscious mind, transforming it into a spiritual mind (John 16:13; Romans 12:2; Ephesians 4:23-24). A spiritually trained conscious mind will become highly alert and a permanent guard that filters and screens all external information before it registers in our subconscious mind. The Holy Spirit of God, Who dwells within us, will flood our spiritual subconscious mind with positive thoughts and directions that can also be recalled and processed at any time by our brain and transmitted to our spiritually conscious mind.

*The Holy Spirit of God gives us a clean, brand new and positive perspective on things.*

The Holy Spirit of God is the Person and power that also guides our subconscious mind to focus on divine thinking and tap into its supernatural zone (1 Corinthians 2:12; John 16:12; 1 John 2:27). Under the guidance of the Holy Spirit of God, our subconscious mind is transformed into a power house of God that inspires, guides, reveals ideas and plans, and gives us directions that will help us achieve our goals, ambitions and ultimate purpose for our life. The power of the Holy Spirit within our subconscious mind triggers our creative energy and thoughts, and finally directs this energy through our conscious, intelligent thinking into the righteous paths of Christ-rooted success. The Holy Spirit's primary goal is for us to be made holy (John 15:26-27, 16:7-11). As we allow God's Holy Word to cleanse our minds of toxic debris from our experiences in life, and help us live a life of holiness with the help of the Holy Spirit, we begin to attain and maintain a proper and wholesome balance between our spirit, soul and body. The power of God's Holy Word and Holy Spirit of God within us helps us reach a healthy state of balance between our spirit and soul (our mind, emotions, thoughts, will and resolve), expressed through our physical form, our body. Without this balance, a healthy state of self: regard, confidence, esteem and worthiness will elude us.

*Through Christ, you have God's awesome victory over the odious spirit of racism and its nasty fruit of racism.*

Hope, joy, love, peace, kindness, goodness, faithfulness, gentleness and happiness would also remain elusive in our lives.

Racist assaults bombard our natural conscious mind with lies that we are inferior and distortions about our true self: worth, esteem and confidence. Our spiritual conscious mind guided by God's Holy Spirit can immediately recognize this and discard such information as junk, thereby preventing it from entering into our Holy Spirit-directed subconscious mind. Our mind now relies on God's Holy Word and Holy Spirit within us for guidance and fortification with true spiritual knowledge of who we truly are in Jesus Christ. Our spirit, now equipped with authentic spiritual knowledge of who we are in Christ, will not allow temporary or permanent residence of any negative thoughts or lies in our heart, conscious and subconscious mind. This is a divine strategy for banishing the lies that the vile spirit of racism tries to deposit on our minds. You have the authority and power of Jesus Christ in you—you have the power of the Holy Spirit in you—you have the power of God's Holy Word in you—and through Christ, you have God's awesome victory over the odious spirit of racism (1 John 5:4; Luke 10:18-19).

*Through Christ, you have God's awesome victory over the odious spirit of racism and its nasty fruit of racism.*

Now, let's continue to walk in Christ's footprints to daily victory over the vile spirit of racism and the nasty activities that it orchestrates against our lives through willing human hosts. Racism can never change who you truly are in Christ. You are the child of the Living God and no evil spirit, including the foul spirit of racism, can ever rule over your spirit and new nature in Christ. Receive and believe this holy truth that racism can never change!

**Chapter Quiz**

1. What must you do on a daily basis to place within your conscious mind a spiritual guard gate against racism or the evil spirit of racism?

---

2. How do you get rid of the 'junk' and lies, which the odious spirit of racism tries to implant within your heart and mind?

---

3. Through Jesus Christ, how can God's Holy Word help you cleanse your heart and mind of any imprint of the evil spirit of racism or negative effect of racism?

---

4. How can the victory that our Lord and Savior Jesus Christ obtained for you on the Cross, give you victory over the vile spirit of racism and its nasty fruit of racism?

---

∞∞∞∞∞∞∞ ♦ ♦ ♦ ♦ ♦ ∞∞∞∞∞∞∞

## Reflections:

_______________________________________________

_______________________________________________

_______________________________________________

_______________________________________________

∞∞∞∞∞∞∞ ♦ ♦ ♦ ♦ ♦ ∞∞∞∞∞∞∞

Chapter References:

1. wordnetweb.princeton.edu
2. Definitons by Sigmund Freud in "The Conscious and Unconscious Mind: The Structure of the Mind According to Freud" By Kendra Cherry: http://psychology.about.com/od/theoriesofpersonality/a/consciousuncon.htm

# CHAPTER 40: Power Thoughts Against Racism

***Who You are in Jesus Christ***

∞∞♦ ♦ ♦ ♦ ♦∞∞

- God is multiracial and every race and ethnic group is made and reflected in His excellent Image.
- Therefore, regardless of your race, ethnicity or nationality, you are made in the excellent Image of the awesome Triune God, and through Jesus Christ, you have become a child of God.
- You are born equal, in humanity and dignity, to every other person, regardless of race, ethnicity or nationality.
- Your racial and ethnic makeup is in God's excellent Image.
- By accepting Jesus Christ into your heart, you receive God's Holy Spirit.

- God's divine grace to us, Jesus Christ, is our unmerited favor from Him which is enough for your spiritual and material success. He has also blessed you with spiritual gifts, talents and great potential.
- God has given you many million-dollar talents and gifts to invest properly, and to receive and share a great harvest in the Name of His Son Jesus Christ, to the glory of His Name.
- You are a special person with a unique purpose in life.
- You are not a mishap, coincidence, mistake or shame.
- You are not illegitimate; Jesus Christ has made you legitimate.
- You are a blessing to yourself, your family, your friends and your enemies (including racists), and to the world.
- The actions of a prejudiced or racist person lack the ultimate power to stop you from achieving your success, unless you allow them.
- The real "You" comes from your spirit that has been redeemed through Jesus Christ and empowered by the Holy Spirit of God; through Jesus Christ, the only Mediator, you have access to God.
- You are always beautiful in the eyes of God your Creator.
- You spiritual and natural gifts and talents, when utilized properly and efficiently, will gloriry God first and then make you highly successful.

- You are elegant in the eyes of all of God's worthy creations.
- You are a special being with a unique purpose in life.

∞∞♦ ♦ ♦ ♦ ♦∞∞

***True Spiritual Knowledge, Understanding, Wisdom***

- God loved you first and offered the amazing Sacrifice of His Son, Jesus Christ, for your eternal salvation.
- By faith you have received Jesus Christ as your Lord and Savior and believed in your heart that He died for you and was raised from the dead by the power of the Holy Spirit; and He, Christ ascended into Heaven and is seated at the right hand of God the Father.
- Therfore, your spirit has become born again in Jesus Christ—and you have become justified and made righteous in Christ.
- Your old self has been crucified with Jesus Christ, and He now lives in you. You are a new creation in Christ and old things have been erased and made brand new. Your spirit has been renewed in Christ.
- Through Christ, you have received the Holy Spirit Who now lives in you.
- Now, the Holy Spirit is helping you begin and continue with your process of sanctification. You have become

consecrated—set apart for God and to do His awesome work.

- The Holy Spirit of God helps you to live holy through Jesus Christ, activate your inherent measure of faith and drive your creativity (in your soul) through your spirit.
- Knowing God through Jesus Christ and understanding your true spiritual nature is the gateway to knowing His purpose for your individual life.
- Through Jesus Christ, God has made you larger than racism.
- Authentic spiritual knowledge empowers true self-knowledge and is a silent gear that pushes against racism until it is permanently stalled and unable to attack or erode your psyche or soul.
- True heavenly knowledge gives you spiritual wisdom for mental resistance against racism and its evils.
- Mental resistance is most effective against racism when your heart and mind are fortified by God's Holy Word.
- True self-knowledge is deeply founded in the knowledge of God, Who is the Fountain and Source of all true knowledge.
- Within your life's journey is your spiritual purpose that God designed for your life.
- God's grace is more than sufficient for you to gain your personal victory over racism.

- You must exercise positive spiritual dominance over racism through spiritual warfare to experience actual victory in your physical environment.
- God's spiritual truth and understanding gives you wisdom to deal victoriously with racism.
- For the power of God's Holy Word against racism to work on your behalf, you must believe it, embrace it and activate the measure of faith in you.
- Racism is no match against the power of God.
- Racism has never been authorized by God.
- Racism will never be authorzed by God.
- Racism is not backed by God.
- The vile spirit of racism has been defeated by Jesus Christ.
- The key to the mantle of spiritual victory over racism lies within you. You have the power of Jesus Christ in you, and through Him you have the indwelling power of the Holy Spirit.

***Conquering Fear***

- Reject fear always!
- God has not given you a spirit of fear, but of love, power and a sound, clear and disciplined mind.

- Fear is not of God, but of the devil, the prince of darkness and the ruler of this world.
- Fear is the devil's weapon, which is designed to cripple your faith and hold you under carnal bondage.
- Fear blinds your spiritual wisdom and fills your mind with lies and distortions about what the evil power of racism and the foul spirit behind it can accomplish in your life.
- The spirit of fear is a weapon of defeat, destruction and bondage of the mind.
- Fear also fuels the power that sustains racism against others.
- To confront real or imagined fear, you need spiritual courage.
- To obtain spiritual courage, you need to read, know and believe God's Holy Word, meditate on it, solidify it in your heart, and declare it with your mouth.
- When you fear humans, who are merely creations of God, you fail to revere the protective, limitless and boundless power of God, the Maker of all humans.
- You are to fear only God by revering His power and glory; do not allow your fear of any man, woman or circumstance to control your life.
- Always reject fear and its vile spirit!
- Fear can be confronted when you are armed with spiritual courage and with the Word of God as your ammunition.

- To master control of fear is not to destroy it, but to hold every fearful thought captive with the Word and promises of God.
- No fearful thought bound or held captive by the Word and promises of God, with complete and unwavering faith, will ever become victorious in your life.
- Fear diminishes your faith and transforms it into double-mindedness and God does not respond to a double-minded person.
- Fear smothers the power of God's spiritual warfare in our lives, because God responds primarily to our faith.
- Your faith must completely replace your fear, for if not, fear will steal your rays of victory, your deliverance "thunder" from God.
- Fear breeds feelings of frustration and accomplishes nothing for you.
- Have faith, for faith overcomes fear and faith cripples fear.
- Your faith dispels fear, because the Word and promises of God within your heart and mind fortify your faith.
- It is not an act of faith, but an act of fear to believe that the power of any man to do evil against you is greater than the power of God to overcome that evil resulting in good for your life.
- To claim God's rays of victory within you, fear must be replaced by faith. Faith will in turn generate hope and

hope will give rise to patience and sustain your journey in the present and into the future, and position you to receive God's miracles in your daily life.

∞∞♦ ♦ ♦ ♦ ♦∞∞

***The Power of Your Faith***

- For your faith to move into spiritual action, you must activate it by accepting Jesus Christ as your Lord, Savior and Redeemer.
- To grow your faith, you need to read, receive and believe the Holy Word of God and His promises; and mediate on His Word daily.
- Unwavering faith is the solid foundation of your trusting relationship with God.
- Unwavering faith requires believing God's Word without doubting; believing that with God, all things are possible.
- Your faith in God's Holy Word fine-focuses on and empowers your spirit, heart, mind, emotions, thoughts, will, resolve and actions against evil, including racism.
- God's powerful guiding spiritual light takes you from the paths of oppression and injustice to freedom and justice.
- When the light of God shines in and on you daily, neither racism nor its evils will be able to darken His paths of triumph for you.
- Focusing your faith against racism is only possible by hearing and meditating on God's Word.

- God's Word reminds you to journey through the rugged challenges and obstacles of life by faith and not by sight.
- Fear will eliminate faith and invite unbelief into your heart and mind, and lead you to defeat by the devil and his foul spirits, including the vile spirit of racism.
- For God to move on your behalf against racism, you must have the faith to believe that He can.
- Your faith must be bigger than racism around you for your individual victory to become reality.
- Faith works from within your spirit and powers your soul, so that your inward spirit is in complete control of your soul and external environment, and you are able to control your internal space in response to your outward person and external circumstances.
- You have the authority that God has given to you through Jesus Christ to bind racism that exists around you and in the world as a whole.
- You have the authority that God has given to you through Jesus Christ to loose God's power from Heaven against racism here on Earth.
- The Word of God powers your built-in faith, and your faith fortifies your spirit, which in turn drives your soul and body.
- No mountain is too high for God to tear down. No form of racism is too intricate for God to untangle, expose or destroy.

- Faith in the Triune God and His Holy Word is the foundation of your spiritual and physical courage.
- Faith defeats the seeds of fear, anxiety, anger, frustration, bitterness, resentment, hate, vengeance and all other negative emotions, thoughts, words and actions.
- God will expose the injustice of racism that you are dealing with, if you trust Him, let go and let Him take over the situation on your behalf.
- God will release you from the oppression of racism by your activated faith in His Holy Word, power, might and glory, through Jesus Christ.

**Chapter Quiz**

1. List at least five power thoughts against racism that are based on God's holy truth that you can apply to gain daily victory over racism.

---

2. In what ways do Holy Word-based power thoughts destroy the burden of the yoke of racism on your mind?

---

3. True or false: Faith is the foundation of your spiritual and physical courage. Explain your answer.

---

4. True or false: Fear is the devil's weapon which is designed to cripple your faith and hold you under carnal bondage. Explain your answer.

______________________________________________________________

∞∞∞∞∞∞∞∞∞∞∞♦ ♦ ♦ ♦ ♦∞∞∞∞∞∞∞∞∞∞∞

**Reflections:**

______________________________________________________________

______________________________________________________________

______________________________________________________________

______________________________________________________________

∞∞∞∞∞∞∞∞∞∞∞♦ ♦ ♦ ♦ ♦∞∞∞∞∞∞∞∞∞∞∞

# Available:

## RAYS OF VICTORY SERIES

ꝏꝏꝏꝏꝏꝏ♦ ♦ ♦ ♦ ♦ꝏꝏꝏꝏꝏꝏ

This Book is:

***A WORKBOOK SERIES***

# FOOTPRINTS OF VICTORY OVER RACISM

## *In the Secret Place With God*

## (Volume 2)

**Illuminating Daily Guideposts for God's Rays of Victory Over Racism**

## By
## Dr. Jacyee Aniagolu-Johnson

**First Paperback Edition**
**ISBN 978-0-9789669-6-6**

# Also Available:

## RAYS OF VICTORY SERIES

∞∞∞∞∞∞♦♦♦♦♦∞∞∞∞∞∞

*WORKBOOK SERIES*

# FOOTPRINTS OF VICTORY OVER RACISM

## *In the Secret Place With God*

## (Volume 1)

**Illuminating Daily Guideposts for God's Rays of Victory Over Racism**

# By
# Dr. Jacyee Aniagolu-Johnson

**First Paperback Edition**
**ISBN 978-0-9789669-5-9**

FOOTPRINTS OF VICTORY OVER RACISM – VOLUME 2

# RAYS OF VICTORY SERIES

∞∞∞∞∞∞∞∞∞∞♦♦♦♦♦∞∞∞∞∞∞∞∞∞∞

## <u>ON THE HAMMOCK</u>:

# WITH THE SWORD OF THE SPIRIT

## *FOR INDIVIDUAL VICTORY OVER RACISM*

## *A Meditation Journal*

*[40 Days of Daily Meditation]*

(Volume 1)

By

Dr. Jacyee Aniagolu-Johnson

∞∞∞∞∞∞∞∞∞∞♦♦♦♦♦∞∞∞∞∞∞∞∞∞∞

**First Paperback Edition**
**ISBN 978-0-9789669-8-0**

FOOTPRINTS OF VICTORY OVER RACISM – VOLUME 2

# RAYS OF VICTORY SERIES

ꝏꝏꝏꝏꝏꝏ♦ ♦ ♦ ♦ ♦ꝏꝏꝏꝏꝏꝏ

## ON THE HAMMOCK:

# WITH THE OIL OF GRACE

## *FOR INDIVIDUAL VICTORY OVER RACISM*

## *A Meditation Journal*

*[40 Days of Daily Meditation]*

(Volume 2)

By

Dr. Jacyee Aniagolu-Johnson

ꝏꝏꝏꝏꝏꝏ♦ ♦ ♦ ♦ ♦ꝏꝏꝏꝏꝏꝏ

**First Paperback Edition**
**ISBN 978-0-9789669-9-7**

FOOTPRINTS OF VICTORY OVER RACISM – VOLUME 2

## RAYS OF VICTORY SERIES

∞∞∞∞∞∞∞∞∞∞∞∞♦♦♦♦♦∞∞∞∞∞∞∞∞∞∞∞∞

# ONE ON ONE WITH GOD

## *FOR VICTORY OVER RACISM*

*Daily Prayer Conversations With God for Individual Victory Over Racism*

## By
## Dr. Jacyee Aniagolu-Johnson

∞∞∞∞∞∞∞∞∞∞∞∞♦♦♦♦♦∞∞∞∞∞∞∞∞∞∞∞∞

**First Paperback Edition:**
**ISBN 978-0-9789669-7-3**

FOOTPRINTS OF VICTORY OVER RACISM – VOLUME 2

# RAYS OF VICTORY SERIES

ꝏꝏꝏꝏꝏꝏ♦ ♦ ♦ ♦ ♦ꝏꝏꝏꝏꝏꝏ

# My Rays of Victory

# *BIBLE STUDY DIARY*

*A Unique Diary for your Signature Penmanship as you Triumph Over Racism*

## By
## Dr. Jacyee Aniagolu-Johnson

ꝏꝏꝏꝏꝏꝏ♦ ♦ ♦ ♦ ♦ꝏꝏꝏꝏꝏꝏ

**First Paperback Edition:**
**ISBN: 978-0-9789669-4-2**

FOOTPRINTS OF VICTORY OVER RACISM – VOLUME 2

## RAYS OF VICTORY SERIES

∞∞∞∞∞∞∞∞∞∞ ♦ ♦ ♦ ♦ ♦ ∞∞∞∞∞∞∞∞∞∞

# 150 POWER THOUGHTS FOR VICTORY OVER RACISM

∞∞∞∞∞∞∞∞∞∞ ♦ ♦ ♦ ♦ ♦ ∞∞∞∞∞∞∞∞∞∞

*The Power of a Christ-rooted Mindset Over Racism*

∞∞∞∞∞∞∞∞∞∞ ♦ ♦ ♦ ♦ ♦ ∞∞∞∞∞∞∞∞∞∞

*Excerpts from "Nailing Racism to the Cross"*

∞∞∞∞∞∞∞∞∞∞ ♦ ♦ ♦ ♦ ♦ ∞∞∞∞∞∞∞∞∞∞

## By

## Dr. Jacyee Aniagolu-Johnson

**First Paperback Edition**
ISBN 978-1-937-230-00-5

FOOTPRINTS OF VICTORY OVER RACISM – VOLUME 2

# RAYS OF VICTORY SERIES

∞∞∞∞∞∞∞∞∞∞♦♦♦♦♦∞∞∞∞∞∞∞∞∞∞

# 150 POWER THOUGHTS
# Diary
# FOR VICTORY OVER RACISM

∞∞∞∞∞∞∞∞∞∞♦♦♦♦♦∞∞∞∞∞∞∞∞∞∞

*A Journal for Power Thoughts Against Racism*

∞∞∞∞∞∞∞∞∞∞♦♦♦♦♦∞∞∞∞∞∞∞∞∞∞

*Excerpts from "Nailing Racism to the Cross"*

∞∞∞∞∞∞∞∞∞∞♦♦♦♦♦∞∞∞∞∞∞∞∞∞∞

## By


## Dr. Jacyee Aniagolu-Johnson



**First Paperback Edition**

ISBN 978-1-937-230-04-3

## RAYS OF VICTORY SERIES

∞∞∞∞∞∞∞∞∞∞∞♦♦♦♦♦∞∞∞∞∞∞∞∞∞∞∞

# 150 SIGN POSTS TO VICTORY OVER RACISM
(Volume 1)

*Empowering Sign Posts for Victory Over Racism*

∞∞∞∞∞∞∞∞∞∞∞♦♦♦♦♦∞∞∞∞∞∞∞∞∞∞∞

*Excerpts from "Nailing Racism to the Cross"*

∞∞∞∞∞∞∞∞∞∞∞♦♦♦♦♦∞∞∞∞∞∞∞∞∞∞∞

## By
## Dr. Jacyee Aniagolu-Johnson

**First Paperback Edition**
ISBN 978-1-937230-01-2

FOOTPRINTS OF VICTORY OVER RACISM – VOLUME 2

## RAYS OF VICTORY SERIES

ooooooooooooo♦♦♦♦♦ooooooooooooo

# 150 SIGN POSTS TO VICTORY OVER RACISM

(Volume 2)

*Empowering Sign Posts for Victory Over Racism*

ooooooooooooo♦♦♦♦♦ooooooooooooo

*Excerpts from "Nailing Racism to the Cross"*

ooooooooooooo♦♦♦♦♦ooooooooooooo

By

Dr. Jacyee Aniagolu-Johnson

First Paperback Edition

ISBN 978-1-937230-02-9

FOOTPRINTS OF VICTORY OVER RACISM – VOLUME 2

## RAYS OF VICTORY SERIES

ꝏꝏꝏꝏꝏꝏ♦♦♦♦♦ꝏꝏꝏꝏꝏꝏ

# 150 SIGN POSTS TO VICTORY OVER RACISM

(Volume 3)

*Empowering Sign Posts for Victory Over Racism*

ꝏꝏꝏꝏꝏꝏ♦♦♦♦♦ꝏꝏꝏꝏꝏꝏ

*Excerpts from "Nailing Racism to the Cross"*

ꝏꝏꝏꝏꝏꝏ♦♦♦♦♦ꝏꝏꝏꝏꝏꝏ

## By
## Dr. Jacyee Aniagolu-Johnson

**First Paperback Edition**
**ISBN 978-1-937230-03-6**

# Rays of Victory Series

*Correspondence:*

Please send Correspondence to:

Marble Tower Publishing

P.O. Box 1654, Laurel, Maryland 20725

OR

Submit a Contact Request Form at:

**www.marbletowerpublishing.com**

**www.ravbookseries.com**

www.ingramcontent.com/pod-product-compliance
Lightning Source LLC
LaVergne TN
LVHW020526100826
845148LV00010B/1358
*9780978966966*